Mastering the Risk Management Framework Version 2

James Broad

DEDICATION

This book is dedicated to my family that allows me to spend so much time projects like this.

CONTENTS

ACKNOWLEDGMENTS

I want to thank the hard working team at the National Institute of Standard and Technology (NIST) and Federal Risk and Authorization Management Program (FedRAMP) for keeping risk management up to date.

1 UPDATES TO THE RMF

Updates to the Risk Management Framework

On December 18th, 2018 the National Institute of Standards and Technology (NIST) released revision 2 of its Special Publication (SP) 800-37 covering the updates to the Risk Management Framework (RMF). The updates provide additional detail to some tasks that have been implied in the past, add an entirely new step (prepare), provide alignment with the Cybersecurity Framework (CSF), increase the integration between security and privacy, and rearrange some of the existing tasks to improve the RMF process overall.

NIST defines seven major objectives that drove the update.
- o To provide closer linkage and communication between the risk management processes and activities at the C-suite or governance level of the organization and the individuals, processes, and activities at the system and operational level of the organization;
- o To institutionalize critical risk management preparatory activities at all risk management levels to facilitate a more effective, efficient, and cost-effective execution of the RMF;
- o To demonstrate how the NIST Cybersecurity Framework [NIST CSF] can be aligned with the RMF and implemented using established NIST risk management processes;
- o To integrate privacy risk management processes into the RMF to better support the privacy protection needs for which privacy programs are responsible;
- o To promote the development of trustworthy secure software and systems by aligning life cycle-based systems engineering processes in NIST Special Publication 800-160, Volume 1 [SP 800-160 v1], with the relevant tasks in the RMF;
- o To integrate security-related, supply chain risk management (SCRM) concepts into the RMF to address untrustworthy suppliers, insertion of counterfeits, tampering, unauthorized production, theft, insertion of malicious code, and poor manufacturing and development practices throughout the SDLC; and
- o To allow for an organization-generated control selection approach to complement the traditional baseline control selection approach and support the use of the consolidated control catalog in NIST Special Publication 800-53, Revision 5.

One of the biggest changes to the RMF is the addition of the prepare step, this step consists of two parts. The first half is the seven tasks for organization to be prepared for conducting the RMF. Two of the seven organizational prepare tasks are optional, while the remaining five are required by the RMF. The prepare step at the system level consists of eleven tasks that are all required by the RMF.

NIST defines five primary objectives for developing the new prepare step. These are illustrated in the following points, as documented by NIST.

- To facilitate effective communication between senior leaders and executives at the organization and mission/business process levels and system owners at the operational level;
- To facilitate organization-wide identification of common controls and the development of organizationally-tailored control baselines, reducing the workload on individual system owners and the cost of system development and asset protection;
- To reduce the complexity of the information technology (IT) and operations technology (OT) infrastructure using Enterprise Architecture concepts and models to consolidate, optimize, and standardize organizational systems, applications, and services;
- To reduce the complexity of systems by eliminating unnecessary functions and security and privacy capabilities that do not address security and privacy risk; and
- To identify, prioritize, and focus resources on the organization's high value assets (HVA) that require increased levels of protection—taking measures commensurate with the risk to such assets.

In addition to the new prepare step, several additional tasks have been added to the framework and some tasks have been moved between the steps to improve process flow. While the institute has introduced a total of twenty-three new tasks throughout the framework, many of the requirements are not totally new. Some tasks have been separated into more than one task, while other tasks that were previously implied are now formally codified in a new task. There are a number of tasks that are totally new and in all cases this new structure improves security and provides more implicit guidance on implementing the framework.

It is also interesting to note that NIST has moved away from its traditional numbering of the steps and tasks of the RMF to a schema that indicates the function of the task. For example, Task 3-1 Security Control Implementation is now I-1 Control implementation. By using this format, it is much easier to identify the goal of each task. Table 1.1 illustrates the new task nomenclature and the nomenclature from revision 1 of the RMF. Table 1.2 illustrates the changes in the steps and tasks between revision 1 and revision 2 of SP 800-37.

Revision 1 Step Number	Revision 2 Letter	Revision 2 Step Name	Notes
	P	Prepare	New Step
1	C	Categorize	
2	S	Select	
3	I	Implement	
4	A	Assess	
5	R	Authorize	
6	M	Monitor	

Table 1.1 RMF Step Titles

R1#	SP 800-37 R1 Task Name	R2 #	SP 800-37 R2 Task Name	Notes
			Prepare	
		P1	Risk Management Roles	New Organization Level
		P2	Risk Management Strategy	New Organization Level
		P3	Risk Assessment—Organization	New Organization Level
		P4	Organizationally-Tailored Control Baselines & Cybersecurity Framework Profiles	New Organization Level Optional
2.1	Common Control Identification	P5	Common Control Identification	Was 2.1 Organization Level
		P6	Impact-Level Prioritization	New Organization Level Optional
		P7	Continuous Monitoring Strategy	New Organization Level
		P8	Mission or Business Focus	New System Level
		P9	System Stakeholders	New System Level
		P10	Asset Identification	New System Level
		P11	Authorization Boundary	New System Level
		P12	Information Types	New System Level
		P13	Information Life Cycle	New System Level
		P14	Risk Assessment—System	New System Level
		P15	Requirements Definition	New System Level
		P16	Enterprise Architecture	New System Level
		P17	Requirements Allocation	New System Level

R1#	SP 800-37 R1 Task Name	R2 #	SP 800-37 R2 Task Name	Notes
1.3	Information System Registration	P18	System Registration	Was 1.3 System Level
Categorize				
1.1	Security Categorization	C1	System Description	Now C2
1.2	Information System Description	C2	Security Categorization	Now C1
		C3	Security Categorization Review & Approval	New
Select				
2.2	Security Control Selection	S1	Control Selection	
		S2	Control Tailoring	New
		S3	Control Allocation	New
		S4	Documentation of Planned Control Implementations	New
2.3	Monitoring Strategy	S5	Continuous Monitoring Strategy	ISCM System Level
2.4	Security Plan Approval	S6	Plan Review & Approval	
Implement				
3.1	Security Control Implementation	I1	Control Implementation	
3.2	Security Control Documentation	I2	Update Control Implementation Information	
Assess				
		A1	Assessor Selection	
4.1	Assessment Preparation	A2	Assessment Plan	
4.2	Security Control Assessment	A3	Control Assessments	
4.3	Security Assessment Report	A4	Assessment Reports	
4.4	Remediation Actions	A5	Remediation Actions	
5.1	Plan of Action & Milestones	A6	Plan of Action & Milestones	Was 5.1
Authorize				
5.2	Security Authorization Package	R1	Authorization Package	
5.3	Risk Determination	R2	Risk Analysis & Determination	

R1#	SP 800-37 R1 Task Name	R2 #	SP 800-37 R2 Task Name	Notes
		R3	Risk Response	New
5.4	Risk Acceptance	R4	Authorization Decision	
		R5	Authorization Reporting	New
			Monitor	
6.1	Information System & Environment Changes	M1	System & Environment Changes	
6.2	Ongoing Security Control Assessments	M2	Ongoing Assessments	
6.3	Ongoing Remediation Actions	M3	Ongoing Risk Response	
6.4	Key Updates	M4	Authorization Package Updates	
6.5	Security Status Reporting	M5	Security & Privacy Reporting	
6.6	Ongoing Risk Determination & Acceptance	M6	Ongoing Authorization	
6.7	Information System Removal & Disposal	M7	System Disposal	

Table 1.2 Task Names

Benefits

By updating the RMF NIST has streamlined the process by focusing on simplification and automation. Other major focuses of this update are to more tightly integrate implementing privacy and security controls, security for Information Technology/Operational Technology (IT/OT) systems, and securing third party supply chains. By updating the RMF the institute notes organizations implementing the framework will be able to realize the following benefits.

- Use the tasks and outputs of the Organization-Level and System-Level *Prepare* step to promote a consistent starting point within organizations to execute the RMF;
- Maximize the use of common controls at the organization level to promote standardized, consistent, and cost-effective security and privacy capability inheritance;
- Maximize the use of shared or cloud-based systems, services, and applications to reduce the number of authorizations needed across the organization;

- Employ organizationally-tailored control baselines to increase the speed of security and privacy plan development and the consistency of security and privacy plan content;

- Employ organization-defined controls based on security and privacy requirements generated from a systems security engineering process;

- Maximize the use of automated tools to manage security categorization; control selection, assessment, and monitoring; and the authorization process;

- Decrease the level of effort and resource expenditures for low-impact systems if those systems cannot adversely affect higher-impact systems through system connections;

- Maximize the reuse of RMF artifacts (e.g., security and privacy assessment results) for standardized hardware/software deployments, including configuration settings;

- Reduce the complexity of the IT/OT infrastructure by eliminating unnecessary systems, system components, and services — employing the least functionality principle; and

- Make the transition to ongoing authorization a priority and use continuous monitoring approaches to reduce the cost and increase the efficiency of security and privacy programs.

Cybersecurity Framework Alignment

Updates to the framework integrate the individual RMF tasks with the tasks in the Cybersecurity Framework (CSF). This allows organizations to relate consistent security and privacy controls across the organizations system/software development lifecycle (SDLC) and risk management response programs. Finally, each control is updated with specific inputs and outputs that assist in more complete integration with program and project management functions.

Illustrative examples

SP 800-37 R2 begins defining each step by identifying tasks, outcomes, and CSF alignment for each task in that step, this is illustrated in figure 1.1.

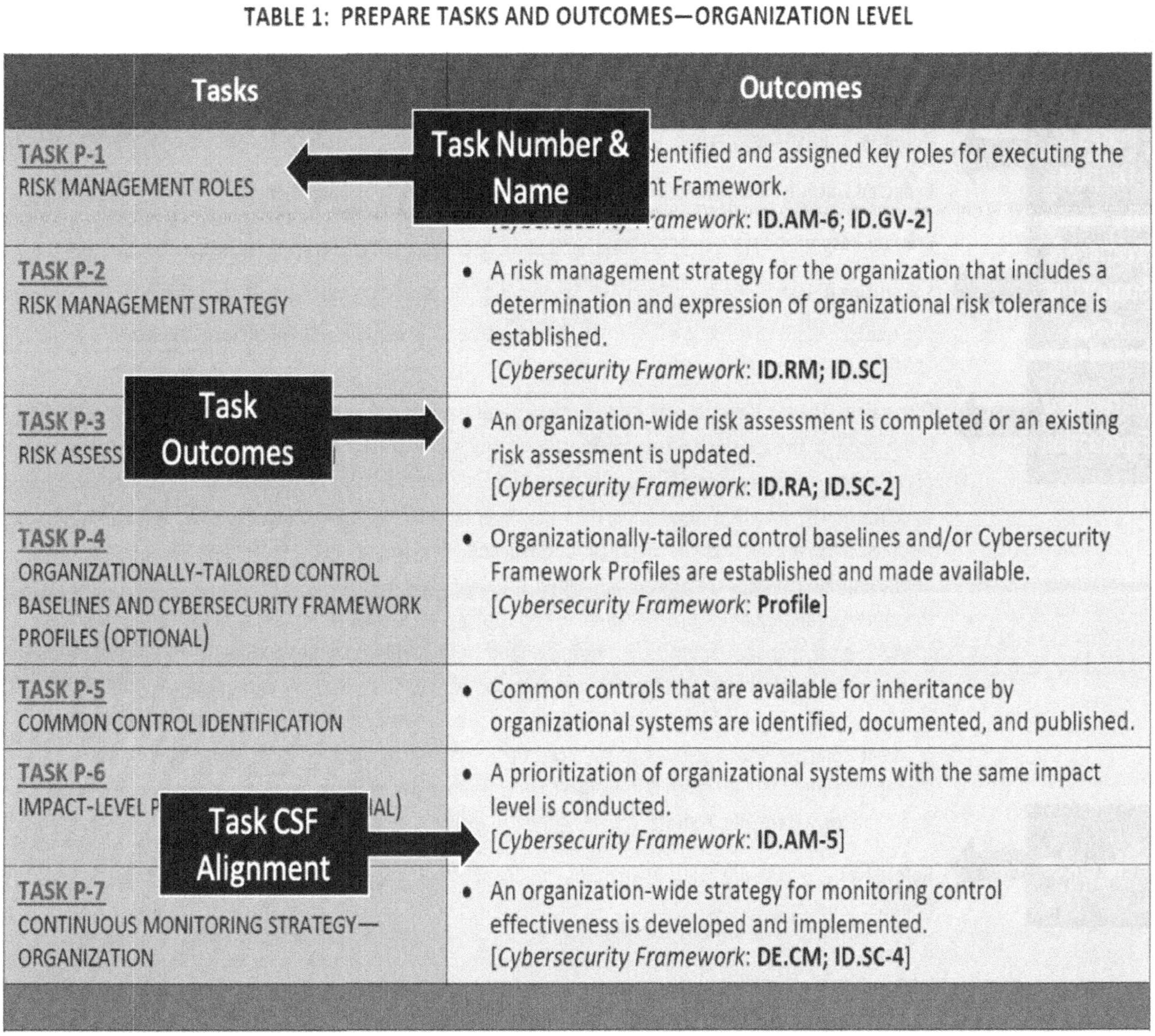

TABLE 1: PREPARE TASKS AND OUTCOMES—ORGANIZATION LEVEL

Tasks	Outcomes
TASK P-1 RISK MANAGEMENT ROLES	• Identified and assigned key roles for executing the ...nt Framework. [Cybersecurity Framework: **ID.AM-6; ID.GV-2**]
TASK P-2 RISK MANAGEMENT STRATEGY	• A risk management strategy for the organization that includes a determination and expression of organizational risk tolerance is established. [Cybersecurity Framework: **ID.RM; ID.SC**]
TASK P-3 RISK ASSESS...	• An organization-wide risk assessment is completed or an existing risk assessment is updated. [Cybersecurity Framework: **ID.RA; ID.SC-2**]
TASK P-4 ORGANIZATIONALLY-TAILORED CONTROL BASELINES AND CYBERSECURITY FRAMEWORK PROFILES (OPTIONAL)	• Organizationally-tailored control baselines and/or Cybersecurity Framework Profiles are established and made available. [Cybersecurity Framework: **Profile**]
TASK P-5 COMMON CONTROL IDENTIFICATION	• Common controls that are available for inheritance by organizational systems are identified, documented, and published.
TASK P-6 IMPACT-LEVEL P... (IAL)	• A prioritization of organizational systems with the same impact level is conducted. [Cybersecurity Framework: **ID.AM-5**]
TASK P-7 CONTINUOUS MONITORING STRATEGY—ORGANIZATION	• An organization-wide strategy for monitoring control effectiveness is developed and implemented. [Cybersecurity Framework: **DE.CM; ID.SC-4**]

The table contains callout labels: "Task Number & Name", "Task Outcomes", and "Task CSF Alignment".

Figure 1.1 Step Example

- The task number & name defines the nomenclature number and illustrative name for the task.
- Task outcome describes the potential outcomes that can be seen as deliverables when the task is successfully completed.
- CSF alignment defines the tasks linkage to the Cybersecurity Framework

An example of the new structure of a control is illustrated in figure 1.2

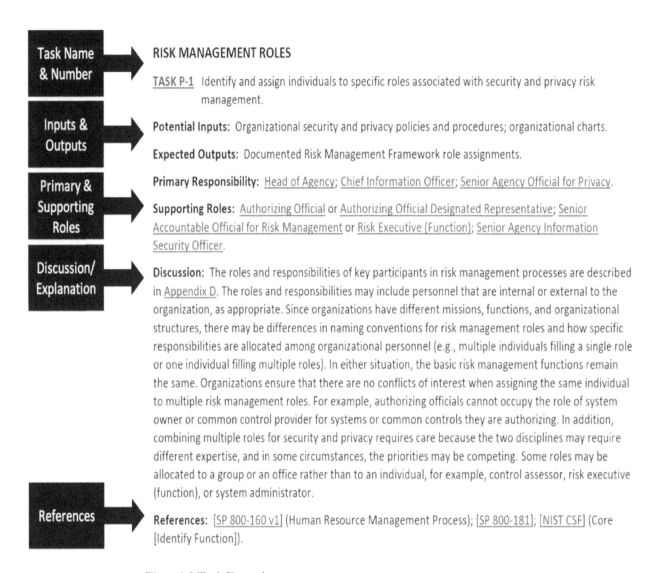

RISK MANAGEMENT ROLES

TASK P-1 Identify and assign individuals to specific roles associated with security and privacy risk management.

Potential Inputs: Organizational security and privacy policies and procedures; organizational charts.

Expected Outputs: Documented Risk Management Framework role assignments.

Primary Responsibility: Head of Agency; Chief Information Officer; Senior Agency Official for Privacy.

Supporting Roles: Authorizing Official or Authorizing Official Designated Representative; Senior Accountable Official for Risk Management or Risk Executive (Function); Senior Agency Information Security Officer.

Discussion: The roles and responsibilities of key participants in risk management processes are described in Appendix D. The roles and responsibilities may include personnel that are internal or external to the organization, as appropriate. Since organizations have different missions, functions, and organizational structures, there may be differences in naming conventions for risk management roles and how specific responsibilities are allocated among organizational personnel (e.g., multiple individuals filling a single role or one individual filling multiple roles). In either situation, the basic risk management functions remain the same. Organizations ensure that there are no conflicts of interest when assigning the same individual to multiple risk management roles. For example, authorizing officials cannot occupy the role of system owner or common control provider for systems or common controls they are authorizing. In addition, combining multiple roles for security and privacy requires care because the two disciplines may require different expertise, and in some circumstances, the priorities may be competing. Some roles may be allocated to a group or an office rather than to an individual, for example, control assessor, risk executive (function), or system administrator.

References: [SP 800-160 v1] (Human Resource Management Process); [SP 800-181]; [NIST CSF] (Core [Identify Function]).

Figure 1.2 Task Example

- o Task Number & Task Name: This section defines the nomenclature number and illustrative name for the task.
- o Potential Inputs and Expected Outputs: The potential input section defines the references, documents and resources that may be used to complete the task. The expected outputs section defines the deliverables that are produced when the task is successfully completed.
- o Primary & Supporting Roles: The primary roles section defines those roles that are held responsible for completing the task. Supporting roles are those roles or individuals that assist in completing the task
- o Discussion: this section provides information on how to successfully complete the task.
- o References: The references section provides the reader with sources that can be used to better understand the task.

2. DESCRIBE RISK MANAGEMENT

Describe Risk Management

The Basic Risk Formula

Risk can be determined based on its most simple calculation;

$$Threat + Vulnerability = Risk$$

In this basic form we can evaluate each component and determine if a risk actually exists. If we have a threat but no vulnerability, then no risk can exist. The opposite is true as well; if there is no threat but a vulnerability exists there is no risk. While this may seem hard to comprehend initially an illustrative example may help. Assume that a home has an open window, this is a vulnerability but by itself there I no real risk. However, add a threat, like a thief now we have the risk of theft. There could be multiple threats resulting in multiple risks, for example an environmental threat, like rain, could cause the risk of water damage using the same vulnerability, the open window. The threat, the thief, could also exploit multiple vulnerabilities, for example an unlocked or open door could be another vulnerability that could be exploited by the thief resulting in a risk.

More advanced risk calculations take in a number of additional factors or variables. Some of the basic additions include environment, and assets. The risk model's environment may drive up the risk level, for example an open window in a high crime neighborhood may have a higher risk score than an open window in a low crime neighborhood. The asset or assets in a home can also impact the risk score as high value assets provide more incentive for the thief to exploit the vulnerability.

While this example focused on risk in a physical environment, the same process is used to determine risk in a technical environment.

Understand security controls

Before understanding risk management, it is important to understand security controls. Security controls are those protections that are put in place to drive down the level of risk. These controls are often called safeguards, or protections. Most people use security controls in their daily lives without thinking about it. For example, there may be a risk that a car is stolen, to counter this risk the owner may put a number of security controls in place including parking in a safe location, locking the car and turning on the cars alarm. These three security controls drive down the risk of the car being taken.

Implementing controls effectively is done by balancing the risk with the cost of the controls. For example, the same car owner may implement the security control of hiring armed guards to protect the car. In most cases this would be excessive and could even be more expensive than the cars value. This is the evaluation made when making risk-based decisions.

Distinguish between risk management and compliance requirements

When developing an organization or system level risk and security program it is important to differentiate between risk management and compliance requirements. These items are two important parts of an organization's overall security program as they have the base intention of improving overall security and reducing exposure to risks.

For an organization to be compliant they will meet all requirements prescribed by law, regulation, policy, and guidance. It is possible for an organization to be compliant law, policy, and regulations and not be secure. Compliance is based on security principles, but an organization can circumvent security and still maintain compliance. An example of this is if there is a compliance requirement to implement a firewall on the organization's perimeter, and that firewall is put in place without any protective rules the organization would be technically complaint, but the organization would be no more secure than not having the firewall at all. In this case, the intent of the compliance rule was missed.

Risk management, on the other hand, looks at the threats and risks to an organization and builds a security program to meet or counter these threats and risks. In the case of risk management metered responses are implemented for known risks and vulnerabilities that may impact the enterprise of the information system in question. This approach evaluates the risks, vulnerabilities, and threats to an organization and its missions and functions, countering these with controls and countermeasures equal to the threat posed to the organization. Risk management is a full discipline to itself and several frameworks exist to assist people in the implementation of risk management, the NIST Risk Management Framework is one of the most widely used processes, or frameworks, for managing organizational and system risk.

Organizations use their risk appetite and tolerance levels to make risk-based determinations on the security controls, processes and procedures that will be implemented. At times this can contradict compliance requirements, for example a specific control may be required by compliance but organizations implementing a risk-based approach may determine that the control required does not reduce risk and decide not to implement the control. Many times, compliance-based requirements may result in a monetary risk that must be considered in the risk determination. Organizations may determine not to implement a control after reviewing the risk reduction provided by the control, the compliance penalty of not implementing the control, and the cost of implementing the control. This is the real differentiator between a risk based and a compliance-based approach to implementing a security program. Organizations must factor both compliance and risk when developing a security program, but by using a risk-based approach an organization can gain the best return on security investment (ROSI) and develop a balanced security program

EXERCISE 2-1

Risk management and compliance are two distinct, but interrelated concepts, in your words define the differences and similarities between risk management and compliance.

_____

_____

_____

_____

Identify and maintain information systems inventory

One on the most important components required to develop a comprehensive enterprise security program is determining what hardware and software components the organization is maintaining. It would be nearly impossible for an organization to secure its information and information systems without knowing exactly what it has. For this reason, an enterprise hardware and software inventory are critical.

A listing of hardware components should include the manufacturer, make, model, serial number(s), Operating System, Firmware settings, and responsible person or custodians contact information. If possible, the components IP address, MAC address, location, purchase date and service information should also be captured. This information is critical in identifying components that would be exposed to vulnerabilities as they are discovered and published. It is also important to identify older and components that are no longer supported that need to be replaced.

Software listings are also critical. While this can be exhaustive the organization should develop and maintain a listing of every software title in use in the organization. This listing should include manufacturer, software name, version, an indicator of type (i.e. operating system, database, etc.), purchase date, license, and assurance/maintenance information. If possible, the database should also contain who purchased the software, the custodian, update status and if the title is still in use.

The hardware and software databases can be individual or combined and can even be combined into the organization's configuration management system. Additions to the hardware and software listings should be processed through the organizations change control or configuration management board and documentation maintained as with any other change. The approved product listing that results from this inventory should be made available to the widest audience needed to perform the organization's mission but not to the entire enterprise as this information could be useful to advisories in their information gathering. System developers and maintainers should be included in those that have access, however, the full listing of who this list is distributed should be made as a risk-based decision by the organization.

It is also important to document any hardware and software that should never be allowed to be implemented or installed. This provides a listing of components that do not comply with the organization's risk profile, allowed processes, protocols, or services or introduce unwarranted risks or vulnerabilities to the organization.

It is critical to an organization to know the components of its network and systems. This helps in determining the exposure to evolving threats and the level of effort that will be required to correct evolving threats. Knowing what you have is also important in identifying rogue devices on the network, or software that has been installed without approval.
The importance of the hardware and software inventory is amplified by its importance in the general security community. The Center for Internet Security Critical Security Controls (CIS CSC), and SysAdmin, Audit, Network, and Security (SANS) publish a listing of the 20 most critical controls, in order of importance. The number 1 and 2 controls are, Inventory of authorized and unauthorized hardware, and Inventory of authorized and unauthorized software. This is illustrated in the Critical Security Controls poster at https://www.sans.org/media/critical-security-controls/critical-controls-poster-2016.pdf.

EXERCISE 2-2

Hardware and software inventories are critical to developing and maintaining a secure environment. What are critical items of information that should be captured and documented in these inventories?

_____

_____

_____

_____

Importance of securing information

Information is critical to the successful completion of the organization's core missions or functions. For an organization to be successful in fulfilling its mission securely it is important that it first know what types of information is maintained by the enterprise. This can be done by developing a database of information types that are processed by the organization's information systems. This may take time to initially develop but once developed new information types and systems processing specific information types can be updated as systems are registered in step 1 of the RMF.

Maintaining this information securely not only impacts the organization but also mission and function partners and individuals may be impacted if this information is not protected. An organization may share the responsibility for protecting information that is used by other organizations to accomplish the functions they are charged with, at times this information is so critical that the mission of that organization could be impacted if the information is unprotected and disclosed. Individuals have the right to have information about them protected by the organizations that gather, store and use this type of information, in this case, there can be harsh penalties for not protecting this information. In either case, failure protection of information may result in the organization or partner organizations not being able to accomplish their missions, personal information being exposed to those without authorization and sensitive information being disclosed to the organization's adversaries.

Not all information should be protected at the same level. For these reasons enterprise risk management program should determine the appropriate level of protection for each of the information types, the organization is responsible for. Information is the new lifeblood of organizations and needs to be protected in a way that is commensurate with the damage that could result from its unauthorized disclosure.

NOTES:

3 DISTINGUISH RMF STEPS

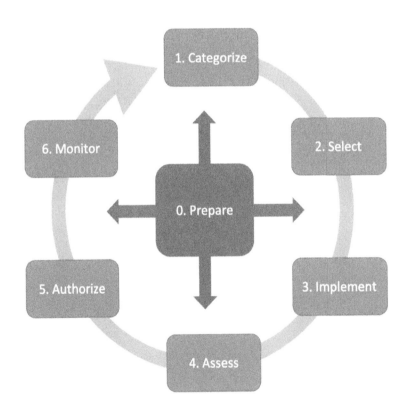

The risk management framework RMF is a cyclical process where each step builds on the previous step, however throughout the process the system being processed can revisit any previous step if needed as changes or new information are discovered. This six-step process should be initiated as early as possible in the systems development.

Understand the RMF

The RMF is a cyclic seven step process that manages an information system from its initial inception through decommissioning and removal. The frameworks steps are introduced in this chapter, while later chapters will detail each step and task fully.

The RMF supports organization wide risk management, where the approval of an individual system is evaluated not only on risks to the individual system but also risks that would be introduced to the organization if the system were to gain approval to operate and be allowed to be promoted into the production environment.

In this case organization-wide risk management focuses on a three-tiered operational model as illustrated in figure 3-1

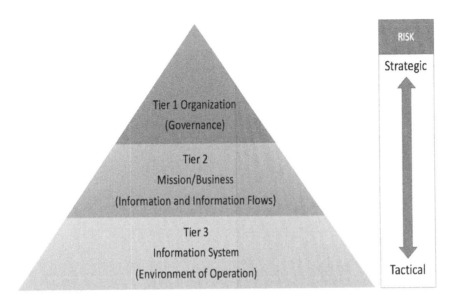

Figure 3-1 Organizational Risk Management

In this model, organizational leadership at tier 1 provides policy, direction, funding, and strategic guidance for the organization. Tier 2 consists of those organizations and systems in organizational mission and business functions, many of the organizations common controls will be developed and employed at tier 2. The RMF is most widely deployed at tier 3, the tier where systems are mostly developed. Evaluating this model strategic decisions are made at tier 1 and more tactical decisions are made at tier 3.

RMF steps

When initially introduced the RMF was composed of six distinct steps that contained the tasks required to implement security controls using an organizationally scoped risk management view

Prepare step

The prepare is sometimes referred to as step 0 and it is composed of two parts that provide RMF process initiation. Seven tasks occur at the organization level and eleven tasks occur at the system level that ensure the organization and system are ready to successfully conduct the remaining steps and tasks in the framework. These tasks ensure the essential activities at the organization, mission and business process, and information system level are carried out prior to information systems beginning step one of the RMF.

Categorize step

This step is the foundation for the RMF and sets the security baseline controls for the system. This is where the system is registered, the categorization is set and the system security plan (SSP) is started. There are three tasks in this step; categorize the information system, describe the information system and register the information system.

Select step

The select step builds upon the categorize by refining the controls selected for the system and determining how these controls will be monitored over the lifetime of the system. There are three tasks in this step; identifying common controls, selecting system security controls, and developing a control monitoring strategy.

Implement Step

The implement leads to identifying the controls required for the system and determining if these need to be adjusted by adding or removing controls. IN this step determination of enterprise or common controls that can be inherited by the system, finally the SSP is approved.

Assess Step

The assess step focuses on developing a security assessment plan that will determine the effectiveness of the implemented controls. Once the system is assessed using this plan, security assessment report is developed, and remediation steps occur.

Authorize Step

In the authorize step risk assessments and determinations are made. These tasks help the Authorizing Official (AO) determine if the system will be issues an authorization to operate (ATO) or a denial of authorization to operate (DATO).

Monitor Step

In the monitor step, the system enters the continuous monitoring stage where the system is monitored for changes and evaluated for new security risks that could impact the organizations risk level or change the system authorization decision. This step also details how to decommission a system.

EXERCISE 3-1

Using your understanding of the RMF answer the following questions.

Strategic decisions about the organizations risk management occur at which tier?

_____

What step does the independent assessment of security controls occur?

_____

How many steps are there in the RMF?

_____

What is the last step in the RMF?

_____

NOTES:

4. THE PREPARE STEP – ORGANIZATIONAL TASKS

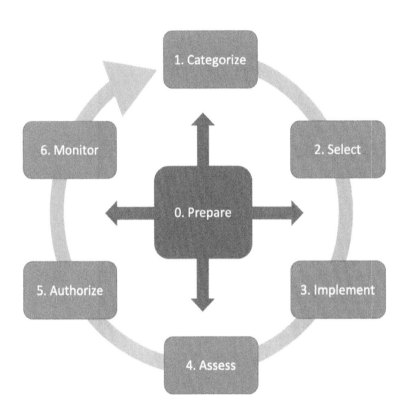

Introduction:

There are several roles, sometimes referred to as positions, defined in the RMF that help ensure successful implementation. For each task one or more role is assigned primary responsibility as well as roles identified as supporting. While the primary role responsible is accountable for the task, unless specifically prohibited, tasks can be delegated. For example, tasks assigned to the information system owner (ISO) are often delegated to the information system security officer (ISSO) however, the task, "making the authorization decision" cannot be delegated. To be effective roles should be assigned in writing.

This section defined each role as well as identifies the primary responsibility and supporting role for each of the tasks in the RMF.

Responsibilities	
Primary Responsibility	Supporting Roles
- Head of Agency - Chief Information Officer - Senior Agency Official for Privacy.	- Authorizing Official or - Authorizing Official Designated Representative - Senior Accountable Official for Risk Management or Risk Executive (Function) - Senior Agency Information Security Officer

SDLC Alignment	
New Systems	Legacy Systems

CSF Alignment	
Profile	CSF Task
	- ID.AM-6 - ID.GV-2

Task Flow	
Inputs	Outputs
- Organizational security and privacy policies and procedures - Organizational charts.	- Documented Risk Management Framework role assignments.

Defining the roles that will be needed to complete each of the tasks defined in the RMF is critical to the successful implementation of this framework at an organization. Roles should be officially assigned and documented using whatever process is normally used in assigning roles. Based on the roles developed by the organizations the tasks that are defined in the RMF can be easily assigned to these roles. While NIST provides a complete listing of recommended roles that can be used in an organization, it is possible that existing organizational structures, job roles, or assignments may fulfil the requirements needed to successfully complete the tasks defined in the process.

It is important to note that using the suggested RMF roles is the easiest way of implementing the framework. Organizations that would like to use their own roles must be detailed in these roles to ensure they meet the requirements for the tasks assigned to each role. For example, some roles can only be filled by government employees, or organizational employees when the RMF is being implemented in non-government organizations. In other cases some tasks cannot be assigned to the same role. While using organizationally specific roles is not prohibited the complexity of ensuring roles meet the requirements defined by NIST, only in specific instance should organizations delineate from the roles that follow.

NIST provides the following instruction on this task

The following roles have been defined by NIST, in SP 800-37 revision 2, to assist an organization in completing the tasks defined in the RMF.

RMF ROLES

Head of Agency (Chief Executive Officer)

The **head of agency** is responsible and accountable for providing information security protections commensurate with the risk to organizational operations and assets, individuals, other organizations, and the Nation—that is, risk resulting from unauthorized access, use, disclosure, disruption, modification, or destruction of information collected or maintained by or on behalf of the agency; and the information systems used or operated by an agency or by a contractor of an agency or other organization on behalf of an agency. The head of agency is also the senior official in an organization with the responsibility for ensuring that privacy interests are protected and that PII is managed responsibly within the organization. The heads of agencies ensure that:
   o   Information security and privacy management processes are integrated with strategic and operational planning processes;
   o   Senior officials within the organization provide information security for the information and systems supporting the operations and assets under their control;
   o   Senior agency officials for privacy are designated who are responsible and accountable for ensuring compliance with applicable privacy requirements, managing privacy risk, and the organization's privacy program; and

- o The organization has adequately trained personnel to assist in complying with security and privacy requirements in legislation, executive orders, policies, directives, instructions, standards, and guidelines.

The head of agency establishes the organizational commitment and the actions required to effectively manage security and privacy risk and protect the missions and business functions being carried out by the organization. The head of agency establishes security and privacy accountability and provides active support and oversight of monitoring and improvement for the security and privacy programs. Senior leadership commitment to security and privacy establishes a level of due diligence within the organization that promotes a climate for mission and business success.

Risk Executive (Function)

The **risk executive (function)** is an individual or group within an organization that provides a comprehensive, organization-wide approach to risk management. The risk executive (function) is led by the senior accountable official for risk management and serves as the common risk management resource for senior leaders, executives, and managers, mission/business owners, chief information officers, senior agency information security officers, senior agency officials for privacy, system owners, common control providers, enterprise architects, security architects, systems security or privacy engineers, system security or privacy officers, and any other stakeholders having a vested interest in the mission/business success of organizations. The risk executive (function) is an inherent U.S. Government function and is assigned to government personnel only.

The risk executive (function) ensures that risk considerations for systems (including authorization decisions for those systems and the common controls inherited by those systems), are viewed from an organization-wide perspective regarding the organization's strategic goals and objectives in carrying out its core missions and business functions. The risk executive (function) ensures that managing risk is consistent throughout the organization, reflects organizational risk tolerance, and is considered along with other types of risk to ensure mission/business success. The risk executive (function) coordinates with senior leaders and executives to:
- o Establish risk management roles and responsibilities;
- o Develop and implement an organization-wide risk management strategy that provides a strategic view of security risks for the organization and that guides and informs organizational risk decisions (including how risk is framed, assessed, responded to, and monitored over time);
- o Provide a comprehensive, organization-wide, holistic approach for addressing risk—an approach that provides a greater understanding of the integrated operations of the organization;
- o Manage threat, vulnerability, and security and privacy risk (including supply chain risk) information for organizational systems and the environments in which the systems operate;

o Establish organization-wide forums to consider all types and sources of risk (including aggregated risk);
o Identify the organizational risk posture based on the aggregated risk from the operation and use of systems and the respective environments of operation for which the organization is responsible;
o Provide oversight for the risk management activities carried out by organizations to help ensure consistent and effective risk-based decisions;
o Develop a broad-based understanding of risk regarding the strategic view of organizations and their integrated operations;
o Establish effective vehicles and serve as a focal point for communicating and sharing risk information among key stakeholders (e.g., authorizing officials and other senior leaders) internally and externally to organizations;
o Specify the degree of autonomy for subordinate organizations permitted by parent organizations regarding framing, assessing, responding to, and monitoring risk;
o Promote cooperation and collaboration among authorizing officials to include authorization actions requiring shared responsibility (e.g., joint authorizations);
o Provide an organization-wide forum to consider all sources of risk (including aggregated risk) to organizational operations and assets, individuals, other organizations, and the Nation;
o Ensure that authorization decisions consider all factors necessary for mission and business success; and
o Ensure shared responsibility for supporting organizational missions and business functions using external providers receives the needed visibility and is elevated to appropriate decision-making authorities.

The risk executive (function) presumes neither a specific organizational structure nor formal responsibility assigned to any one individual or group within the organization. Heads of agencies or organizations may choose to retain the risk executive (function) or to delegate the function. The risk executive (function) requires a mix of skills, expertise, and perspectives to understand the strategic goals and objectives of organizations, organizational missions/business functions, technical possibilities and constraints, and key mandates and guidance that shape organizational operations. To provide this needed mixture, the risk executive (function) can be filled by a single individual or office (supported by an expert staff) or by a designated group (e.g., a risk board, executive steering committee, executive leadership council). The risk executive (function) fits into the organizational governance structure in such a way as to facilitate efficiency and effectiveness.

Chief Information Officer

The *chief information officer* is an organizational official responsible for designating a senior agency information security officer; developing and maintaining security policies, procedures, and control techniques to address security requirements; overseeing personnel with significant responsibilities for security and ensuring that the personnel are adequately trained; assisting senior organizational officials concerning their security responsibilities; and reporting to the head of the agency on the effectiveness of the organization's security program, including progress of remedial actions. The chief information officer, with the support of the senior accountable official for risk management, the risk executive (function), and the senior agency information security officer, works closely with authorizing officials and their designated representatives to help ensure that:

- o An organization-wide security program is effectively implemented resulting in adequate security for all organizational systems and environments of operation;
- o Security and privacy (including supply chain) risk management considerations are integrated into programming/planning/budgeting cycles, enterprise architectures, the SDLC, and acquisitions;
- o Organizational systems and common controls are covered by approved system security plans and possess current authorizations;
- o Security activities required across the organization are accomplished in an efficient, cost-effective, and timely manner; and
- o There is centralized reporting of security activities.

The chief information officer and authorizing officials determine the allocation of resources dedicated to the protection of systems supporting the organization's missions and business functions based on organizational priorities. For information systems that process personally identifiable information, the chief information officer and authorizing officials coordinate any determination about the allocation of resources dedicated to the protection of those systems with the senior agency official for privacy. For selected systems, the chief information officer may be designated as an authorizing official or a co-authorizing official with other senior organizational officials. The role of chief information officer is an inherent U.S. Government function and is assigned to government personnel only.

Information Owner/Steward

The information owner or steward is an organizational official with statutory, management, or operational authority for specified information and the responsibility for establishing the policies and procedures governing its generation, collection, processing, dissemination, and disposal. In information-sharing environments, the information owner/steward is responsible for establishing the rules for appropriate use and protection of the information and retains that responsibility even when the information is shared with or provided to other organizations. The owner/steward of the information processed, stored, or transmitted by a system may or may not be the same individual as the system owner. An individual system may contain information from multiple information owners/stewards. Information owners/stewards provide input to system owners regarding the security and privacy requirements and controls for the systems where the information is processed, stored, or transmitted.

Senior Information Security Officer

The senior agency information security officer is an organizational official responsible for carrying out the chief information officer security responsibilities under FISMA, and serving as the primary liaison for the chief information officer to the organization's authorizing officials, system owners, common control providers, and system security officers. The senior agency information security officer is also responsible for coordinating with the senior agency official for privacy to ensure coordination between privacy and information security programs. The senior agency information security officer possesses the professional qualifications, including training and experience, required to administer security program functions; maintains security duties as a primary responsibility; and heads an office with the specific mission and resources to assist the organization in achieving trustworthy, secure information and systems in accordance with the requirements in FISMA. The senior agency information security officer may serve as authorizing official designated representative or as a security control assessor. The role of senior agency information security officer is an inherent U.S. Government function and is therefore assigned to government personnel only. Organizations may also refer to the senior agency information security officer as the senior information security officer or chief information security officer.

Authorizing Official

The authorizing official is a senior official or executive with the authority to formally assume responsibility and accountability for operating a system; providing common controls inherited by organizational systems; or using a system, service, or application from an external provider. The authorizing official is the only organizational official who can accept the security and privacy risk to organizational operations, organizational assets, and individuals. Authorizing officials typically have budgetary oversight for the system or are responsible for the mission and/or business operations supported by the system. Accordingly, authorizing officials are in management positions with a level of authority commensurate with understanding and accepting such security and privacy risks. Authorizing officials approve plans, memorandums of agreement or understanding, plans of action and milestones, and determine whether significant changes in the information systems or environments of operation require reauthorization.

Authorizing officials coordinate their activities with common control providers, system owners, chief information officers, senior agency information security officers, senior agency officials for privacy, system security and privacy officers, control assessors, senior accountable officials for risk management/risk executive (function), and other interested parties during the authorization process. With the increasing complexity of the mission/business processes in an organization, partnership arrangements, and the use of shared services, it is possible that a system may involve co-authorizing officials. If so, agreements are established between the co-authorizing officials and documented in the security and privacy plans. Authorizing officials are responsible and accountable for ensuring that authorization activities and functions that are delegated to authorizing official designated representatives are carried out as specified. For federal agencies, the role of authorizing official is an inherent U.S. Government function and is assigned to government personnel only.

Authorizing Official Designated Representative

The authorizing official designated representative is an organizational official designated by the authorizing official who is empowered to act on behalf of the authorizing official to coordinate and conduct the day-to-day activities associated with managing risk to information systems and organizations. This includes carrying out many of the activities related to the execution of the RMF. The only activity that cannot be delegated by the authorizing official to the designated representative is the authorization decision and signing of the associated authorization decision document (i.e., the acceptance of risk).

Common control provider

The common control provider is an individual, group, or organization that is responsible for the implementation, assessment, and monitoring of common controls (i.e., controls inherited by organizational systems). Common control providers also are responsible for ensuring the documentation of organization-defined common controls in security and privacy plans (or equivalent documents prescribed by the organization); ensuring that required assessments of the common controls are conducted by qualified assessors with an appropriate level of independence; documenting assessment findings in control assessment reports; and producing plans of action and milestones for controls having deficiencies. Security and privacy plans, security and privacy assessment reports, and plans of action and milestones for common controls (or summary of such information) are made available to the system owners of systems inheriting common controls after the information is reviewed and approved by the authorizing officials accountable for those common controls.

The senior agency official for privacy is responsible for designating which privacy controls may be treated as common controls. Privacy controls that are designated as common controls are documented in the organization's privacy program plan. The senior agency official for privacy has oversight responsibility for common controls in place or planned for meeting applicable privacy requirements and managing privacy risks and is responsible for assessing those controls. At the discretion of the organization, privacy controls that are designated as common controls may be assessed by an independent assessor. In all cases, however, the senior agency official for privacy retains responsibility and accountability for the organization's privacy program, including any privacy functions performed by independent assessors. Privacy plans and privacy control assessment reports are made available to systems owners whose systems inherit privacy controls that are designated as common controls.

Information system owner

The *information system owner* is an organizational official responsible for the procurement, development, integration, modification, operation, maintenance, and disposal of an information system. The information system owner is responsible for addressing the operational interests of the user community (i.e., users who require access to the information system to satisfy mission, business, or operational requirements) and for ensuring compliance with information security requirements. In coordination with the information system security officer, the information system owner is responsible for the development and maintenance of the security plan and ensures that the system is deployed and operated in accordance with the agreed-upon security controls. In coordination with the information owner/steward, the information system owner is also responsible for deciding who has access to the system (and with what types of privileges or access rights) and ensures that system users and support personnel receive the requisite security training (e.g., instruction in rules of behavior). Based on guidance from the authorizing official, the information system owner informs appropriate organizational officials of the need to conduct the security authorization, ensures that the necessary resources are available for the effort, and provides the required information system access, information, and documentation to the security control assessor. The information system owner receives the security assessment results from the security control assessor. After taking appropriate steps to reduce or eliminate vulnerabilities, the information system owner assembles the authorization package and submits the package to the authorizing official or the authorizing official designated representative for adjudication.

SYSTEM SECURITY OR PRIVACY OFFICER

The system security or privacy officer124 is an individual responsible for ensuring that the security and privacy posture is maintained for an organizational system and works in close collaboration with the system owner. The system security or privacy officer also serves as a principal advisor on all matters, technical and otherwise, involving the controls for the system. The system security or privacy officer has the knowledge and expertise to manage the security or privacy aspects of an organizational system and, in many organizations, is assigned responsibility for the day-to-day system security or privacy operations. This responsibility may also include, but is not limited to, physical and environmental protection; personnel security; incident handling; and security and privacy training and awareness.

The system security or privacy officer may be called on to assist in the development of the system-level security and privacy policies and procedures and to ensure compliance with those policies and procedures. In close coordination with the system owner, the system security or privacy officer often plays an active role in the monitoring of a system and its environment of operation to include developing and updating security and privacy plans, managing and controlling changes to the system, and assessing the security or privacy impact of those changes.

When the system security officer and system privacy officer are separate roles, the system security officer is generally responsible for aspects of the system that protect information and information systems from unauthorized system activity or behavior to provide confidentiality, integrity, and availability. The system privacy officer is responsible for aspects of the system that ensure compliance with privacy requirements and manage the privacy risks to individuals associated with the processing of PII. The responsibilities of system security officers and system privacy officers overlap regarding aspects of the system that protect the security of PII.

Security or Privacy Architect

The security or privacy architect is an individual, group, or organization responsible for ensuring that stakeholder protection needs and the corresponding system requirements necessary to protect organizational missions and business functions and individuals' privacy are adequately addressed in the enterprise architecture including reference models, segment architectures, and solution architectures (systems supporting mission and business processes). The security or privacy architect serves as the primary liaison between the enterprise architect and the systems security or privacy engineer and coordinates with system owners, common control providers, and system security or privacy officers on the allocation of controls. Security or privacy architects, in coordination with system security or privacy officers, advise authorizing officials, chief information officers, senior accountable officials for risk management or risk executive (function), senior agency information security officers, and senior agency officials for privacy on a range of security and privacy issues. Examples include establishing authorization boundaries; establishing security or privacy alerts; assessing the severity of deficiencies in the system or controls; developing plans of action and milestones; creating risk mitigation approaches; and potential adverse effects of identified vulnerabilities or privacy risks.

When the security architect and privacy architect are separate roles, the security architect is generally responsible for aspects of the enterprise architecture that protect information and information systems from unauthorized system activity or behavior to provide confidentiality, integrity, and availability. The privacy architect is responsible for aspects of the enterprise architecture that ensure compliance with privacy requirements and manage the privacy risks to individuals associated with the processing of PII. Security and privacy architect responsibilities overlap regarding aspects of the enterprise architecture that protect the security of PII.

System Security or Privacy Engineer

The systems security or privacy engineer is an individual, group, or organization responsible for conducting systems security or privacy engineering activities as part of the SDLC. Systems security and privacy engineering is a process that captures and refines security and privacy requirements for systems and ensures that the requirements are effectively integrated into systems and system elements through security or privacy architecting, design, development, and configuration. Systems security or privacy engineers are part of the development team—designing and developing organizational systems or upgrading existing systems along with ensuring continuous monitoring requirements are addressed at the system level. Systems security or privacy engineers employ best practices when implementing controls including software engineering methodologies; system and security or privacy engineering principles; secure or privacy-enhancing design, secure or privacy-enhancing architecture, and secure or privacy-enhancing coding techniques. Systems security or privacy engineers coordinate security and privacy activities with senior agency information security officers, senior agency officials for privacy, security and privacy architects, system owners, common control providers, and system security or privacy officers.

When the systems security engineer and privacy engineer are separate roles, the systems security engineer is generally responsible for those activities associated with protecting information and information systems from unauthorized system activity or behavior to provide confidentiality, integrity, and availability. The privacy engineer is responsible for those activities associated with ensuring compliance with privacy requirements and managing the privacy risks to individuals associated with the processing of PII. The responsibilities of systems security engineers and privacy engineers overlap regarding activities associated with protecting the security of PII.

Control Assessor

The control assessor is an individual, group, or organization responsible for conducting a comprehensive assessment of implemented controls and control enhancements to determine the effectiveness of the controls (i.e., the extent to which the controls are implemented correctly, operating as intended, and producing the desired outcome with respect to meeting the security and privacy requirements for the system and the organization). For systems, implemented system-specific controls and system-implemented parts of hybrid controls are assessed. For common controls, implemented common controls and common control-implemented parts of hybrid controls are assessed. The system owner and common control provider rely on the security and privacy expertise and judgment of the assessor to assess the implemented controls using the assessment procedures specified in the security and privacy assessment plans. Multiple control assessors who are differentiated by their expertise in specific control requirements or technologies may be required to conduct the assessment effectively. Prior to initiating the control assessment, assessors review the security and privacy plans to facilitate development of the assessment plans. Control assessors provide an assessment of the severity of the deficiencies discovered in the system, environment of operation, and common controls and can recommend corrective actions to address the identified vulnerabilities. For system-level control assessments, control assessors do not assess inherited controls, and only assess the system-implemented portions of hybrid controls. Control assessors prepare security and privacy assessment reports containing the results and findings from the assessment.

The required level of assessor independence is determined by the authorizing official based on laws, executive orders, directives, regulations, policies, standards, or guidelines. When a control assessment is conducted in support of an authorization decision or ongoing authorization, the authorizing official makes an explicit determination of the degree of independence required. Assessor independence is a factor in preserving an impartial and unbiased assessment process; determining the credibility of the assessment results; and ensuring that the authorizing official receives objective information to make an informed, risk-based authorization decision.

The senior agency official for privacy is responsible for assessing privacy controls and for providing privacy information to the authorizing official. At the discretion of the organization, privacy controls may be assessed by an independent assessor. However, in all cases, the senior agency official for privacy retains responsibility and accountability for the privacy program of the organization, including any privacy functions performed by the independent assessors.

Chief Acquisition Officer

The chief acquisition officer is an organizational official designated by the head of an agency to advise and assist the head of agency and other agency officials to ensure that the mission of the agency is achieved through the management of the agency's acquisition activities. The chief acquisition officer monitors the performance of acquisition activities and programs; establishes clear lines of authority, accountability, and responsibility for acquisition decision making within the agency; manages the direction and implementation of acquisition policy for the agency; and establishes policies, procedures, and practices that promote full and open competition from responsible sources to fulfill best value requirements considering the nature of the property or service procured. The Chief Acquisition Officer coordinates with mission or business owners, authorizing officials, senior accountable official for risk management, system owners, common control providers, senior agency information security officer, senior agency official for privacy, and risk executive (function) to ensure that security and privacy requirements are defined in organizational procurements and acquisitions.

Enterprise Architect

The enterprise architect is an individual or group responsible for working with the leadership and subject matter experts in an organization to build a holistic view of the organization's missions and business functions, mission/business processes, information, and information technology assets. With respect to information security and privacy, enterprise architects:

- o Implement an enterprise architecture strategy that facilitates effective security and privacy solutions;
- o Coordinate with security and privacy architects to determine the optimal placement of systems/system elements within the enterprise architecture and to address security and privacy issues between systems and the enterprise architecture;
- o Assist in reducing complexity within the IT infrastructure to facilitate security;
- o Assist with determining appropriate control implementations and initial configuration baselines as they relate to the enterprise architecture;
- o Collaborate with system owners and authorizing officials to facilitate authorization boundary determinations and allocation of controls to system elements;
- o Serve as part of the Risk Executive (function); and
- o Assist with integration of the organizational risk management strategy and system-level security and privacy requirements into program, planning, and budgeting activities, the SDLC, acquisition processes, security and privacy (including supply chain) risk management, and systems engineering processes.

Mission or Business Owner

The mission or business owner is the senior official or executive within an organization with specific mission or line of business responsibilities and that has a security or privacy interest in the organizational systems supporting those missions or lines of business. Mission or business owners are key stakeholders that have a significant role in establishing organizational mission and business processes and the protection needs and security and privacy requirements that ensure the successful conduct of the organization's missions and business operations. Mission and business owners provide essential inputs to the risk management strategy, play an active part in the SDLC, and may also serve in the role of authorizing official.

Senior Accountable Official for Risk Management

The *senior accountable official for risk management* is the individual that leads and manages the risk executive (function) in an organization and is responsible for aligning information security and privacy risk management processes with strategic, operational, and budgetary planning processes. The senior accountable official for risk management is the head of the agency or an individual designated by the head of the agency. The senior accountable official for risk management determines the organizational structure and responsibilities of the risk executive (function), and in coordination with the head of the agency, may retain the risk executive (function) or delegate the function to another organizational official or group. The senior accountable official for risk management is an inherent U.S. Government function and is assigned to government personnel only.

Senior Agency Official for Privacy

The senior agency official for privacy is the senior official or executive with agency-wide responsibility and accountability for ensuring compliance with applicable privacy requirements and managing privacy risk. Among other things, the senior agency official for privacy is responsible for:

- o Coordinating with the senior agency information security officer to ensure coordination of privacy and information security activities;
- o Reviewing and approving the categorization of information systems that create, collect, use, process, store, maintain, disseminate, disclose, or dispose of personally identifiable information;
- o Designating which privacy controls will be treated as program management, common, system-specific, and hybrid privacy controls;
- o Identifying assessment methodologies and metrics to determine whether privacy controls are implemented correctly, operating as intended, and sufficient to ensure compliance with applicable privacy requirements and manage privacy risks;

- o Reviewing and approving privacy plans for information systems prior to authorization, reauthorization, or ongoing authorization;
- o Reviewing authorization packages for information systems that create, collect, use, process, store, maintain, disseminate, disclose, or dispose of personally identifiable information to ensure compliance with privacy requirements and manage privacy risks;
- o Conducting and documenting the results of privacy control assessments to verify the continued effectiveness of all privacy controls selected and implemented at the agency; and
- o Establishing and maintaining a privacy continuous monitoring program to maintain ongoing awareness of privacy risks and assess privacy controls at a frequency sufficient to ensure compliance with privacy requirements and manage privacy risks.

The role of senior agency official for privacy is an inherent U.S. Government function and is therefore assigned to government personnel only.

System Administrator

The system administrator is an individual, group, or organization responsible for setting up and maintaining a system or specific system elements. System administrator responsibilities include, for example, installing, configuring, and updating hardware and software; establishing and managing user accounts; overseeing or conducting backup, recovery, and reconstitution activities; implementing controls; and adhering to and enforcing organizational security and privacy policies and procedures. The system administrator role includes other types of system administrators (e.g., database administrators, network administrators, web administrators, and application administrators).

System Owner

The system owner is an organizational official responsible for the procurement, development, integration, modification, operation, maintenance, and disposal of a system. The system owner is responsible for addressing the operational interests of the user community (i.e., users who require access to the system to satisfy mission, business, or operational requirements) and for ensuring compliance with security requirements. In coordination with the system security and privacy officers, the system owner is responsible for the development and maintenance of the security and privacy plans and ensures that the system is operated in accordance with the selected and implemented controls.

In coordination with the information owner/steward, the system owner decides who has access to the system (and with what types of privileges or access rights). The system owner ensures that system users and support personnel receive the requisite security and privacy training. Based on guidance from the authorizing official, the system owner informs organizational officials of the need to conduct the authorization, ensures that resources are available for the effort, and provides the required system access, information, and documentation to control assessors. The system owner receives the security and privacy assessment results from the control assessors. After taking appropriate steps to reduce or eliminate vulnerabilities or security and privacy risks, the system owner assembles the authorization package and submits the package to the authorizing official or the authorizing official designated representative for adjudication.

System User

The system user is an individual or (system) process acting on behalf of an individual that is authorized to access information and information systems to perform assigned duties. System user responsibilities include, but are not limited to, adhering to organizational policies that govern acceptable use of organizational systems; using the organization-provided information technology resources for defined purposes only; and reporting anomalous or suspicious system behavior.

System Security or Privacy Engineer

The systems security or privacy engineer is an individual, group, or organization responsible for conducting systems security or privacy engineering activities as part of the SDLC. Systems security and privacy engineering is a process that captures and refines security and privacy requirements for systems and ensures that the requirements are effectively integrated into systems and system elements through security or privacy architecting, design, development, and configuration. Systems security or privacy engineers are part of the development team— designing and developing organizational systems or upgrading existing systems along with ensuring continuous monitoring requirements are addressed at the system level. Systems security or privacy engineers employ best practices when implementing controls including software engineering methodologies; system and security or privacy engineering principles; secure or privacy-enhancing design, secure or privacy-enhancing architecture, and secure or privacy-enhancing coding techniques. Systems security or privacy engineers coordinate security and privacy activities with senior agency information security officers, senior agency officials for privacy, security and privacy architects, system owners, common control providers, and system security or privacy officers.

When the systems security engineer and privacy engineer are separate roles, the systems security engineer is generally responsible for those activities associated with protecting information and information systems from unauthorized system activity or behavior to provide confidentiality, integrity, and availability. The privacy engineer is responsible for those activities associated with ensuring compliance with privacy requirements and managing the privacy risks to individuals associated with the processing of PII. The responsibilities of systems security engineers and privacy engineers overlap regarding activities associated with protecting the security of PII.

RMF Tasks to Roles

Table 4-1 illustrates the primary responsibility and supporting roles for each task. In some cases, only one role is responsible for a task while in other many roles may share responsibility for a specific task. When a task is shared between multiple roles it is the organizations responsibility to determine the assignment of responsibility for that specific task. In most cases the responsibility for completing a task may be delegated by the role with primary responsibility, for example many tasks assigned to an information system owner may be delegated to the Information Systems Security Officer (ISSO). However, some tasks may not be delegated, and in these cases this restriction is defined in the task, for example making an authorization decision is a task that cannot be delegated.

RMF Task	Primary Responsibility	Supporting Roles
TASK P-1 Risk Management Roles Identify and assign individuals to specific roles associated with security and privacy risk management.	• Head of Agency • Chief Information Officer • Senior Agency Official for Privacy	• Authorizing Official or Authorizing Official Designated Representative • Senior Accountable Official for Risk Management or Risk Executive (Function) • Senior Agency Information Security Officer
TASK P-2 Risk Management Strategy Establish a risk management strategy for the organization that includes a determination of risk tolerance.	• Head of Agency	• Senior Accountable Official for Risk Management or Risk Executive (Function) • Chief Information Officer • Senior Agency Information Security Officer • Senior Agency Official for Privacy
TASK P-3 Risk Assessment— Organization	• Senior Accountable Official for Risk Management or Risk	• Chief Information Officer • Authorizing Official or Authorizing Official Designated

RMF Task	Primary Responsibility	Supporting Roles
Assess organization-wide security and privacy risk and update the risk assessment results on an ongoing basis.	Executive (Function) • Senior Agency Information Security Officer • Senior Agency Official for Privacy	Representative • Mission or Business Owner
TASK P-4 Organizationally-Tailored Control Baselines and Cybersecurity Framework Profiles (Optional) Establish, document, and publish organizationally-tailored control baselines and/or Cybersecurity Framework Profiles.	• Mission or Business Owner • Senior Accountable Official for Risk Management or Risk Executive (Function)	• Chief Information Officer • Authorizing Official or Authorizing Official Designated Representative • Senior Agency Information Security Officer • Senior Agency Official for Privacy
TASK P-5 Common Control Identification Identify, document, and publish organization-wide common controls that are available for inheritance by organizational systems.	• Senior Agency Information Security Officer • Senior Agency Official for Privacy	• Mission or Business Owner • Senior Accountable Official for Risk Management or Risk Executive (Function) • Chief Information Officer • Authorizing Official or Authorizing Official Designated Representative • Common Control Provider • System Owner
TASK P-6 Impact-Level Prioritization (Optional) Prioritize organizational systems with the same impact level.	• Senior Accountable Official for Risk Management or Risk Executive (Function)	• Senior Agency Information Security Officer • Senior Agency Official for Privacy • Mission or Business Owner • System Owner • Chief Information Officer • Authorizing Official or Authorizing Official Designated Representative
TASK P-7 Continuous Monitoring Strategy—Organization Develop and implement an organization-wide strategy for continuously monitoring control effectiveness.	Senior Accountable Official for Risk Management or Risk Executive (Function)	Chief Information Officer • Senior Agency Information Security Officer • Senior Agency Official for Privacy • Mission or Business Owner • System Owner • Authorizing Official or

RMF Task	Primary Responsibility	Supporting Roles
		Authorizing Official Designated Representative
TASK P-8 Mission or Business Focus Identify the missions, business functions, and mission/business processes that the system is intended to support.	• Mission or Business Owner	• Authorizing Official or Authorizing Official Designated Representative • System Owner • Information Owner or Steward • Chief Information Officer • Senior Agency Information Security Officer • Senior Agency Official for Privacy
TASK P-9 System Stakeholders Identify stakeholders who have an interest in the design, development, implementation, assessment, operation, maintenance, or disposal of the system.	• Mission or Business Owner • System Owner	• Chief Information Officer • Authorizing Official or Authorizing Official Designated Representative • Information Owner or Steward • Senior Agency Information Security Officer • Senior Agency Official for Privacy • Chief Acquisition Officer
TASK P-10 Asset Identification Identify assets that require protection.	• System Owner	• Authorizing Official or Authorizing Official Designated Representative • Mission or Business Owner • Information Owner or Steward • Senior Agency Information Security Officer • Senior Agency Official for Privacy • System Administrator
TASK P-11 Authorization Boundary Determine the authorization boundary of the system.	• Authorizing Official	• Chief Information Officer • Mission or Business Owner • System Owner • Senior Agency Information Security Officer • Senior Agency Official for Privacy • Enterprise Architect
TASK P-12 Information Types Identify the types of information to be	• System Owner • Information Owner or Steward	• System Security Officer • System Privacy Officer • Mission or Business Owner

RMF Task	Primary Responsibility	Supporting Roles
processed, stored, and transmitted by the system.		
TASK P-13 Information Life Cycle Identify and understand all stages of the information life cycle for each information type processed, stored, or transmitted by the system.	• Senior Agency Official for Privacy • System Owner • Information Owner or Steward	• Chief Information Officer • Mission or Business Owner • Security Architect • Privacy Architect • Enterprise Architect • Systems Security Engineer • Privacy Engineer
TASK P-14 Risk Assessment—System Conduct a system-level risk assessment and update the risk assessment results on an ongoing basis.	• System Owner • System Security Officer • System Privacy Officer	• Senior Accountable Official for Risk Management or Risk Executive (Function) • Authorizing Official or Authorizing Official Designated Representative • Mission or Business Owner • Information Owner or Steward • System Security Officer
TASK P-15 Requirements Definition Define the security and privacy requirements for the system and the environment of operation.	• Mission or Business Owner • System Owner • Information Owner or Steward • System Privacy Officer	• Authorizing Official or Authorizing Official Designated Representative • Senior Agency Information Security Officer • Senior Agency Official for Privacy • System Security Officer • Chief Acquisition Officer • Security Architect • Privacy Architect • Enterprise Architect
TASK P-16 Enterprise Architecture Determine the placement of the system within the enterprise architecture.	• Mission or Business Owner • Enterprise Architect • Security Architect • Privacy Architect	• Chief Information Officer • Authorizing Official or Authorizing Official Designated Representative • Senior Agency Information Security Officer • Senior Agency Official for Privacy • System Owner • Information Owner or Steward
TASK P-17 Requirements Allocation Allocate security and	• Security Architect • Privacy Architect • System Security Officer	• Chief Information Officer • Authorizing Official or Authorizing Official Designated

RMF Task	Primary Responsibility	Supporting Roles
privacy requirements to the system and to the environment of operation.	• System Privacy Officer	Representative • Mission or Business Owner • Senior Agency Information Security Officer • Senior Agency Official for Privacy • System Owner
TASK P-18 System Registration Register the system with organizational program or management offices.	• System Owner	• Mission or Business Owner • Chief Information Officer • System Security Officer • System Privacy Officer
TASK C-1 System Description Document the characteristics of the system.	System Owner	• Authorizing Official or Authorizing Official Designated Representative • Information Owner or Steward • System Security Officer • System Privacy Officer
TASK C-2 Security Categorization Categorize the system and document the security categorization results.	• System Owner • Information Owner or Steward	• Senior Accountable Official for Risk Management or Risk Executive (Function) • Chief Information Officer • Senior Agency Information Security Officer • Authorizing Official or Authorizing Official Designated Representative • System Security Officer • System Privacy Officer
TASK C-3 Security Categorization Review and Approval Review and approve the security categorization results and decision.	• Authorizing Official or Authorizing Official Designated Representative • Senior Agency Official for Privacy (for systems processing PII)	• Senior Accountable Official for Risk Management or Risk Executive (Function) • Chief Information Officer • Senior Agency Information Security Officer
TASK S-1 Control Selection Select the controls for the	• System Owner • Common Control Provider	• Authorizing Official or Authorizing Official Designated Representative

RMF Task	Primary Responsibility	Supporting Roles
system and the environment of operation.		• Information Owner or Steward • Systems Security Engineer • Privacy Engineer • System Security Officer • System Privacy Officer
TASK S-2 Control Tailoring Tailor the controls selected for the system and the environment of operation.	• System Owner • Common Control Provider	• Authorizing Official or Authorizing Official Designated Representative • Information Owner or Steward • Systems Security Engineer • Privacy Engineer • System Security Officer • System Privacy Officer
TASK S-3 Control Allocation Allocate security and privacy controls to the system and to the environment of operation.	• Security Architect • Privacy Architect • System Security Officer • System Privacy Officer	• Chief Information Officer • Authorizing Official or Authorizing Official Designated Representative • Mission or Business Owner • Senior Agency Information Security Officer • Senior Agency Official for Privacy • System Owner
TASK S-4 Documentation of Planned Control Implementations Document the controls for the system and environment of operation in security and privacy plans.	• System Owner • Common Control Provider	• Authorizing Official or Authorizing Official Designated Representative • Information Owner or Steward • Systems Security Engineer • Privacy Engineer • System Security Officer • System Privacy Officer
TASK S-5 Continuous Monitoring Strategy — System Develop and implement a system-level strategy for monitoring control effectiveness that is consistent with and supplements the organizational continuous monitoring strategy.	• System Owner • Common Control Provider	• Senior Accountable Official for Risk Management or Risk Executive (Function) • Chief Information Officer • Senior Agency Information Security Officer • Senior Agency Official for Privacy • Authorizing Official or Authorizing Official Designated Representative • Information Owner or Steward

RMF Task	Primary Responsibility	Supporting Roles
		• Security Architect • Privacy Architect • Systems Security Engineer • Privacy Engineer • System Security Officer
TASK S-6 Plan Review and Approval Review and approve the security and privacy plans for the system and the environment of operation.	• Authorizing Official or Authorizing Official Designated Representative	• Senior Accountable Official for Risk Management or Risk Executive (Function) • Chief Information Officer • Senior Agency Information Security Officer • Senior Agency Official for Privacy • Chief Acquisition Officer
TASK I-1 Control Implementation Implement the controls in the security and privacy plans.	• System Owner • Common Control Provider	• Information Owner or Steward • Security Architect • Privacy Architect • Systems Security Engineer • Privacy Engineer • System Security Officer • System Privacy Officer • Enterprise Architect • System Administrator
TASK I-2 Update Control Implementation Information Document changes to planned control implementations based on the "as-implemented" state of controls.	• System Owner • Common Control Provider	• Information Owner or Steward • Security Architect • Privacy Architect • Systems Security Engineer • Privacy Engineer • System Security Officer • System Privacy Officer • Enterprise Architect • System Administrator
TASK A-1 Assessor Selection Select the appropriate assessor or assessment team for the type of control assessment to be conducted.	• Authorizing Official or Authorizing Official Designated Representative	• Chief Information Officer • Senior Agency Information Security Officer • Senior Agency Official for Privacy
TASK A-2 Assessment Plan Develop, review, and approve plans to assess	• Authorizing Official or Authorizing Official Designated Representative • Control Assessor	• Senior Agency Information Security Officer • Senior Agency Official for Privacy

RMF Task	Primary Responsibility	Supporting Roles
implemented controls.		• System Owner • Common Control Provider • Information Owner or Steward • System Security Officer • System Privacy Officer
TASK A-3 Control Assessments Assess the controls in accordance with the assessment procedures described in assessment plans.	• Control Assessor	• Authorizing Official or Authorizing Official Designated Representative • System Owner • Common Control Provider • Information Owner or Steward • Senior Agency Information Security Officer • Senior Agency Official for Privacy • System Security Officer • System Privacy Officer
TASK A-4 Assessment Reports Prepare the assessment reports documenting the findings and recommendations from the control assessments.	• Control Assessor	• System Owner • Common Control Provider • System Security Officer
TASK A-5 Remediation Actions Conduct initial remediation actions on the controls and reassess remediated controls.	• System Owner • Common Control Provider • Control Assessor	• Authorizing Official or Authorizing Official Designated Representative • Senior Agency Information Security Officer • Senior Agency Official for Privacy • Senior Accountable Official for Risk Management or Risk Executive (Function) • Information Owner or Steward • Systems Security Engineer • Privacy Engineer • System Security Officer • System Privacy Officer
TASK A-6 Plan of Action and Milestones Prepare the plan of action and milestones based on	• System Owner • Common Control Provider	• Information Owner or Steward • System Security Officer • System Privacy Officer • Senior Agency Information Security Officer

RMF Task	Primary Responsibility	Supporting Roles
the findings and recommendations of the assessment reports.		• Senior Agency Official for Privacy • Chief Acquisition Officer • Control Assessor
TASK R-1 Authorization Package Assemble the authorization package and submit the package to the authorizing official for an authorization decision.	• System Owner • Common Control Provider	• System Security Officer • System Privacy Officer • Senior Agency Information Security Officer • Senior Agency Official for Privacy • Control Assessor
TASK R-2 Risk Analysis and Determination Analyze and determine the risk from the operation or use of the system or the provision of common controls.	• Authorizing Official or Authorizing Official Designated Representative	• Senior Accountable Official for Risk Management or Risk Executive (Function) • Senior Agency Information Security Officer • Senior Agency Official for Privacy
TASK R-3 Risk Response Identify and implement a preferred course of action in response to the risk determined.	• Authorizing Official or Authorizing Official Designated Representative	• Senior Accountable Official for Risk Management or Risk Executive (Function) • Senior Agency Information Security Officer • Senior Agency Official for Privacy • System Owner or Common Control Provider • Information Owner or Steward • Systems Security Engineer • Privacy Engineer • System Security Officer • System Privacy Officer
TASK R-4 Authorization Decision Determine if the risk from the operation or use of the information system or the provision or use of common controls is acceptable.	• Authorizing Official	• Senior Accountable Official for Risk Management or Risk Executive (Function) • Chief Information Officer • Senior Agency Information Security Officer • Senior Agency Official for Privacy • Authorizing Official Designated Representative

RMF Task	Primary Responsibility	Supporting Roles
TASK R-5 Authorization Reporting Report the authorization decision and any deficiencies in controls that represent significant security or privacy risk.	• Authorizing Official or Authorizing Official Designated Representative	• System Owner or Common Control Provider • Information Owner or Steward • System Security Officer • System Privacy Officer • Senior Agency Information Security Officer • Senior Agency Official for Privacy
TASK M-1 System and Environment Changes Monitor the information system and its environment of operation for changes that impact the security and privacy posture of the system.	• System Owner or Common Control Provider • Senior Agency Information Security Officer • Senior Agency Official for Privacy	• Senior Accountable Official for Risk Management or Risk Executive (Function) • Authorizing Official or Authorizing Official Designated Representative • Information Owner or Steward • System Security Officer • System Privacy Officer
TASK M-2 Ongoing Assessments Assess the controls implemented within and inherited by the system in accordance with the continuous monitoring strategy.	• Control Assessor	• Authorizing Official or Authorizing Official Designated Representative • System Owner or Common Control Provider • Information Owner or Steward • System Security Officer • System Privacy Officer • Senior Agency Information Security Officer • Senior Agency Official for Privacy
TASK M-3 Ongoing Risk Response Respond to risk based on the results of ongoing monitoring activities, risk assessments, and outstanding items in plans of action and milestones.	• Authorizing Official • System Owner • Common Control Provider	• Senior Accountable Official for Risk Management or Risk Executive (Function) • Senior Agency Information Security Officer • Senior Agency Official for Privacy; Authorizing Official Designated Representative • Information Owner or Steward • System Security Officer • System Privacy Officer • Systems Security Engineer • Privacy Engineer

RMF Task	Primary Responsibility	Supporting Roles
		• Security Architect • Privacy Architect
TASK M-4 Authorization Package Updates Update plans, assessment reports, and plans of action and milestones based on the results of the continuous monitoring process.	• System Owner • Common Control Provider	• Information Owner or Steward • System Security Officer • System Privacy Officer • Senior Agency Official for Privacy • Senior Agency Information Security Officer
TASK M-5 Security and Privacy Reporting Report the security and privacy posture of the system to the authorizing official and other organizational officials on an ongoing basis in accordance with the organizational continuous monitoring strategy.	• System Owner • Common Control Provider • Senior Agency Information Security Officer • Senior Agency Official for Privacy	• System Security Officer • System Privacy Officer
TASK M-6 Ongoing Authorization Review the security and privacy posture of the system on an ongoing basis to determine whether the risk remains acceptable.	• Authorizing Official	• Senior Accountable Official for Risk Management or Risk Executive (Function) • Chief Information Officer • Senior Agency Information Security Officer • Senior Agency Official for Privacy • Authorizing Official Designated Representative
TASK M-7 System Disposal Implement a system disposal strategy and execute required actions when a system is removed from operation.	• System Owner	• Authorizing Official or Authorizing Official Designated Representative • Information Owner or Steward • System Security Officer • System Privacy Officer • Senior Accountable Official for Risk Management or Risk Executive (Function) • Senior Agency Information

RMF Task	Primary Responsibility	Supporting Roles
		Security

Table 3-1 RMF Tasks to Roles

NIST SP 800-37 Text

RISK MANAGEMENT ROLES

TASK P-1 Identify and assign individuals to specific roles associated with security and privacy risk management.

Potential Inputs: Organizational security and privacy policies and procedures; organizational charts.

Expected Outputs: Documented Risk Management Framework role assignments.

Primary Responsibility: Head of Agency; Chief Information Officer; Senior Agency Official for Privacy.

Supporting Roles: Authorizing Official or Authorizing Official Designated Representative; Senior Accountable Official for Risk Management or Risk Executive (Function); Senior Agency Information Security Officer.

Discussion: The roles and responsibilities of key participants in risk management processes are described in Appendix D. The roles and responsibilities may include personnel that are internal or external to the organization, as appropriate. Since organizations have different missions, functions, and organizational structures, there may be differences in naming conventions for risk management roles and how specific responsibilities are allocated among organizational personnel (e.g., multiple individuals filling a single role or one individual filling multiple roles). In either situation, the basic risk management functions remain the same. Organizations ensure that there are no conflicts of interest when assigning the same individual to multiple risk management roles. For example, authorizing officials cannot occupy the role of system owner or common control provider for systems or common controls they are authorizing. In addition, combining multiple roles for security and privacy requires care because the two disciplines may require different expertise, and in some circumstances, the priorities may be competing. Some roles may be allocated to a group or an office rather than to an individual, for example, control assessor, risk executive (function), or system administrator.

References: [SP 800-160 v1] (Human Resource Management Process); [SP 800-181]; [NIST CSF] (Core

[Identify Function]).

EXERCISE #-#

What role is responsible for risk acceptance?

_____

What role starts the risk management process?

_____

TASK P2 RISK MANAGEMENT STRATEGY

Introduction

The organizational risk management strategy evaluates threats and vulnerabilities that may impact the enterprise. Risks are assessed based on the impact that they will have at the organization level. Once the organization defines the risk management strategy, information system owners can frame the information systems they are responsible for using the defined process and strategy.

Responsibilities

Primary Responsibility	Supporting Roles
- Head of Agency	- Senior Accountable Official for Risk Management or Risk Executive (Function) - Chief Information Officer - Senior Agency Information - Security Officer - Senior Agency Official for Privacy

SDLC Alignment	
New Systems	Legacy Systems

CSF Alignment	
Profile	CSF Task
	- ID.RM - ID.SC

Task Flow	
Inputs	Outputs
Organizational mission statement - Organizational policies - Organizational risk assumptions, constraints, priorities and trade-offs.	- Risk management strategy and statement of risk tolerance inclusive of information security and privacy risk.

Objectives:

- o Understand organizational risk management tasks
- o Define the components of the risk management model

Risk management is practiced across all three of the tiers in the enterprise risk management model as defined in NIST SP 800-39, Enterprise Risk Management. Organizations at each level of the model manage and monitor risk using the strategy and processes developed or defined at tier 1.

Enterprise risk management process begins with tier 1 organizations Framing the risk. The way the organization frames the enterprise risk results in a risk management strategy that addresses the way that an organization will assess, respond and monitor risk. This is illustrated in figure 4-1.

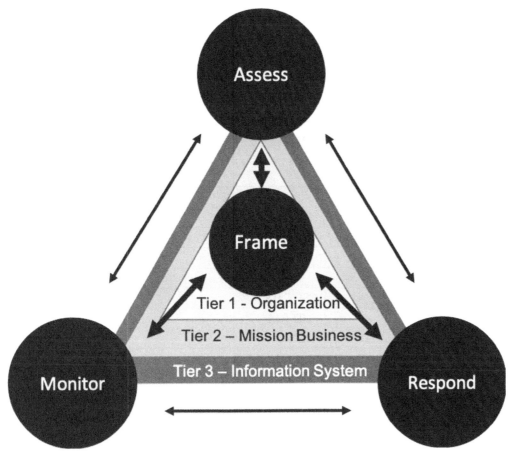

Figure 4-0-1 Enterprise Risk Management

This results in an organizational risk management program that ensures that risks will be managed within the risk tolerance levels of the enterprise.

Risk assessment: Information generated during the risk assessment may influence the original assumptions, change the constraints regarding appropriate risk responses, identify additional tradeoffs, or shift priorities. For example, the characterization of adversaries (including representative tactics, techniques, and procedures), or sources of vulnerability information may not be consistent with how some organizations conduct their missions/business functions; a source of threat/vulnerability information that is useful for one mission/business function could, in fact, be useful for others; or organizational guidance on assessing risk under uncertainty may be too onerous, or insufficiently defined, to be useful for one or more mission/business functions.

Risk response: Information uncovered during the development of alternative courses of action could reveal that risk framing has removed or failed to uncover some potentially high-payoff alternatives from consideration. This situation may challenge organizations to revisit original assumptions or investigate ways to change established constraints.

Risk monitoring: Security control monitoring by organizations could indicate that a class of controls, or a specific implementation of a control, is relatively ineffective, given investments in people, processes, or technology. This situation could lead to changes in assumptions about which types of risk responses are preferred by organizations.

Monitoring of the operational environment could reveal changes in the threat landscape (e.g., changes in the tactics, techniques, and procedures observed across all organizational information systems; increasing frequency and/or intensity of attacks against specific missions/business functions) that cause organizations to revisit original threat assumptions and/or to seek different sources of threat information. Significant advances in defensive or proactive operational and technical solutions could generate the need to revisit the investment strategy identified

during the framing step. Monitoring of legal/regulatory environments could also influence changes in assumptions or constraints. Also, monitoring of risk being incurred might result in the need to reconsider the organizational risk tolerance if the existing statement of risk tolerance does not appear to match the operational realities.

RISK MANAGEMENT STRATEGY

TASK P-2 Establish a risk management strategy for the organization that includes a determination of risk tolerance.

Potential Inputs: Organizational mission statement; organizational policies; organizational risk assumptions, constraints, priorities and trade-offs.

Expected Outputs: Risk management strategy and statement of risk tolerance inclusive of information security and privacy risk.

Primary Responsibility: Head of Agency.

Supporting Roles: Senior Accountable Official for Risk Management or Risk Executive (Function); Chief Information Officer; Senior Agency Information Security Officer; Senior Agency Official for Privacy.

Discussion: Risk tolerance is the degree of risk or uncertainty that is acceptable to an organization. Risk tolerance affects all parts of the organization's risk management process, having a direct impact on the risk management decisions made by senior leaders or executives throughout the organization and providing important constraints on those decisions. The risk management strategy guides and informs risk-based decisions including how security and privacy risk is framed, assessed, responded to, and monitored. The risk management strategy may be composed of a single document, or separate security and privacy risk management documents. The risk management strategy makes explicit the threats, assumptions, constraints, priorities, trade-offs, and risk tolerance used for making investment and senior leaders and executives are to manage security and privacy risks (including supply chain risks) to organizational operations, organizational assets, individuals, other organizations, and the Nation. The risk management strategy includes an expression of organizational risk tolerance; acceptable risk assessment methodologies and risk response strategies; a process for consistently evaluating security and privacy risks organization-wide; and approaches for monitoring risk over time. As organizations define and implement the risk management strategies, policies, procedures, and processes, it is important that they include SCRM considerations. The risk management strategy for security and privacy connects security and privacy programs with the management control systems established in the organization's Enterprise Risk Management strategy.

References: [SP 800-30]; [SP 800-39] (Organization Level); [SP 800-160 v1] (Risk Management, Decision Management, Quality Assurance, Quality Management, Project Assessment and Control Processes); [SP 800-161]; [IR 8062]; [IR 8179] (Criticality Analysis Process B); [NIST CSF] (Core [Identify Function]).

TASK P3 RISK ASSESSMENT - ORGANIZATION

After defining the organizational risk assessment strategy, risk assessments must be completed. In this task the responsible organizational officials complete the risk assessments based on enterprise threats and vulnerabilities.

Responsibilities	
Primary Responsibility	Supporting Roles
- Senior Accountable Official for Risk Management or Risk Executive (Function) - Senior Agency Information Security Officer - Senior Agency Official for Privacy.	- Chief Information Officer - Mission or Business Owner - Authorizing Official or Authorizing Official Designated Representative

SDLC Alignment	
New Systems	Legacy Systems

CSF Alignment	
Profile	CSF Task
	- ID.RA - ID.SC-2

Task Flow	
Inputs	Outputs
- Risk management strategy - Mission or business objectives - Current threat information; system-level security and privacy risk assessment results - Supply chain risk assessment results - Previous organization-level security and privacy risk assessment results - Information sharing agreements or memoranda of understanding - Security and privacy information from continuous monitoring.	- Assess organization-wide security and privacy risk and update the risk assessment results on an ongoing basis

All risks have the ability to impact the organization, but their impacts can be dramatically different. For example risks that impact a single system with no direct support to the organizational mission normally has less of an impact the enterprise than large systems that with direct linkage to that mission. When risk professionals assess the risk to the enterprise they must frame the threats and vulnerabilities through the lens of enterprise risks.

Using the risk assessment strategy, the risk assessment professional conducts risk assessments to determine the threats and vulnerabilities that can impact the organization at the enterprise level. Using risk assessments, security control assessments, audits, continuous monitoring results, enterprise hardware and software inventories, environment details, and other information is evaluated to determine vulnerabilities that could possibly be exploited by threats.

When the risk professional conducts enterprise risk assessments they must consider the totality of risk the organization faces from a number of different variables. This includes the risks from operating the information systems at all tiers of the enterprise, exchanging information with internal and external partners, from the use of third party suppliers, and the use of external providers.

To conduct a thorough enterprise risk assessment it is critical to understand the mission or missions of the organization as this is the focus of the risk assessment. Threats and vulnerabilities should be viewed through the lens of how these would impact the mission or missions that the organization is responsible for accomplishing. Risks that directly impact these missions must be viewed as more critical than risks that have little or no impact on this.

Like all risks, enterprise risks are based on the basic calculation of vulnerabilities plus threats equals risks. The enterprise risk professional must determine the threats that will attempt to compromise the enterprise information or missions, as well as the vulnerabilities that exist in the enterprise. The FedRAMP program office has developed an impressive listing of threats that can serve as a starting point for determining the threats that may impact an enterprise. This listing, while lengthy, should be expanded to meet the threats to the organization. The FedRAMP listing is detailed in table 4-2.

Threat Name	Description
Alteration	Alteration of data, files, or records.
Audit Compromise	An unauthorized user gains access to the audit trail and could cause audit records to be deleted or modified, or prevents future audit records from being recorded, thus masking a security relevant event.
Bomb	An intentional explosion.
Communications Failure	Cut of fiber optic lines, trees falling on telephone lines.
Compromising Emanations	Eavesdropping can occur via electronic media directed against large scale electronic facilities that do not process classified National Security Information.
Cyber Brute Force	Unauthorized user could gain access to the information systems by random or systematic guessing of passwords, possibly supported by password cracking utilities.

Threat Name	Description
Data Disclosure Attack	An attacker uses techniques that could result in the disclosure of sensitive information by exploiting weaknesses in the design or configuration.
Data Entry Error	Human inattention, lack of knowledge, and failure to cross-check system activities could contribute to errors becoming integrated and ingrained in automated systems.
Denial of Service Attack	An adversary uses techniques to attack a single target rendering it unable to respond and could cause denial of service for users of the targeted information systems.
Distributed Denial of Service Attack	An adversary uses multiple compromised information systems to attack a single target and could cause denial of service for users of the targeted information systems.
Earthquake	Seismic activity can damage the information system or its facility.
Electromagnetic Interference	Disruption of electronic and wire transmissions could be caused by high frequency (HF), very high frequency (VHF), and ultra-high frequency (UHF) communications devices (jamming) or sun spots.
Espionage	The illegal covert act of copying, reproducing, recording, photographing or intercepting to obtain sensitive information .
Fire	Fire can be caused by arson, electrical problems, lightning, chemical agents, or other unrelated proximity fires.
Floods	Water damage caused by flood hazards can be caused by proximity to local flood plains. Flood maps and base flood elevation should be considered.
Fraud	Intentional deception regarding data or information about an information system could compromise the confidentiality, integrity, or availability of an information system.
Hardware or Equipment Failure	Hardware or equipment may fail due to a variety of reasons.
Hardware Tampering	An unauthorized modification to hardware that alters the proper functioning of equipment in a manner that degrades the security functionality the asset provides.
Hurricane	A category 1, 2, 3, 4, or 5 land falling hurricane could impact the facilities that house the information systems.
Malicious Software	Software that damages a system such a virus, Trojan, or worm.
Phishing Attack	Adversary attempts to acquire sensitive information such as usernames, passwords, or SSNs, by pretending to be communications from a legitimate/trustworthy source. Typical attacks occur via email, instant messaging, or comparable means; commonly directing users to Web sites that appear to be legitimate sites, while actually stealing the entered information.
Power Interruptions	Power interruptions may be due to any number of reasons such as electrical grid failures, generator failures, uninterruptable power supply failures (e.g. spike, surge, brownout, or blackout).
Procedural Error	An error in procedures could result in unintended consequences.
Procedural Violations	Violations of standard procedures.
Resource Exhaustion	An errant (buggy) process may create a situation that exhausts critical resources preventing access to services.
Sabotage	Underhand interference with work.
Scavenging	Searching through disposal containers (e.g. dumpsters) to acquire unauthorized data.
Severe Weather	Naturally occurring forces of nature could disrupt the operation of an information system by freezing, sleet, hail, heat, lightning, thunderstorms, tornados, or snowfall.
Social Engineering	An attacker manipulates people into performing actions or divulging confidential information, as well as possible access to computer systems or facilities.
Software Tampering	Unauthorized modification of software (e.g. files, programs, database records) that alters the proper operational functions.
Terrorist	An individual performing a deliberate violent act could use a variety of agents to damage the information system, its facility, and/or its operations.
Theft	An adversary could steal elements of the hardware.
Time and State	An attacker exploits weaknesses in timing or state of functions to perform actions that would otherwise be prevented (e.g. race conditions, manipulation user state).

Threat Name	Description
Transportation Accidents	Transportation accidents include train derailments, river barge accidents, trucking accidents, and airlines accidents. Local transportation accidents typically occur when airports, sea ports, railroad tracks, and major trucking routes occur in close proximity to systems facilities. Likelihood of HAZMAT cargo should be determined when considering the probability of local transportation accidents.
Unauthorized Facility Access	An unauthorized individual accesses a facility which may result in comprises of confidentiality, integrity, or availability.
Unauthorized Systems Access	An unauthorized user accesses a system or data.
Volcanic Activity	A crack, perforation, or vent in the earth's crust followed by molten lava, steam, gases, and ash forcefully ejected into the atmosphere.

Table 4-2 Threat Examples

After determining the listing of possible threats, next a listing of vulnerabilities must be compiled. These vulnerabilities are based on the specific logical and physical environment and architecture of the organization. This includes specific hardware, software, configuration settings, policies and procedures implemented. Using this information, risk management professionals can conduct research and determine possible vulnerabilities that could be exploited by the threats identified earlier.

Enterprise level risk assessments can also benefit from examining and aggregating risk assessments conducted at lower levels including at the system (tier 3) and business process levels (tier 2). Additional information can be compiled from system level assessments, results from continuous monitoring, and strategic risk considerations.

The risk professional must also consider the variability of the enterprise environment as it exists. Care should be taken to assess the risk of different locations, missions, business processes, technologies, environments (both physical and logical),
Must consider the variability of environment that may exist (and the need to account for this variability)
-different locations
-different missions
-different business processes

Risk assessments must be completed on the organizations supply chain.

These risk assessments results may be used to help the organization establish the Cybersecurity Framework profile.

NIST SP 800-37 Text
RISK ASSESSMENT—ORGANIZATION   **TASK P-3** Assess organization-wide security and privacy risk and update the risk assessment results on

an ongoing basis.

Potential Inputs: Risk management strategy; mission or business objectives; current threat information; system-level security and privacy risk assessment results; supply chain risk assessment results; previous organization-level security and privacy risk assessment results; information sharing agreements or memoranda of understanding; security and privacy information from continuous monitoring.

Expected Outputs: Organization-level risk assessment results.

Primary Responsibility: Senior Accountable Official for Risk Management or Risk Executive (Function); Senior Agency Information Security Officer; Senior Agency Official for Privacy.

Supporting Roles: Chief Information Officer; Mission or Business Owner; Authorizing Official or Authorizing Official Designated Representative.

Discussion: Risk assessment at the organizational level leverages aggregated information from system-level risk assessment results, continuous monitoring, and any strategic risk considerations relevant to the organization. The organization considers the totality of risk from the operation and use of its information systems, from information exchange and connections with other internally and externally owned systems, and from the use of external providers. For example, the organization may review the risk related to its enterprise architecture and information systems of varying impact levels residing on the same network and whether higher impact systems are segregated from lower impact systems or systems operated and maintained by external providers. The organization may also consider the variability of environments that may exist within the organization (e.g., different locations serving different missions/business processes) and the need to account for such variability in risk assessments. Risk assessments of the organization's supply chain may be conducted as well. Risk assessment results may be used to help organizations establish a Cybersecurity Framework Profile.

References: [SP 800-30]; [SP 800-39] (Organization Level, Mission/Business Process Level); [SP 800-161]; [IR 8062].

TASK P4 ORGANIZATIONALLY-TAILORED CONTROL BASELINES AND CYBERSECURITY FRAMEWORK PROFILES (OPTIONAL)

Responsibilities	
Primary Responsibility	Supporting Roles
- Senior Accountable Official for Risk Management or Risk Executive (Function) - Senior Agency Information Security Officer - Senior Agency Official for Privacy.	- Chief Information Officer - Mission or Business Owner - Authorizing Official or Authorizing Official Designated Representative

SDLC Alignment	
New Systems	Legacy Systems
N/A	N/A

CSF Alignment	
Profile	CSF Task
	- Profile

Task Flow	
Inputs	Outputs
- Risk management strategy - Mission or business objectives - Current threat information; system-level security and privacy risk assessment results - Supply chain risk assessment results - Previous organization-level security and privacy risk assessment results - Information sharing agreements or memoranda of understanding - Security and privacy information from continuous monitoring.	- Assess organization-wide security and privacy risk and update the risk assessment results on an ongoing basis

Objective:

Security control baselines provide the system owner with a set of security controls that serve as a starting point for the controls required to reduce the risk of operating the information system and provide the needed security protections. NIST provides three default baselines based on the categorization of the information system, these three baselines are low, moderate, and high. The Committee on National Security Systems (CNSS) developed an additional set of baselines that provides a more granular approach to default baselines providing 27 different baselines based on defining the categorization (low, moderate, or high) from each of the security objectives, confidentiality, integrity, and availability. This results in a set of baselines that range from low, low, low (low for confidentiality, low of availability, and low for integrity) to high, high, high.

NOTE: At the time of this books publishing the NIST document SP 800-53B has not been published and is not available in draft form.

Many times, these baselines provide adequate coverage for most information systems, however some organizations may require specifically tailored baselines that are specifically developed for the systems, technology or environments that the organization operates under. When an organization has a specific mission, specific needs, or plans to operate in specific environments it may be beneficial to develop specific control baselines for systems that meet these specific conditions. By doing this the enterprise assists the information system owners in identifying security control baselines that can be used as a more specific starting point for the controls that will drive down the risks associated with a specific configuration, technology or environment. These organizationally-tailored baselines will contain a set of fully defined controls, control enhancements, and organizationally defined variables. This will increase the speed of developing secure systems while reducing the cost and time needed to develop the most effective set of security controls.

An alternative to developing a baseline is the development of overlays. Overlays are listings of security controls that have been identified to be added or removed from an information system after a baseline has been selected. The use of organizationally-tailored overlays and organizationally-tailored baselines results in the same outcome, a set of security controls that is developed for a specific situation that results in driving down the risks of operating that type of system.

Tailored baselines and overlays are designed to address the custom security and privacy needs of different types of missions, business functions, operations, systems, technology, environments, operating modes, statutory or regulatory requirements, sensitivity or data, or other specific need. Organizations are not limited in the number of baselines or overlays that they develop, however the number developed should meet the diversity of the environment and be an amount that can be effectively managed.

The development of these baselines and overlays should include the identification of organizationally defined variables. The details for the assignment and selection of these variables should be included whenever possible. If needed the supplemental guidance that details the implementation details for the controls specific to the baseline can be expanded on to assist the implementor of the control to better understand the controls and ensure it is executed correctly

Baselines and overlays can also be developed outside the organization. For example, developers of specific technologies and operating systems may provide custom developed security baselines. Externally developed baselines and overlays may be required by laws, executive orders, directives, regulations, policies, or standards. There may also be situations when a baseline is required by a community, technology, asset criticality, information confidentiality or criticality, or environment.

The development of organizationally-tailored baselines can also assist the organization in developing one or more Cybersecurity Framework Policies. By developing the profiles, the framework core is used to align the cybersecurity outcomes with mission or business requirements, risk tolerance, and resources of the organization. This can help with making system level risk-based decisions resulting in an overall improvement in security and risk management.

NIST SP 800-37 Text

ORGANIZATIONALLY-TAILORED CONTROL BASELINES AND CYBERSECURITY FRAMEWORK PROFILES (Optional)

TASK P-4 Establish, document, and publish organizationally-tailored control baselines and/or Cybersecurity Framework Profiles.

Potential Inputs: Documented security and privacy requirements directing the use of organizationally-tailored control baselines; mission or business objectives; enterprise architecture; security architecture; privacy architecture; organization- and system-level risk assessment results; list of common control providers and common controls available for inheritance; NIST Special Publication 800-53B control baselines.

Expected Outputs: List of approved or directed organizationally-tailored control baselines; [NIST CSF] Profiles.

Primary Responsibility: Mission or Business Owner; Senior Accountable Official for Risk Management or Risk Executive (Function).

Supporting Roles: Chief Information Officer; Authorizing Official or Authorizing Official Designated Representative; Senior Agency Information Security Officer; Senior Agency Official for Privacy.

Discussion: To address the organizational mission or business need for specialized sets of controls to reduce risk, organizationally-tailored control baselines may be developed for organization-wide use. [SP 800-160 v1]. Organizations can use the tailored control baseline concept when there is divergence from the specific assumptions used to create the initial control baselines in [SP 800-53B]. This would include, for example, situations when the organization has specific security or privacy risks, has specific mission or business needs, or plans to operate in environments that are not addressed in the initial baselines. An organizationally-tailored baseline provides a fully specified set of controls, control enhancements, and supplemental guidance derived from established control baselines described in [SP 800-53B]. The tailoring process can also be guided and informed by the requirements engineering process described in [

Organizationally-tailored baselines and overlays complement the NIST control baselines by providing an opportunity to add or eliminate controls to accommodate organizational requirements while continuing to protect information commensurate with risk. Organizations can use tailored baselines and overlays to customize control baselines by describing control applicability and by providing interpretations for specific technologies; types of missions or business functions, operations, systems, environments of operation, and operating modes; and statutory or regulatory requirements. Multiple customized baselines may be useful for organizations with heterogeneous systems (e.g., organizations that maintain systems with different operating or processing characteristics, or mission or business characteristics).

Organizationally-tailored baselines can establish organization-defined control parameter values for assignment or selection statements in controls and control enhancements that are agreeable to specific communities of interest and can also extend the supplemental guidance where necessary. Tailored baselines may be more stringent or less stringent than the baselines identified in [SP 800-53B] and are applied to multiple systems.

Tailored baselines developed outside the organization may also be mandated for use by certain laws, executive orders, directives, regulations, policies, or standards. In some situations, tailoring actions may be restricted or limited by the developer of the tailored baseline or by the issuing authority for the tailored baseline. Tailored baselines (or overlays) have been developed by communities of interest for cloud and shared systems, services, and applications; industrial control systems; privacy; national security systems; weapons and space-based systems; high value assets;58 mobile device management; federal public key infrastructure; and privacy risks.

Organizations may also benefit from developing one or more Cybersecurity Framework *Profiles*. A Cybersecurity Framework Profile uses the Subcategories in the Framework Core to align cybersecurity outcomes with mission or business requirements, risk tolerance, and resources of the organization. The prioritized list of cybersecurity outcomes developed at the organization and mission/business process levels can be helpful in facilitating consistent, risk-based decisions at the system level. The Subcategories identified in the applicable Cybersecurity Framework Profiles can also be used to guide and inform the development of the tailored control baselines described above.

References: [SP 800-53]; [SP 800-53B]; [SP 800-160 v1] (Business or Mission Analysis and Stakeholder Needs and Requirements Definition Processes); [NIST CSF] (Core, Profiles).

TASK P-5 COMMON CONTROL IDENTIFICATION

Responsibilities	
Primary Responsibility	Supporting Roles
- Senior Agency Information Security Officer - Senior Agency Official for Privacy	- Mission or Business Owner; Senior Accountable Official for Risk Management or Risk Executive (Function) - Chief Information Officer; Authorizing Official or Authorizing Official Designated Representative - Common Control Provider - System Owner.

SDLC Alignment	
New Systems	Legacy Systems
N/A	N/A

CSF Alignment	
Profile	CSF Task
	ID.AM-5

Task Flow	
Inputs	Outputs
- Documented security and privacy requirements; existing common control providers and associated security and privacy plans; information security and privacy program plans - Organization- and system-level security and privacy risk assessment results	- List of common control providers and common controls available for inheritance - Security and privacy plans (or equivalent documents) providing a description of the common control implementation (including inputs, expected behavior, and expected outputs).

A common control is a security control that has been developed and is available to one or more systems as an inheritable control. Common controls are typically developed at tier 1 or 2 of the organization, but in some cases tier 3 systems can be a common control provider.

The development of common controls in an organization is a major advantage of the RMF as it allows security controls to be developed once and be used by a number of systems, removing the responsibility for the common controls implementation from system owners. This reduces the number of controls that the system owner will be responsible for implementing, reducing the cost of security control implementation, speeding the development of the system, and providing consistency for the common control across the organization.

Inheritance of common controls is dependent on some factors. First, the common controls should be security control that is listed in the organizations control catalog, for many this is NIST SP 800-53, and could be enhanced by adding controls that are unique to the enterprise but should align with the families in NIST SP 800-53. Then, controls the common controls must have a valid authorization to operate (ATO). Next, the common controls being inherited must provide the levels of protection required by the information system inheriting the controls. Additionally, the system owner should be aware of the expiration date of the common controls to ensure the date of expiration is not before the expected approval of the system inheriting the control. Finally, if the date is before the expected system ATO issuance, or even shortly after, it is important that the system owner work with the common control provider (CCP) to ensure a reauthorization is underway. If a common control that is being inherited by an information system has an ATO that expires, it becomes the system owner's responsibility to find another CCP or implement the security control themselves.

The CCP may be an internal organization such as a business process owner, organizational entity, or information system. Organizational CCPS may come from differing levels in the organization including corporate organizations, departments, agencies, bureaus, subcomponents and even from individual programs and systems. It is also possible that the CCP is an entity outside the organization, such as a cloud service provider (CSP), or security service vendor such as a provider of external vulnerability scanning or penetration testing. It is important that the entity responsible for tracking the CCPs is aware of all of the providers of common controls for the organization.

The identification of common controls is the primary responsibility of organizational leadership and should be completed as part of the organization preparing for implementation of the risk management framework (RMF). Common controls are allocated to a one or more organizational entities that are designated as CCP. In most cases a single CCP is the most effective way of implementing common controls, however multiple CCPs may be needed to cover different hosting locations, system architectures, organizational structures, or technologies. For example, identity and access control may be provided by different CCPs based on operating systems, or physical security may be provided by different CCPs based on geographic location. In cases where multiple CCPS are offering the same controls, it is important to identify any dependencies for inheritance.

Clear cataloging of common controls is important so that information system owners can identify the controls that are available for inheritance, including any restrictions. One way of efficiently doing this is by providing a listing of the available common controls and the respective CCP as well as ATO expiration dates. A less effective way is to have the CCPS make their ATO documentation available in a common location, such as a file share or online location.

System owners inheriting common controls are not required to assess the inherited controls but should conduct due diligence in reviewing the inherited controls. The CCP should make basic documentation available to system owners inheriting the controls including, at a minimum, the security plan, the security assessment reports, the plan of actions and milestones, and the ATO documentation including any caveats levied on the ATO. Likewise, the CCP is not required to have any visibility into the information systems inheriting controls.

If the approval status of the common controls changes it is the responsibility of the CCP to notify the system owners inheriting the controls. This could be a change in the POA&M status of any of the inherited controls, changes in threats to the controls, new vulnerabilities in the controls or changes in the common controls ATO status.

CCPs are required to follow all of the requirements for a system when progressing through the RMF, including following an information security continuous monitoring program (ISCM). System owners inheriting controls from a CCP should be made aware of the outcome of the ISCM, including any controls that is failing to provide the level of protection documented in the CCPs ATO package.

System owners should identify inherited common controls in their system security plan (SSP) and security controls traceability matrix (SCTM). The CCP should be clearly identified and ant documentation associated with the ATO (SSP, SAR, POA&M, and ATO documents) should be included in the systems ATO package or be referenced and be available to the security control assessor (SCA), the authorizing official (AO), and other approved stakeholders.

There are times that a common control will not fully protect an information system. This could be because the common controls do not implement stringent enough protections form the system owner, or the control is intestinally split between the CCP and the information system. In these cases, the controls are implemented, in part, by both the CCP and the system owner becoming a hybrid control. For controls that do not provide the level of protection required by the system the information system owner will accept the control as provided by the CCP and then add additional enhancements to the control at the system level. For the controls that are split between the CCP and the system owner part of the controls is provided by the CCP and part is provided by the system owner. In this case the CCP may provide training and templates for some controls and the system owner will be responsible for having personnel attend the training and complete the forms. In the case of a hybrid control, the system owner must identify in the portions of the controls that are the responsibility of the CCP and the parts that are the responsibility of the system owner. For the portions the CCP is responsible for, all of the common control requirements stated earlier apply.

Common, and hybrid are two of the three types of controls available to the information system owner. The third type of control is the system security control, that is fully implemented, documented and maintained by the information system owner. These controls are fully the responsibility of the system owner when implementing the RMF.

COMMON CONTROL IDENTIFICATION

TASK P-5 Identify, document, and publish organization-wide common controls that are available for inheritance by organizational systems.

Potential Inputs: Documented security and privacy requirements; existing common control providers and associated security and privacy plans; information security and privacy program plans; organization- and system-level security and privacy risk assessment results.

Expected Outputs: List of common control providers and common controls available for inheritance; security and privacy plans (or equivalent documents) providing a description of the common control implementation (including inputs, expected behavior, and expected outputs).

Primary Responsibility: Senior Agency Information Security Officer; Senior Agency Official for Privacy.

Supporting Roles: Mission or Business Owner; Senior Accountable Official for Risk Management or Risk Executive (Function); Chief Information Officer; Authorizing Official or Authorizing Official Designated Representative; Common Control Provider; System Owner.

Discussion: Common controls are controls that can be inherited by one or more information systems. [SP 800-53] control family, for example, physical and environmental protection controls, system boundary and monitoring controls, personnel security controls, policies and procedures, acquisition controls, account and identity management controls, audit log and accountability controls, or complaint management controls for receiving privacy inquiries from the public. Organizations identify and select the set of common controls and allocate those controls to the organizational entities designated as common control providers. Common controls may differ based upon a variety of factors, such as hosting location, system architecture, and the structure of the organization. The organization-wide list of common controls takes these factors into account. Common controls can also be identified at different levels of the organization (e.g., corporate, department, or agency level; bureau or subcomponent level; or individual program level). Organizations may establish one or more lists of common controls that can be inherited by information systems. A requirement may not be fully met by a common control. In such cases, the control is considered a hybrid control and is noted as such by the organization, including specifying which parts of the control requirement are provided for inheritance by the common control and which parts are to be provided at the system level. When there are multiple sources of common controls, organizations specify the common control provider (i.e., who is providing the controls and through what venue, for example, shared services, specific systems, or within a specific type of architecture) and which systems or types of systems can inherit the controls. Common control listings are communicated to system owners, so they are aware of the security and privacy capabilities that are available from the organization through inheritance. System owners are not required to assess common controls that are inherited by their systems or document common control implementation details; that is the responsibility of the common control providers. Likewise, common control providers are not required to have visibility into the system-level details of those systems that are inheriting the common controls they are providing.

Risk assessment results can be used when identifying common controls to determine if the controls available for inheritance satisfy the security and privacy requirements for organizational systems and the environments in which those systems operate (including the identification of potential single points of failure). When the common controls provided by the organization are determined to be insufficient for the information systems inheriting those controls, system owners can supplement the common controls with system-specific or hybrid controls to achieve the required protection for their systems or accept greater risk with the acknowledgement and approval of the organization.

Common control providers execute the RMF steps to implement, assess, and monitor the controls designated as common controls. Common control providers may also be system owners when the common controls are resident within an information system. Organizations select senior officials or executives to serve as authorizing officials for common controls. The senior agency official for privacy is responsible for designating common privacy controls and for documenting them in the organization's privacy program plan. Authorizing officials are responsible for accepting security and privacy risk resulting from the use of common controls inherited by organizational systems.

Common control providers are responsible for documenting common controls in security and privacy plans (or equivalent documents prescribed by the organization); ensuring that the common controls are implemented and assessed for effectiveness by qualified assessors and that assessment findings are documented in assessment reports; producing a plan of action and milestones for common controls determined to have unacceptable deficiencies and targeted for remediation; receiving authorization for the common controls from the designated authorizing official; and monitoring control effectiveness on an ongoing basis. Plans, assessment reports, and plans of action and milestones for common controls (or a summary of such information) are made available to system owners and can be used by authorizing officials to guide and inform authorization decisions for systems inheriting common controls. For information about the authorization of common controls, see Task R-4 and Appendix F.

References: [SP 800-53].

TASK P6 IMPACT-LEVEL PRIORITIZATION (OPTIONAL)

Responsibilities	
Primary Responsibility	Supporting Roles
- Senior Accountable Official for Risk Management or Risk Executive (Function)	- Senior Agency Information Security Officer - Senior Agency Official for Privacy - Mission or Business Owner - System Owner; Chief Information Officer - Authorizing Official or Authorizing Official Designated Representative

SDLC Alignment	
New Systems	Legacy Systems
N/A	N/A

CSF Alignment	
Profile	CSF Task
	ID.AM-5

Task Flow	
Inputs	Outputs
- Security categorization information for organizational systems - System descriptions organization- and system-level risk assessment results - Mission or business objectives - Cybersecurity Framework Profiles.	- Organizational systems prioritized into low-, moderate-, and high-impact sub-categories.

Determine impact-level prioritization

Prior to accomplishing this optional task, the enterprises information systems must be categorized using the high-water mark process to determine their security categorization. At the individual information system level, this is task C-2, Security Categorization, of the RMF in the Categorize step. For that reason, the categorization process will not be covered in this task.

The NIST categorization process will result each system being categorized as low impact, moderate impact or high impact. For many organizations this level of categorization will be adequate to determine the starting point for the selection of the baseline set of security controls based on information types and risk.

Some organizations may require more granularity in the selection method of baselines based on impact designations and to make risk-based decisions including determining the baseline sets of security controls. In these cases, the organization can expand upon the base categorization levels, to provide the needed level of granularity. In these cases, the new designations can be used to align a system with a specific organizationally-tailored security control baseline or overlay. In other cases, it can be used to prioritize the allocation or resources to higher impact systems.

Specific information systems in one baseline categorization may be more critical to the organizations mission to others in the same baseline categorization. In these cases, the systems that have more impact to the mission may get a specific indicator to identify this priority. For example, the moderate categorization can be divided by the organization. NIST SP 800-37 provides one suggestion in that the moderate category is divided into low-moderate, moderate-moderate, and high-moderate. In this case the high-moderate categorization would be a higher priority, possibly with an extended set of security controls, than the moderate-moderate, and low-moderate baselines.

This tailoring is defined by the organization and should fit the needs of the enterprise. For example, the organization could use additional factors, like information criticality, in this sub categorization like moderate-PII, moderate-sensitive, moderate-public. It is important that the sub categorization is accomplished to provide the level of detail and specificity the organization needs and provide the tools to make more informed risk-based decisions and selections.

Prioritizations in the determination of sub categories can also be used to identify those systems that are critical or essential to the operation of the organization, for example moderate-critical. They can also be used when the baseline categorization does not reflect the aggregation of information at the same level that may cause the information system to be more critical. In the case of aggregation, a large number of information that is categorized at the low impact level may actually put the system, and enterprise, at a higher level of risk, in these cases the system may benefit from sub level categorization like low-aggregation, or high-low.

Care must be taken when developing sub categories to ensure that too many sub categories are not created. This could be complex for the system developers, security professionals, risk managers, and others to navigate and may become unwieldly to manage. Organizational leadership, including the risk executive (function) should be closely involved in the development and approval of sub categories.

The use of Cybersecurity Framework profiles can assist the organization in the development of sub-categories by using the applicable CSF profile aligned to the organizations mission and business objectives. These objectives can be used to distinguish different sub categorization levels based on the associated CSF profile.

In any case the development of impact level prioritization and the associated sub categorizations should be an organizational decision and used when needed. It can be helpful in determining which specific security control baseline to use and to order information system based on priority and criticality to the organizations mission. Used incorrectly the number of sub categories can become unnecessarily large, and complex to use and manage. Care should be taken to ensure the development of this prioritization makes implementation of the RMF simpler and development of systems more secure.

NIST SP 800-37 Text

IMPACT-LEVEL PRIORITIZATION (Optional)
TASK P-6 Prioritize organizational systems with the same impact level.

Potential Inputs: Security categorization information for organizational systems; system descriptions; organization- and system-level risk assessment results; mission or business objectives; Cybersecurity Framework Profiles.

Expected Outputs: Organizational systems prioritized into low-, moderate-, and high-impact sub-categories.

Primary Responsibility: Senior Accountable Official for Risk Management or Risk Executive (Function).

Supporting Roles: Senior Agency Information Security Officer; Senior Agency Official for Privacy; Mission or Business Owner; System Owner; Chief Information Officer; Authorizing Official or Authorizing Official Designated Representative.

Discussion: This task is carried out *only* after organizational systems have been categorized (see Task C1). This task requires organizations to first apply the high-water mark concept to each of their information systems categorized in accordance with [FIPS 199] and [FIPS 200]. The application of the high-water mark concept results in systems designated as low impact, moderate impact, or high impact. Organizations desiring additional granularity in their impact designations for risk-based decision making can use this task to prioritize their systems within each impact level.63 For example, an organization may decide to prioritize its moderate-impact systems by assigning each moderate system to one of three new subcategories: *low-moderate* systems, *moderate-moderate* systems, and *high-moderate* systems. The high-moderate systems assume a higher priority than the moderate-moderate systems and low-moderate systems assume a lower priority than the moderate-moderate systems. The prioritization of its moderate systems gives organizations an opportunity to make more informed decisions regarding control selection and the tailoring of control baselines when responding to identified risks.

Impact-level prioritization can also be used to determine those systems that are critical or essential to organizational missions and business operations and therefore, organizations can focus on the factors of complexity, aggregation, and system interconnections. Such systems can be identified, for example, by prioritizing high-impact systems into *low-high* systems, *moderate-high* systems, and *high-high* systems. Impact-level prioritizations can be conducted at any level of the organization and are based on security categorization data reported by individual system owners. Impact-level prioritization may necessitate the development of organizationally-tailored baselines to designate the appropriate set of controls for the additional, more granular impact levels.

Cybersecurity Framework *Profiles* can be used by organizations to support the impact-level prioritization task. The mission and business objectives and prioritized outcomes defined in applicable Cybersecurity Framework Profiles can help distinguish relative priority between systems with the same impact level. Cybersecurity Framework Profiles can be organized around the priority of mission/business objectives of an organization, and those objectives are assigned a relative priority among them. For example, human and environmental safety objectives may be the two most important objectives relevant to a Profile's context. In this example, when performing Task P-6, a system that relates to a human safety objective may be prioritized higher than a system that has the same impact levels but does not relate to the human safety objective.

References: [FIPS 199]; [FIPS 200]; [SP 800-30]; [SP 800-39] (Organization and System Levels); [SP 800-59]; [SP 800-60 v1]; [SP 800-60 v2]; [SP 800-160 v1] (System Requirements Definition Process); [IR 8179] (Criticality Analysis Process B); [CNSSI 1253]; [NIST CSF] (Core [Identify Function]; Profiles).

TASK P7 CONTINUOUS MONITORING STRATEGY - ORGANIZATION

Responsibilities	
Primary Responsibility	Supporting Roles
- Senior Accountable Official for Risk Management or Risk Executive (Function).	- Chief Information Officer - Senior Agency Information Security Officer - Senior Agency Official for Privacy - Mission or Business Owner - System Owner - Authorizing Official - Authorizing Official Designated Representative

SDLC Alignment	
New Systems	Legacy Systems
N/A	N/A

CSF Alignment	
Profile	CSF Task
	ID.AM-5

Task Flow	
Inputs	Outputs
- Risk management strategy; organization- and system-level risk assessment results; organizational security and privacy policies	- An implemented organizational continuous monitoring strategy

A monitoring strategy establishes the proposed method and frequency of security control monitoring using both independent and system initiated assessments, audits and monitoring through the systems lifecycle. This strategy should define how each of the security controls will be validated to ensure it is working as designed, providing the correct level of protection, and developing the correct output. This assessment strategy should be detailed enough to ensure each portion of control fully implemented. Assessment results should be detailed enough to result in a complete assessment of the viability of the control and its ability to provide the correct level of protection. These findings should detail the portions of the controls working correctly, those that are not working as required and those that are not implemented. Assessment procedures should be documented in the continuous monitoring strategy, the security plan, or both.

The monitoring strategy should detail the frequency, or how often a control will be assessed. This frequency should first be drawn from the organizational Information Security Continuous Monitoring Strategy (ISCM), the organizations policy documentation, and all applicable laws, guidance and regulations. In those areas where this guidance cannot be found the system owner can look for community security guidelines, best business practices and vendor security implementation guides. The frequency of assessment of controls that are more perishable, provide organizational protections or those controls that are listed on a Plan of Actions and Milestones (POA&M) will be higher than those controls that do not fall into these categories. The frequency of security control assessment should be documented in the continuous monitoring strategy, the security plan, or both.

The continuous monitoring strategy document should contain a table that allows easy reference to the frequency of assessment of each required control. These frequencies include, but are not limited to, continuous and ongoing, daily, weekly, monthly, quarterly, semiannual, annual and every 2 or more years. An example of what a portion of this document could look like is illustrated in table 4-3

Row #	Control #	Control Name	Control Description
		Continuous & Ongoing	
1	SI-4	Information System Monitoring	The organization: a. Monitors the information system to detect: 1. Attacks and indicators of potential attacks in accordance with [Assignment: organization-defined monitoring objectives]; and 2. Unauthorized local, network, and remote connections; b. Identifies unauthorized use of the information system through [Assignment: organization-defined techniques and methods]; c. Deploys monitoring devices: (i) strategically within the information system to collect organization-determined essential information; and (ii) at ad hoc locations within the system to track specific types of transactions of interest to the organization; …
		Weekly	
2	AU-6a	Audit Review, Analysis, & Reporting	System Owners must review and analyze information system audit records for indications of inappropriate or unusual activity.
		Monthly	
3	RA-5d	Vulnerability Scanning	System Owners must mitigate all discovered high-risk vulnerabilities within 30 days and mitigate moderate vulnerability risks in 90 days. CSPs must send their ISSO updated artifacts

4	CA-7g	Continuous Monitoring Security State	every 30 days to show evidence that outstanding high-risk vulnerabilities have been mitigated.
			System Owners must report the security state of the system to their own organizational officials on a monthly basis.

Table 4-3, Continuous monitoring frequency

Configuration Management and Control Processes

A sound configuration management program ensures that systems are configured, or built, within the approved standard. When a system is designed, and the initial security documentation is created, the configuration of the system including software installed, version, hardware make model and type and general settings of the system are noted in the system configuration management plan and possibly the security. As the system is developed any changes to this baseline are noted in the baseline configuration is updated. Configuration management begins no later than step two of the RMF and continues throughout entire lifecycle.

Strict configuration management control should be maintained route system lifecycle that have been implemented are not impact buy changes to the system. It should be possible anytime in the system lifecycle to track all changes through the configuration management plan back to the original baseline that was authorized during the RMF.

Change management boards or configuration control boards should be comprised of individuals throughout the organization that would be considered stakeholders any information system that is being monitored. This often includes security personnel, System administrators, network administrators, help desk personnel, finance professionals, and members of the organizational leadership. This group Will evaluate changes proposed by system owners to ensure destruction of the information system, the organizational network environment, other systems or business processes are not impacted by the proposed change.

When making the changes it is important that the system owner develop plans that would allow the system to be reverted to its previous state should something go wrong during or after the change is implemented.

Security Impact Analyses on Proposed or Actual Changes

Reviewing proposed changes to a system for security impact is accomplished by security personnel optimally before the proposed change is presented to the configuration management board or change control board, and before the change is actually made. If this is not possible the security member or members of those boards would review the proposed change during or after the meeting. No decision on the change should be made to the system until a full security impact analysis is completed on the requested change and determination is made that change will not cause an unacceptable increase risk to the system, the business unit or, the organization.

The impact analysis must be conducted by an individual or team that has technical and administrative experience to evaluate the changes to the system at the smallest detail. Changes to the system can impact configuration settings, ports and protocols, disable security configurations and change file systems just to name a few things that might be impacted by a change. The individual or team must be able to identify and document these changes and if necessary adjust organizational procedures or policies to ensure the system maintains its approval and the enterprise risk posture is not impacted beyond an acceptable state.

The results of this analysis must be documented and cataloged in the board meeting minutes as well as in the configuration management plan as well as the security plan.

Assessment of Security Controls Employed and Inherited

Approved changes to the system may require full assessment of the impacted controls. The impact assessment conducted in this step determines the amount of the impacted security controls that will need to be assessed up to and including the entirety of the impacted controls. This applies to controls implemented by the system, inherited controls and hybrid controls.

Those controls assessed in this step should be assessed by an independent control assessor to assist with ongoing authorization, however this is not required. If the system owner conducts the assessment the results may come under increased scrutiny during the ongoing authorization

Security Status Reporting

Changes made to the information system through the continuous monitoring process must be reported to organizational officials including the authorizing official. The reporting process, including the report format, report structure, report frequency and report audience should be set at the enterprise level in the organizations ISCM strategy and program. If the enterprise has not yet accomplished this task, the security status reporting process is the responsibility of the system owner.

Contents of the security status reports should inform leadership of significant changes to the systems security status. This should include changes to the Plan of Actions & Milestones (POA&M), results of changes requested, approved and implemented by the change management and configuration control process, and changes to the systems environment. Changes to the environment can be physical, logical or even changes to the threat landscape.

The main outcomes of the reporting process is informing organizational leadership of changes to systems and the environment the systems operate in. This helps leadership ensure security requirements are progressing as required including compliance with POA&M and ATO restrictions. Leaders will use this information to continue to authorize systems, update organizations policy, and provide funding and projects to meet organizational security deficiencies.

NIST SP 800-37 Text
CONTINUOUS MONITORING STRATEGY—ORGANIZATION **TASK P-7** Develop and implement an organization-wide strategy for continuously monitoring control effectiveness. **Potential Inputs:** Risk management strategy; organization- and system-level risk assessment results; organizational security and privacy policies. **Expected Outputs:** An implemented organizational continuous monitoring strategy. **Primary Responsibility:** Senior Accountable Official for Risk Management or Risk Executive (Function). **Supporting Roles:** Chief Information Officer; Senior Agency Information Security Officer; Senior Agency Official for Privacy; Mission or Business Owner; System Owner; Authorizing Official or Authorizing Official Designated Representative. **Discussion:** An important aspect of risk management is the ability to monitor the security and privacy posture across the organization and the effectiveness of controls implemented within or inherited by organizational systems on an ongoing basis.64 An effective organization-wide continuous monitoring strategy is essential to efficiently and cost-effectively carry out such monitoring. Continuous monitoring strategies can also include supply chain risk considerations, for example, regularly reviewing supplier

foreign ownership, control, or influence (FOCI), monitoring inventory forecasts, or requiring on-going audits of suppliers. The implementation of a robust and comprehensive continuous monitoring program helps an organization understand the security and privacy posture of its information systems. It also facilitates ongoing authorization after the initial system or common control authorizations. This includes the potential for changing missions or business functions, stakeholders, technologies, vulnerabilities, threats, risks, and suppliers of systems, components, or services.

The organizational continuous monitoring strategy addresses monitoring requirements at the organization, mission/business process, and information system levels. The continuous monitoring strategy identifies the minimum monitoring frequency for implemented controls across the organization; defines the ongoing control assessment approach; and describes how ongoing assessments are to be conducted (e.g., addressing the use and management of automated tools, and instructions for ongoing assessment of controls for which monitoring cannot be automated). The continuous monitoring strategy may also define security and privacy reporting requirements including recipients of the reports. The criteria for determining the minimum frequency for control monitoring is established in collaboration with organizational officials (e.g., senior accountable official for risk management or risk executive [function)]; senior agency information security officer; senior agency official for privacy; chief information officer; system owners; common control providers; and authorizing officials or their designated representatives). An organizational risk assessment can be used to guide and inform the frequency of monitoring.

The use of automation facilitates a greater frequency and volume of control assessments as part of the monitoring process. The ongoing monitoring of controls using automated tools and supporting databases facilitates near real-time risk management for information systems and supports ongoing authorization and efficient use of resources. The senior accountable official for risk management or the risk executive (function) approves the continuous monitoring strategy including the minimum frequency with which controls are to be monitored.

References: [SP 800-30]; [SP 800-39] (Organization, Mission or Business Process, System Levels); [SP 800-53]; [SP 800-53A]; [SP 800-137]; [SP 800-161]; [IR 8011 v1]; [IR 8062]; [NIST CSF] (Core [Identify, Detect Functions]); [CNSSI 1253].

NOTES:

5. THE PREPARE STEP – SYSTEM TASKS

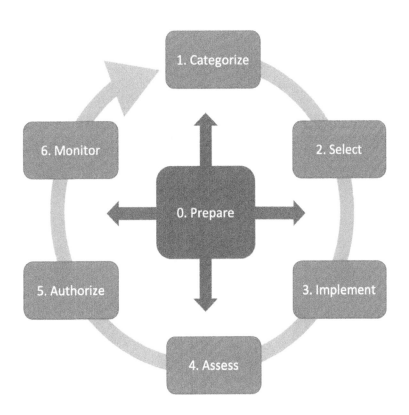

TASK P8 MISSION OR BUSINESS FOCUS

Responsibilities	
Primary Responsibility	Supporting Roles
- Mission or Business Owner	- Authorizing Official or Authorizing Official Designated Representative - System Owner - Information Owner or Steward - Chief Information Officer - Senior Agency Information Security Officer - Senior Agency Official for Privacy

SDLC Alignment	
New Systems	Legacy Systems
- Initiation (concept/requirements definition)	- Operations/Maintenance

CSF Alignment	
Profile	CSF Task
	- Profile -Implementation Tiers -ID.BE

Task Flow	
Inputs	Outputs
- Organizational mission statement - Organizational policies - Mission/business process information - System stakeholder information - Cybersecurity Framework Profiles - Requests for proposal or other acquisition documents - Concept of operations.	- Missions, business functions - Mission/business processes that the system will support

Understand organizational and mission operations

To develop a solid risk management program, organizational leadership, risk managers, and security personnel must know the essential functions and missions of the organization. By identifying these functions those information types and systems that support this mission can be identified. Systems that directly support the organization's mission will be placed at higher levels of risk and go under greater levels of scrutiny when going through tailoring, assessment, authorization and continuous monitoring. Systems with less or no impact on the organization's mission can undergo less scrutiny when completing these tasks and steps. This is a critical function of a risk management process, to tailor the security to a system based on its information types and impact to the organization's mission.

The mission of an organization is often stated in its mission statement, for example, the following is the mission statement of the U.S. Navy.

"The mission of the Navy is to maintain, train and equip combat-ready Naval forces capable of winning wars, deterring aggression and maintaining freedom of the seas."

https://www.navy.com/about/mission.1.html

The functions of the U.S. Navy are also defined in Title 10 of the U.S. Code as Control of the Sea and Power Projection. Therefore, systems that support that mission should be prioritized higher in the organization's risk registry and undergo more intensive evaluations and reviews during the RMF process. Those systems that do not directly support the mission or functions of the Navy can be evaluated and would likely result in a lower risk assessment in relation to the impact that could come to the organization.

At lower levels in the organization, at tier 2 for example, business units and mission support functions have specific functions that must be completed to make those organizations successful. These functions often support the overall organizational function in some way. For example the human resource business unit processes personnel actions, benefits, Payroll and other functions in support of the business. Likewise those supporting common control sets often support the enterprise mission at tier 2. An example for this latter case is an Active Directory (AD) system could support the enterprise identity and access management program and process.

At tier 3, the system level, it is important to understand how a specific system supports the organizational functions at tier 1 or 2. Systems directly supporting the organizations primary mission are often more critical than those supporting functions that are not aligned with the organizations primary function. Systems directly supporting the organizations mission could be expected to have more security controls assigned and expect the assessment of these controls to be more broadly examined using a more rigorous process of assessment.

As a system owner or security or risk professional you should review the input documents for this step to determine the specific organizational functions a system supports. This includes reviewing the organizational mission statement, organizational policies, concepts of operations and other documents.

NIST SP 800-37 Text
MISSION OR BUSINESS FOCUS
TASK P-8 Identify the missions, business functions, and mission/business processes that the system is intended to support.
Potential Inputs: Organizational mission statement; organizational policies; mission/business process information; system stakeholder information; Cybersecurity Framework Profiles; requests for proposal or other acquisition documents; concept of operations.
Expected Outputs: Missions, business functions, and mission/business processes that the system will support.
Primary Responsibility: Mission or Business Owner.
Supporting Roles: Authorizing Official or Authorizing Official Designated Representative; System Owner; Information Owner or Steward; Chief Information Officer; Senior Agency Information Security Officer; Senior Agency Official for Privacy.
System Development Life Cycle Phase: New – Initiation (concept/requirements definition). Existing – Operations/Maintenance.
Discussion: Organizational missions and business functions influence the design and development of the mission or business processes that are created to carry out those missions and business functions. The prioritization of missions and business functions drives investment strategies, funding decisions, resource prioritization, and risk decisions—and thus affects the existing enterprise architecture and development of the associated security and privacy architectures. Information is elicited from stakeholders to acquire a more thorough understanding of the missions, business functions, and mission/business processes of the organization from a system security and privacy perspective.
References: [SP 800-39] (Organization and Mission/Business Process Levels); [SP 800-64]; [SP 800-160 v1] (Business or Mission Analysis, Portfolio Management, and Project Planning Processes); [NIST CSF] (Core [Identify Function]); [IR 8179] (Criticality Analysis Process B).

EXERCISE 5.1

Using web research determine the mission of the United States Air Force Academy.

_____

_____

_____

_____

TASK P9 SYSTEMS STAKEHOLDERS

Responsibilities	
Primary Responsibility	Supporting Roles
- Mission or Business Owner - System Owner	- Chief Information Officer - Authorizing Official or Authorizing Official Designated Representative - Information Owner or Steward Senior Agency Information Security Officer - Senior Agency Official for Privacy - Chief Acquisition Officer

SDLC Alignment	
New Systems	Legacy Systems
- Initiation (concept/requirements definition)	- Operations/Maintenance

CSF Alignment	
CSF Number	CSF Task
	- ID.AM - ID.BE

Task Flow	
Inputs	Outputs
- Organizational mission statement; - Mission or business objectives - Missions, business functions, and mission/business processes that the system will support - Other mission/business process information - Organizational security and privacy policies and procedures - Organizational charts; information about individuals or groups (internal and external) that have an interest in and decision-making responsibility for the system	- List of system stakeholders

For the purpose of this task, stakeholders are those individuals or groups that are impacted by the development, operation, maintenance, or disposal of an information system. The BusinessDictionary defines a stakeholder as, "A person, group or organization that has interest or concern in an organization". (BusinessDictionary) These individuals or groups have a "stake" in the operation of the system (or common control set) and are impacted in some way by the system.

The RMF includes individuals, organizations and representatives as possible stakeholders. They have some interest in the information system through one or more steps or outputs of the system development lifecycles and by relation at one or more steps in the RMF.

A stakeholder may be interested in systems developed by the organization in house, in systems developed by third parties outside the organization, or both. For this reason, some stakeholders are impacted by one or more aspects of the systems supply chain. Stakeholders may have interest in the components being used to develop an in house developed system or may be impacted by the system or supplier developing a system outside the organization, often called third party system development.

As systems of interest may be inside the organization and outside the organization, stakeholders can come from both within and outside the organization. They can be in the same organization or organizational unit, in the same organization but different organizational units, or outside the organization itself. The main commonality between stakeholders is that they are impacted in some way by the information system.

Not all stakeholders are equal in relation to the information system. Some stakeholders may have direct input on the development of the system. Stakeholders can also have major or minor impact on a system, for example the authorizing official (AO) would be a major stakeholder of an information system. For this reason, the information system owner should develop a listing of all identified stakeholders and their associated level. The process for determining the level of impact should be determined by the organization as a policy or process, however if that does not exist it will be the responsibility of the information system owner to develop the rules and levels that apply to system stakeholders. A simple way to start is by using two levels, minor and major stakeholders, and expand from there if needed.

NIST SP 800-37 Text

SYSTEM STAKEHOLDERS

TASK P-9 Identify stakeholders who have an interest in the design, development, implementation, assessment, operation, maintenance, or disposal of the system.

Potential Inputs: Organizational mission statement; mission or business objectives; missions, business functions, and mission/business processes that the system will support; other mission/business process information; organizational security and privacy policies and procedures; organizational charts; information about individuals or groups (internal and external) that have an interest in and decision-making responsibility for the system.

Expected Outputs: List of system stakeholders.

Primary Responsibility: Mission or Business Owner; System Owner.

Supporting Roles: Chief Information Officer; Authorizing Official or Authorizing Official Designated Representative; Information Owner or Steward; Senior Agency Information Security Officer; Senior Agency Official for Privacy; Chief Acquisition Officer.

System Development Life Cycle Phase: New – Initiation (concept/requirements definition).

Existing – Operations/Maintenance.

Discussion: Stakeholders include individuals, organizations, or representatives that have an interest in the system throughout the system life cycle—for design, development, implementation, delivery, operation, and sustainment of the system. It also includes all aspects of the supply chain. Stakeholders may reside in the same organization or they may reside in different organizations in situations when there is a common interest by those organizations in the information system. For example, this may occur during the development, operation, and maintenance of cloud-based systems, shared service systems, or any system where organizations may be adversely impacted by a breach or a compromise to the system or for a variety of considerations related to the supply chain. Communication among stakeholders is important during every step in the RMF and throughout the SDLC to ensure that security and privacy requirements are satisfied, concerns and issues are addressed expeditiously, and risk management processes are carried out effectively.

References: [SP 800-39] (Organization Level); [SP 800-64]; [SP 800-160 v1] (Stakeholder Needs and Requirements Definition and Portfolio Management Processes); [SP 800-161]; [NIST CSF] (Core [Identify Function]).

EXERCISE 5.2

Consider a project you have worked on in the past. Besides those directly working on the project, what positions would you consider to be stakeholders in the project?

_____

_____

_____

_____

TASK P10 ASSET IDENTIFICATION

Responsibilities	
Primary Responsibility	Supporting Roles
- System Owner	- Authorizing Official or Authorizing Official Designated Representative - Mission or Business Owner - Information Owner or Steward - Senior Agency Information - Security Officer - Senior Agency Official for Privacy - System Administrator

SDLC Alignment	
New Systems	Legacy Systems
- Initiation (concept/requirements definition)	- Operations/Maintenance

CSF Alignment	
CSF Number	CSF Task
	ID.AM

Task Flow	
Inputs	Outputs
- Missions, business functions, and mission/business processes the information system will support - Business impact analyses - Internal stakeholders; system stakeholder information - System information - Information about other systems that interact with the system	- Set of assets to be protected

Assets are critical to the successful operation of an enterprise and the accomplishment of its mission or objective. After all, it is impossible to protect the enterprise assets if all assets are not known. Generally, it is accepted that an asset is anything of value and can be tangible or intangible.

Tangible assets are those assets that most people are familiar with. These are physical; in simple terms, these are assets a person can touch or hold. Physical assets include buildings, computers, networks, humans, and other non-digital things.

Intangible assets are less familiar to most people. These include things that cannot be touched and exist as ideas or as digital information. Included in this category are things like software, firmware, procedures, digital information, and image or reputation.

Information itself is one of the most significant assets that organizations are charged to protect in modern system design and operation. Controlled information, including privacy, classified, healthcare, and business-critical information is often some of the most protected of information assets. It is essential that information owners, information stewards, and other key stakeholders within the organization determine the levels of protection for information assets. These levels provide the basis for making risk-based decisions concerning safeguarding this information. Information deemed to be more sensitive or critical to the enterprise is a higher risk and offered more protection. This higher level of protection often results in a more significant number of controls that are implemented and maintained at a higher level of rigor and depth.

Organizational assets, tangible or intangible, should be inventoried and maintained in an enterprise level database. Often the most effective way to accomplish this is to develop an enterprise level configuration management database (CMDB) or asset management database (AMDB) that is part of the enterprise configuration management or asset management program. This database or another inventory system should identify those assets that require protection, how to protect the assets, their business functions, system interconnections, and other vital elements.

NIST SP 800-37 Text
ASSET IDENTIFICATION **TASK P-10** Identify assets that require protection. **Potential Inputs:** Missions, business functions, and mission/business processes the information system will support; business impact analyses; internal stakeholders; system stakeholder information; system information; information about other systems that interact with the system. **Expected Outputs:** Set of assets to be protected. **Primary Responsibility:** System Owner. **Supporting Roles:** Authorizing Official or Authorizing Official Designated Representative; Mission or Business Owner; Information Owner or Steward; Senior Agency Information Security Officer; Senior Agency Official for Privacy; System Administrator. **System Development Life Cycle Phase:** New – Initiation (concept/requirements definition). Existing – Operations/Maintenance. **Discussion:** Assets are tangible and intangible items that are of value to achievement of mission or business objectives. Tangible assets are physical in nature and include physical/environmental elements (e.g., non-digital information, structures, facilities), human elements, and

technology/machine elements (e.g., hardware elements, mechanisms, and networks). In contrast, intangible assets are not physical in nature and include mission and business processes, functions, digital information and data, firmware, software, and services. Information assets can be tangible or intangible assets, and can include the information needed to carry out missions or business functions, to deliver services, and for system management/operation; controlled unclassified information and classified information; and all forms of documentation associated with the information system. Intangible assets can also include the image or reputation of an organization, and the privacy interests of the individuals whose information will be processed by the system. The organization defines the scope of stakeholder assets to be considered for protection. The assets that require protection are identified based on stakeholder concerns and the contexts in which the assets are used. This includes the missions or business functions of the organization; the other systems that interact with the system; and stakeholders whose assets are utilized by the mission or business functions or by the system. Assets can be documented in the system security and privacy plans.

References: [SP 800-39] (Organization Level); [SP 800-64]; [SP 800-160 v1] (Stakeholder Needs and Requirements Definition Process); [IR 8179] (Criticality Analysis Process C); [NIST CSF] (Core [Identify Function]); [NARA CUI].

EXERCISE 5.3

Assets can be both tangible and intangible. Describe one tangible asset and one intangible asset you may encounter when working on an information system.

_____

_____

_____

_____

TASK P11 AUTHORIZATION BOUNDARY

Responsibilities	
Primary Responsibility	Supporting Roles
- Authorizing Official	- Chief Information Officer - System Owner - Mission or Business Owner - Senior Agency Information Security Officer - Senior Agency Official for Privacy - Enterprise Architect.

SDLC Alignment	
New Systems	Legacy Systems

| - Initiation (concept/requirements definition) | - Operations/Maintenance |

CSF Alignment	
CSF Number	CSF Task

Task Flow	
Inputs	Outputs
- System design documentation - network diagrams - system stakeholder information - asset information - network and/or enterprise architecture diagrams - organizational structure (charts, information)	- Documented authorization boundary

Determining system boundaries can seem to be a delicate balance between an art and a science. System boundaries that are too large will result in systems that are hard to implement and cumbersome to process through the RMF. When organizations defined boundaries that create small systems the number of systems that must be processed through the RMF increases. For these reasons establishing well-defined and well-planned system boundaries can result in effective and efficient implementations in the RMF. Many things can help defining information system boundaries. For example, information systems should be under the control of a single authorizing the official, support a common goal, and be under the same direct management or control. In addition to being under the same direct management or control System boundaries can be determined if the information system:

- Support the same mission/business objectives or functions and essentially the same operating characteristics and information security requirements; and
- Reside in the same general operating environment (or in the case of a distributed information system, reside in various locations with similar operating environments).

Many times, organizations may take the approach of combining many smaller subsystems into a single larger system where these subsystems remain independent but fall under the same authorization boundary. In these cases, security controls can often be applied to only those subsystems that require additional protection, if subsystems contain protections to inshore information does not cross subsystem boundaries. This combination of independent subsystems is often referred to as "a system of systems". Conversely, individual subsystems may be accredited individually, with each system being processed through the RMF on its own.

It is also possible that an application or piece of software is authorized as an individual system. In these cases, the software boundary is the authorization boundary and this authorization boundary would follow the same general rules as any other information system. In many cases, these application authorizations Will benefit from Controls inherited not only from the organization here one and tier 2 but also from the underlying operating system that operates accurately as another information system. For example, and organizations generic Windows desktop used by the general user population could be the common control provider for many of the controls inherited by the application for software as it processes through the RMF.

Complex systems create unique challenges for security personnel in relation to determining the bounds of the authorization. These systems are often made of Full large and small components and often contain static and dynamic subsystems. Establishing correct authorization boundaries can be a difficult task where organizations can create boundaries that are too small, creating too many systems to authorize or too large and complex creating systems that are hard to process through the RMF, figure 5-1 illustrates this challenge.

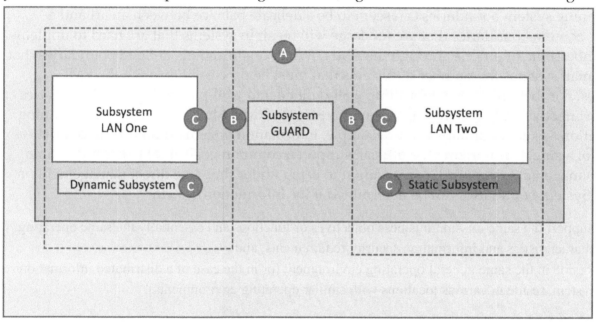

Figure 5-1, Complex System

In this case, the organization could create an organization boundary represented by the letter "A" where LAN One, LAN Two, System Guard, Dynamic Subsystem, and Static Subsystem are all part of one system boundary. They could also elect to create two systems as indicated by the letter "B", with one system being LAN One and the Dynamic Subsystem and the other system being LAN Two and the Static Subsystem. Yet another option would be each of these components being its own system as indicated by the letter "C". There are other ways that the authorization boundary could be drawn from these systems, this illustrates the challenge of defining suitable authorization boundaries.

Net-centric and cloud architectures create new challenges when portions of a system may be hosted by an external entity. In these cases, there must be a level of trust between the system owner and external provider. Several factors complicate creating systems in net-centric and cloud environments including the following.

- The delineation between what is owned by the external entity and the organization may be somewhat blurred (e.g., organization-owned platform executing external entity-developed service/application software or firmware);
- The degree of control the organization has over the external entity providing/supporting the subsystems/services may be very limited;
- The nature and content of the subsystems may be subject to rapid change; and
- The subsystems/services may be of such critical nature that they need to be incorporated into organizational information systems very rapidly.

NIST SP 800-37 Text

AUTHORIZATION BOUNDARY

TASK P-11 Determine the authorization boundary of the system.

Potential Inputs: System design documentation; network diagrams; system stakeholder information; asset information; network and/or enterprise architecture diagrams; organizational structure (charts, information).

Expected Outputs: Documented authorization boundary.

Primary Responsibility: Authorizing Official.

Supporting Roles: Chief Information Officer; System Owner; Mission or Business Owner; Senior Agency Information Security Officer; Senior Agency Official for Privacy; Enterprise Architect.

System Development Life Cycle Phase: New – Initiation (concept/requirements definition). Existing – Operations/Maintenance.

Discussion: Authorization boundaries establish the scope of protection for information systems (i.e., what the organization agrees to protect under its management control or within the scope of its responsibilities). Authorization boundaries are determined by authorizing officials with input from the system owner based on mission, management, or budgetary responsibility (see Appendix F). A clear delineation of authorization boundaries is important for accountability and for security categorization, especially in situations where lower-impact systems are connected to higher-impact systems, or when external providers are responsible for the operation or maintenance of a system. Each system includes a set of elements (i.e., information resources)65 organized to achieve one or more purposes and to support the organization's missions and business processes. Each system element is implemented in a way that allows the organization to satisfy specified security and privacy requirements. System elements include human elements, technology/machine elements, and physical/environmental elements.

The term system is used to define the set of system elements, system element interconnections, and the environment that is the focus of the RMF implementation (see Figure 5). The system is included in a single authorization boundary to ensure accountability. For systems processing PII, the privacy and security programs collaborate to develop a common understanding of authorization boundaries. To

---

conduct effective risk assessments and select appropriate controls, privacy and security programs provide a clear and consistent understanding of what constitutes the authorization boundary. Understanding the authorization boundary and what will occur beyond it may influence controls selected and how they are implemented. For example, if a function of the system includes sharing PII externally, robust encryption controls may be selected for PII transmitted from the system. Similarly, for systems either partially or wholly managed, maintained, or operated by external providers, an agreement clearly describing authorization boundaries ensures accountability. Privacy and security programs collaborate with providers to develop a common understanding of authorization boundaries. Formal agreements with external providers (e.g. contracts) may be used to delineate what constitutes authorization boundaries. Understanding such boundaries facilitates the selection of appropriate controls to manage supply chain risk.

References: [SP 800-18]; [SP 800-39] (System Level); [SP 800-47]; [SP 800-64]; [SP 800-160 v1] (System Requirements Definition Process); [NIST CSF] (Core [Identify Function]).

EXERCISE 5.4

What is a disadvantage of setting the system boundary too large? What is a disadvantage of setting the boundary too small?

_____

_____

_____

_____

TASK P12 INFORMATION TYPES

Responsibilities	
Primary Responsibility	Supporting Roles
- System Owner - Information Owner or Steward	- Mission or Business Owner - System Security Officer - System Privacy Officer

SDLC Alignment	
New Systems	Legacy Systems
- Initiation (concept/requirements definition)	- Operations/Maintenance

CSF Alignment	
CSF Number	CSF Task
	ID.AM-6

Task Flow	
Inputs	Outputs
- System design documentation - Assets to be protected - Mission/business process information - System design documentation	- A list of information types for the system

By determining the information types, the information system can be developed with the correct security profile. This is accomplished by determining the categorization of individual information types that will be processed by the information system as well as categorizing the information system itself.

The most straightforward and basic way to categorize an information system starts with identifying the types of information that will be processed, stored, transmitted of displayed by the information system. The basic information types can be found in NIST SP 800-60, volumes 1 and 2, documents that are indispensable in defining the impact levels for information systems. Using these documents will result in a quantifiable and defendable provisional impact level.

A word of caution is needed at this point. SP 800-60 was developed using the Office of Management and Budget's (OMB) Business Reference Model (BRM) published in 2007. This results in four lines of business
- The purpose of government (services for citizens);
- The mechanisms the government uses to achieve its purpose (mode of delivery);
- The support functions necessary to conduct government operations (support delivery of services); and

- The resource management functions that support all areas of the government's business (management of government resources).

These four lines of business are further decomposed into 39 (FEA) lines of business. The FEA lines are further decomposed into 177 information types. Although this is a high number it is possible that many information types are missing, in this case the organization developing the information system will need to come to consensus of the impact levels of these undocumented information types. It should go without saying these new information types should be documented following the organizations policies and procedures.

Determining the provisional impact level for an information system begins with identifying every information type that will be stored, processed, transmitted or displayed by the system. This listing can then be used with SP 800-60 volume 2 to determine each individual information types impact level for the individual security objectives confidentiality, integrity and availability, commonly known as the "CIA triad".

For example, let's assume the system being developed supports information technology security services. Through meetings, research and debate it has been determined that this system will store, process, transmit or display the following three information types (while this short listing of information types is unrealistic for real information systems it serves well for illustration).
- Information Security Information Type
- Infrastructure Maintenance Information Type
- System and Network Monitoring Information Type

SP 800-60 volume 2 is used to determine the impact levels for each of the security objectives. Working through these three information types, we determine the impact levels as follows.

Information Security Information Type
Security Category = {(confidentiality, Low), (integrity, Moderate), (availability, Low)}

Infrastructure Maintenance Information Type
Security Category = {(confidentiality, Low), (integrity, Low), (availability, Low)}

System and Network Monitoring Information Type

Security Category = {(confidentiality, Moderate), (integrity, Moderate), (availability, Low)}

There are special factors to consider when developing the security objectives impact levels and these are often defined in SP 800-60 volume 2 in the paragraphs titles "special factors". These cases often modify the security objectives impact level up or down based on specific criteria. In our example there are no special factors to consider so this will not be addressed. Once all of the information types for the system have been identified it is common to display these in table 5-1 as follows.

Information Type	Confidentiality	Integrity	Availability
Information Security	Low	Moderate	Low
Infrastructure Maintenance	Low	Low	Low
System and Network Monitoring	Moderate	Moderate	Low

Table 5-1 Information Type Categorization Example

NIST SP 800-37 Text

INFORMATION TYPES

TASK P-12 Identify the types of information to be processed, stored, and transmitted by the system.

Potential Inputs: System design documentation; assets to be protected; mission/business process information; system design documentation.

Expected Outputs: A list of information types for the system.

Primary Responsibility: System Owner; Information Owner or Steward.

Supporting Role: Mission or Business Owner; System Security Officer; System Privacy Officer. System Development Life Cycle Phase: New – Initiation (concept/requirements definition). Existing – Operations/Maintenance.

Discussion: Identifying the types of information needed to support organizational missions, business functions, and mission/business processes is an important step in developing security and privacy plans for the system and a precondition for determining the security categorization. [NARA CUI] defines the information types that require protection as part of its Controlled Unclassified Information (CUI) program, in accordance with laws, regulations, or governmentwide policies. Organizations may define additional information types needed to support organizational missions, business functions, and mission/business processes that are not defined in the CUI Registry or in [SP 800-60 v2]. Identified information types are confirmed by the information owners or stewards and documented in the system security and privacy plans.

References: [OMB A-130]; [NARA CUI]; [SP 800-39] (System Level); [SP 800-60 v1]; [SP 800-60 v2]; [NIST CSF] (Core [Identify Function]).

EXERCISE 5.5

Using NIST SP 800-60 Volume 2, determine the categorization for the Agricultural Innovation and Services Information Type with no special factors affecting the impact determination?

_____

_____

_____

_____

TASK P13 INFORMATION LIFECYCLE

Responsibilities	
Primary Responsibility	Supporting Roles
- Senior Agency Official for Privacy - System Owner - Information Owner or Steward.	- Chief Information Officer - Mission or Business Owner; Security Architect - Privacy Architect - Enterprise Architect - Systems Security Engineer - Privacy Engineer

SDLC Alignment	
New Systems	Legacy Systems
– Initiation (concept/requirements definition).	- Operations/Maintenance

CSF Alignment	
CSF Number	CSF Task
	- ID.AM-3 - ID.AM-4

Task Flow	
Inputs	Outputs
- Missions, business functions, and mission/business processes the system will support; system stakeholder information - Authorization boundary information - Information about other systems that interact with the system (e.g., information exchange/connection agreements) - System design documentation - System element information - List of system information types	- Documentation of the stages through which information passes in the system, such as a data map or model illustrating how information is structured or is processed by the system throughout its life cycle - Such documentation includes, for example, data flow diagrams, entity relationship diagrams, database schemas, and data dictionaries

The classification of information and information types is the basis for the categorization of the information system and the baseline controls that will be identified. This information passes through the system and how it flows and is processed can impact the assessment of risk for the system and the organization. Understanding how information travels through the system is critical to protecting the system and information. To facilitate this understanding the information system owner can develop data maps that illustrate the flow of data through the system and how that data is transformed as it passes through the system. This transformation can impact the stage of the information lifecycle.

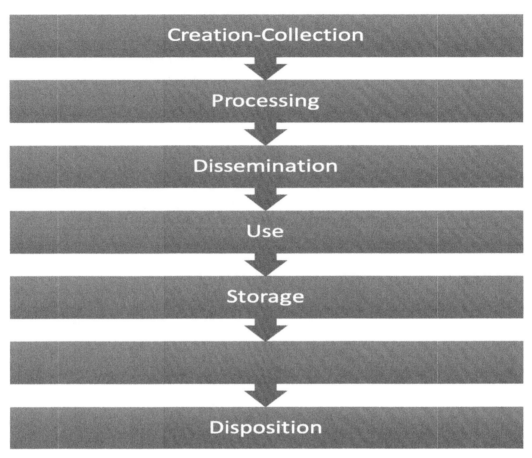

Figure 5-0-2 Information Lifecycle

Development of data flows can also help the system owner understand how his or her system interacts with other systems helping to define system boundaries and interconnection requirements. Information may be ingested from other systems or collected or created by the information system itself. The information may enter the system at one stage in the information life cycle and leave the system in a different stage depending on how it is processed by the information system. The creation or transformation of information by the system should be detailed in the systems data flow diagram.

The information lifecycle is normally described as six stages that information passes through. These stages are creation or collection, processing, dissemination, use, storage, and disposition, to include destruction and deletion. The system owner must understand the different requirements needed to protect information at different stages in the information lifecycle. A good example is when a system will be responsible for the disposition of information, the system owner must understand that information types retention requirements and the processes required to successfully delete the information from the systems media types, such as hard drives.

The system owner is responsible for the protection of each information type at every stage in the information lifecycle that is handled by the information system. For this reason, the information system owner must have a basic understanding of the six stages the information passes through as it moves through the information lifecycle.

NIST SP 800-37 Text

INFORMATION LIFE CYCLE

TASK P-13 Identify and understand all stages of the information life cycle for each information type processed, stored, or transmitted by the system.

Potential Inputs: Missions, business functions, and mission/business processes the system will support; system stakeholder information; authorization boundary information; information about other systems that interact with the system (e.g., information exchange/connection agreements); system design documentation; system element information; list of system information types.

Expected Outputs: Documentation of the stages through which information passes in the system, such as a data map or model illustrating how information is structured or is processed by the system throughout its life cycle. Such documentation includes, for example, data flow diagrams, entity relationship diagrams, database schemas, and data dictionaries.

Primary Responsibility: Senior Agency Official for Privacy; System Owner; Information Owner or Steward.

Supporting Roles: Chief Information Officer; Mission or Business Owner; Security Architect; Privacy Architect; Enterprise Architect; Systems Security Engineer; Privacy Engineer.

System Development Life Cycle Phase: New – Initiation (concept/requirements definition). Existing – Operations/Maintenance.

Discussion: The information life cycle describes the stages through which information passes, typically characterized as creation or collection, processing, dissemination, use, storage, and disposition, to include destruction and deletion [OMB A-130]. Identifying and understanding how each information type is processed during all stages of the life cycle helps organizations identify considerations for protecting the information, informs the organization's security and privacy risk assessments, and informs the selection and implementation of controls. Identification and understanding of the information life cycle facilitates the employment of practices to help ensure, for example, that organizations have the authority to collect or create information, develop rules related to the processing of information in accordance with its impact level, create agreements for information sharing, and follow retention schedules for the storage and disposition of information.

Using tools such as a data map enables organizations to understand how information is being processed so that organizations can better assess where security and privacy risks could arise and where controls could be applied most effectively. It is important for organizations to consider the appropriate delineation of the authorization boundary and the information system's interaction with other systems because the way information enters and leaves the system can affect the security and privacy risk assessments. The elements of the system are identified with sufficient granularity to support such risk assessments.

Identifying and understanding the information life cycle is particularly relevant for the assessment of security and privacy risks since information may be processed by a system in any of the SDLC phases. For example, in the testing and integration phase of the SDLC, processing actual (i.e., live) data would likely raise security and privacy risks, but using substitute (i.e., synthetic) data may allow an equivalent benefit in terms of system testing while reducing risk.

References: [OMB A-130]; [OMB M-13-13]; [NARA RECM]; [NIST CSF] (Core [Identify Function]); [IR 8062].

EXERCISE 5.6

Describe one of the six stages of the information lifecycle.

TASK P14 RISK ASSESSMENT - SYSTEM

Responsibilities	
Primary Responsibility	Supporting Roles
- System Owner - System Security Officer - System Privacy Officer	- Senior Accountable Official for Risk Management or Risk Executive (Function) - Authorizing Official or Authorizing Official Designated Representative - Mission or Business Owner - Information Owner or Steward - Control Assessor

SDLC Alignment	
New Systems	Legacy Systems
- Initiation (concept/requirements definition).	- Operations/Maintenance

CSF Alignment	
CSF Number	CSF Task
	- ID.RA - ID.SC-2

Task Flow	
Inputs	Outputs
- Assets to be protected - Missions, business functions, and mission/business processes the system will support - Business impact analyses or criticality analyses - System stakeholder information - Information about other systems that interact with the system; provider information - Threat information - Data map; system design documentation - Cybersecurity Framework Profiles - Risk management strategy - Organization-level risk assessment results	- Security and privacy risk assessment reports

Assessing risk is a process that must occur at every tier of the organization, including conducting risk assessments at the information system, or Tier 3, level. This is done to ensure that each type of risk is addressed based on the sensitivity of the information processed by that information system and the criticality the system has to accomplishment of the organizational mission.

Expansion of the basic risk model is required to fully address the assessment of risk at the information system level. The basic risk model is Threat + Vulnerability = Risk and works very well to define basic risks but can be expanded to be more detailed as illustrated in figure 5-3.

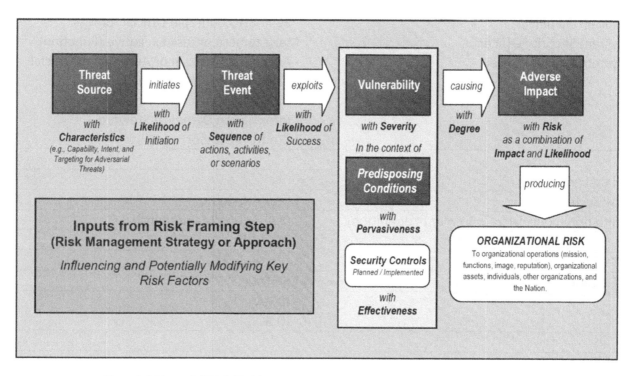

Figure 5-3 Expanded Risk Model

This model is a simplified version of the one defined in NIST SP 800-30, Risk Assessments. However even this simplistic model provides a much more detailed picture of risk is defined. In this case a threat source initiates a threat event that will exploit a vulnerability causing an adverse impact on an asset that will produce an organizational risk. It is also evident that the there is a required likelihood that the threat event will be initiated and also a likelihood that the exploit will actually be successful in exploiting the vulnerability.

Each organizational asset must be assessed to provide a risk assessment result or score. The assets can then be prioritized based on this score that the impact that the information systems loss of exploitation would have on the organization. Loss can be different based on the type of asset including tangible and intangible assets and should be evaluated on differing levels of loss up to and including total loss. A number of factors affect the prioritization of the assets value, NIST provides some assets for illustrative purposes and includes the following.

- Asset value
- Physical consequences
- Cost of replacement
- Criticality
- Impact on image or reputation

- Trust by users, by collaborating organizations, or by mission or business partners, and defining levels of assurance.

The prioritization once complete provides a listing of assets listed in order of their impact on the organizations mission of other risk rating and assists in the allocation of scares resources. This listing can also assist risk managers in identifying high value assets or systems that should be required to more strictly comply with control allocation, implementation and more rigorous and inclusive control assessment. Higher impact system should be meet higher assurance levels while lower impact systems should not be held to the same assurance levels and requirements based on results of the risk assessment and a risk-based approach to implementation and development.

Risk assessments should also be conducted to assess the information system for the processing of Personally Identifiable Information (PII) often called privacy information. These assessments would address the impact of the loss of one or more of the security objectives (confidentiality, availably, or integrity) if compromised by a threat source. The loss or compromise of PII or privacy information could cause detrimental impact on the organization by causing individuals to lose trust in the system processing the PII or may result in fines or penalties for such losses.

NIST defines a number of illustrative contextual factors that can impact privacy risk assessments. It is important to understand that the following list is just examples of these factors and is not exhaustive.
- The sensitivity level of the PII, including specific elements or in aggregate
- The types of organizations using or interacting with the system and individuals' perceptions about the organizations with respect to privacy
- Individuals' understanding about the nature and purpose of the processing
- The privacy interests of individuals, technological expertise or demographic characteristics that influence their understanding or behavior

Organizations must include third party suppliers and other sources of outsourced information services including outsourced data systems, information services and cloud service providers in risk assessments to provide a full picture of the risk that the organization faces. This would include third party developers, implementors, and operators of information systems. At times it is advisable to ask for, and review, risk assessments of outsourced providers including assessments of the supply chain.

Risk assessments should occur throughout the system, or software, development lifecycle (SDLC) and can occur at any step in the risk management framework. In these cases, the risk assessment results inform:
- Security and privacy requirements definition
- Categorization decisions
- The selection, tailoring, implementation, and assessment of controls
- Authorization decisions
- Potential courses of action and prioritization for risk responses

- Continuous monitoring strategy

NIST SP 800-37 Text
RISK ASSESSMENT—SYSTEM **TASK P-14** Conduct a system-level risk assessment and update the risk assessment results on an ongoing basis. **Potential Inputs:** Assets to be protected; missions, business functions, and mission/business processes the system will support; business impact analyses or criticality analyses; system stakeholder information; information about other systems that interact with the system; provider information; threat information; data map; system design documentation; Cybersecurity Framework Profiles; risk management strategy; organization-level risk assessment results. **Expected Outputs:** Security and privacy risk assessment reports. **Primary Responsibility:** System Owner; System Security Officer; System Privacy Officer. **Supporting Roles:** Senior Accountable Official for Risk Management or Risk Executive (Function); Authorizing Official or Authorizing Official Designated Representative; Mission or Business Owner; Information Owner or Steward; Control Assessor. **System Development Life Cycle Phase:** New – Initiation (concept/requirements definition). Existing – Operations/Maintenance. **Discussion:** This task may require that organizations conduct security and privacy risk assessments to ensure that each type of risk is fully assessed. Assessment of security risk includes identification of threat sources67 and threat events affecting assets, whether and how the assets are vulnerable to the threats, the likelihood that an asset vulnerability will be exploited by a threat, and the impact (or consequence) of loss of the assets. As a key part of the risk assessment, assets are prioritized based on the adverse impact or consequence of asset loss. The meaning of loss is defined for each asset type to enable a determination of the loss consequence (i.e., the adverse impact of the loss). Loss consequences may be tangible (e.g., monetary, industrial casualties) or intangible (e.g., reputation) and constitute a continuum that spans from partial loss to total loss relative to the asset. Interpretations of information loss may include, for example, loss of possession, destruction, or loss of precision or accuracy. The loss of a function or service may be interpreted as a loss of control, loss of accessibility, loss of the ability to deliver normal function, performance, or behavior, or a limited loss of capability resulting in a level of degradation of function, performance, or behavior. Physical consequences of compromise can include unscheduled production downtime, industrial equipment damage, casualties at the site, environmental disasters and public safety threats. Prioritization of assets is based on asset value, physical consequences, cost of replacement, criticality, impact on image or reputation, or trust by users, by collaborating organizations, or by mission or business partners. The asset priority translates to precedence in allocating resources, determining strength of

mechanisms, and defining levels of assurance.

Privacy risk assessments are conducted to determine the likelihood that a given operation the system is taking when processing PII could create an adverse effect on individuals—and the potential impact on individuals.68 These adverse effects can arise from unauthorized activities that lead to the loss of confidentiality, integrity, or availability in information systems processing PII, or may arise as a byproduct of authorized activities. Privacy risk assessments are influenced by contextual factors. Contextual factors can include, but are not limited to, the sensitivity level of the PII, including specific elements or in aggregate; the types of organizations using or interacting with the system and individuals' perceptions about the organizations with respect to privacy; individuals' understanding about the nature and purpose of the processing; and the privacy interests of individuals, technological expertise or demographic characteristics that influence their understanding or behavior. The privacy risks to individuals may affect individuals' decisions to engage with the system thereby impacting mission or business objectives, or create legal liability, reputational risks, or other types of risks for the organization. Impacts to the organization are not privacy risks. However, these impacts can guide and inform organizational decision-making and influence prioritization and resource allocation for risk response.

Risk assessments are also conducted to determine the potential that the use of an external provider for the development, implementation, maintenance, management, operation, or disposition of a system, system element, or service could create a loss, and the potential impact of that loss. The impact may be immediate (e.g., physical theft) or on-going (e.g., the ability of adversaries to replicate critical equipment because of theft). The impact may be endemic (e.g., limited to a single system) or systemic (e.g., including any system that uses a specific type of system component). Supply chain risk assessments consider vulnerabilities which may arise related to the disposition of a system or system element and from the use of external providers. Vulnerabilities in the supply chain may include a lack of traceability or accountability leading to the potential use of counterfeits, insertion of malware, or poor-quality systems. The use of external providers may result in a loss of visibility and control over how systems, system elements, and services are developed, deployed, and maintained. A clear understanding of the threats, vulnerabilities, and potential impacts of an adverse supply chain event can help organizations appropriately balance supply chain risk with risk tolerance. Supply chain risk assessments can include information from supplier audits, reviews, and supply chain intelligence. Organizations develop a strategy for collecting information, including a strategy for collaborating with providers on supply chain risk assessments. Such collaboration helps organizations leverage information from providers, reduce redundancy, identify potential courses of action for risk responses, and reduce the burden on providers.

Risk assessments are conducted throughout the SDLC and support various RMF steps and tasks. Risk assessment results are used to inform security and privacy requirements definition; categorization decisions; the selection, tailoring, implementation, and assessment of controls; authorization decisions; potential courses of action and prioritization for risk responses; and continuous monitoring strategy. Organizations determine the form of risk assessment conducted (including the scope, rigor, and formality of such assessments) and method of reporting results.

References: [FIPS 199]; [FIPS 200]; [SP 800-30]; [SP 800-39] (Organization Level); [SP 800-59]; [SP 800-60 v1]; [SP 800-60 v2]; [SP 800-64]; [SP 800-160 v1] (Stakeholder Needs and Requirements Definition and Risk Management Processes); [SP 800-161] (Assess); [IR 8062]; [IR 8179]; [NIST CSF] (Core [Identify Function]); [CNSSI 1253].

EXERCISE 5.7

Describe the expanded risk model as illustrated in this section.

_____

_____

_____

_____

Task P15 Requirements Definition

Responsibilities	
Primary Responsibility	Supporting Roles
- Mission or Business Owner - System Owner - Information Owner or Steward - System Privacy Officer.	- Authorizing Official or Authorizing Official Designated Representative - System Security Officer - Senior Agency Information Security Officer - Senior Agency Official for Privacy - Chief Acquisition Officer; Security Architect - Privacy Architect - Enterprise Architect.

SDLC Alignment	
New Systems	Legacy Systems
- Initiation (concept/requirements definition)	- Operations/Maintenance

CSF Alignment	
CSF Number	CSF Task
	- IDGV
	- PR.IP

Task Flow	
Inputs	Outputs
- System design documentation - Organization- and system-level risk assessment results - Known set of stakeholder assets to be protected - Missions, business functions, and mission/business processes the system will support - Business impact analyses or criticality analyses - System stakeholder information - Data map of the information life cycle for PII - Cybersecurity Framework Profiles - Information about other systems that interact with the system	- Documented security and privacy requirements

- Supply chain information - Threat information - Laws, executive orders, directives, regulations, or policies that apply to the system - Risk management strategy	

Protection needs are an expression of the protection capability required for the system in order to reduce security and privacy risk to an acceptable level while supporting mission or business needs. Protection needs include the security characteristics of the system and the security behavior of the system in its intended operational environment and across all system life cycle phases. The protection needs reflect the priorities of stakeholders, results of negotiations among stakeholders in response to conflicts, opposing priorities, contradictions, and stated objectives, and thus, are inherently subjective. The protection needs are documented to help ensure that the reasoning, assumptions, and constraints associated with those needs are available for future reference and to provide traceability to the security and privacy requirements.

The protection needs of an asset are defined as the protection capability required to reduce the security and privacy risks to an acceptable level while still enabling the accomplishment of the organizational mission or other business needs as defined and approved by organizational stakeholders. These include the security characteristics of the system throughout all phases of the SDLC. According to NIST protection needs are, "are documented to help ensure that the reasoning, assumptions, and constraints associated with those needs are available for future reference and to provide traceability to the security and privacy requirements".

Security and privacy requirements on the other hand are more formal, granular and detailed methods of protecting the systems and information throughout the SDLC. These requirements are mandated by a number of different sources including the following.
- Laws
- Executive orders
- Directives
- Regulations
- Policies
- Standards
- Mission and business needs
- Risk assessments

These requirements assist in the selection of baseline controls and the tailoring of those baseline controls to be as effective as possible in protecting the organization, the information system and the information.

Some organization find it helpful to use the NIST Cybersecurity Framework (CSF) to assist in defining the security requirements and defining those requirements as CSF profiles. When done correctly these CSF profiles can be helpful in developing organizationally defined baseline controls sets.

NIST SP 800-37 Text

REQUIREMENTS DEFINITION

TASK P-15 Define the security and privacy requirements for the system and the environment of operation.

Potential Inputs: System design documentation; organization- and system-level risk assessment results; known set of stakeholder assets to be protected; missions, business functions, and mission/business processes the system will support; business impact analyses or criticality analyses; system stakeholder information; data map of the information life cycle for PII; Cybersecurity Framework Profiles; information about other systems that interact with the system; supply chain information; threat information; laws, executive orders, directives, regulations, or policies that apply to the system; risk management strategy.

Expected Outputs: Documented security and privacy requirements.

Primary Responsibility: Mission or Business Owner; System Owner; Information Owner or Steward; System Privacy Officer.

Supporting Roles: Authorizing Official or Authorizing Official Designated Representative; System Security Officer; Senior Agency Information Security Officer; Senior Agency Official for Privacy; Chief Acquisition Officer; Security Architect; Privacy Architect; Enterprise Architect.

System Development Life Cycle Phase: New – Initiation (concept/requirements definition). Existing – Operations/Maintenance.

Discussion: Protection needs are an expression of the protection capability required for the system in order to reduce security and privacy risk to an acceptable level while supporting mission or business needs. Protection needs include the security characteristics of the system and the security behavior of the system in its intended operational environment and across all system life cycle phases. The protection needs reflect the priorities of stakeholders, results of negotiations among stakeholders in response to conflicts, opposing priorities, contradictions, and stated objectives, and thus, are inherently subjective. The protection needs are documented to help ensure that the reasoning, assumptions, and constraints associated with those needs are available for future reference and to

---

provide traceability to the security and privacy requirements. Security and privacy requirements constitute a formal, more granular expression of protection needs across all SDLC phases, the associated life cycle processes, and protections for the assets associated with the system. Security and privacy requirements are obtained from many sources (e.g., laws, executive orders, directives, regulations, policies, standards, mission and business needs, or risk assessments). Security and privacy requirements are an important part of the formal expression of the required characteristics of the system.72 The security and privacy requirements guide and inform the selection of controls for a system and the tailoring activities associated with those controls.

Organizations can use the Cybersecurity Framework to manage security and privacy requirements and express those requirements in Cybersecurity Framework *Profiles* defined for the organization. For instance, multiple requirements can be aligned and even deconflicted using the *Function-Category-Subcategory* structure of the Framework Core. The Profiles can then be used to inform the development of organizationally-tailored control baselines described in the RMF *Prepare-Organization Level* step, Task P-4.

References: [SP 800-39] (Organization Level); [SP 800-64]; [SP 800-160 v1] (Stakeholder Needs and Requirements Definition Process); [SP 800-161] (Multi-Tiered Risk Management); [IR 8179]; [NIST CSF] (Core [Protect, Detect, Respond, Recover Functions]; Profiles).

EXERCISE 5.8

In your own words describe protection needs.

_____

_____

_____

_____

TASK P16 ENTERPRISE ARCHITECTURE

Responsibilities	
Primary Responsibility	Supporting Roles
- Mission or Business Owner - Enterprise Architect - Security Architect - Privacy Architect.	- Chief Information Officer - Authorizing Official or Authorizing Official Designated Representative - Senior Agency Information Security Officer - Senior Agency Official for Privacy - System Owner - Information Owner or Steward

SDLC Alignment	
New Systems	Legacy Systems
- New – Initiation (concept/requirements definition)	- Existing – Operations/Maintenance

CSF Alignment	
CSF Number	CSF Task

Task Flow	
Inputs	Outputs
- Security and privacy requirements - Organization- and system-level risk assessment results - Enterprise architecture information - Security architecture information - Privacy architecture information - Asset information	- Updated enterprise architecture - Updated security architecture - Updated privacy architecture - Plans to use cloud-based systems and shared systems, services, or applications

The enterprise and information security architecture play an important role in not only the RMF but also in the organization's risk management strategy. These architectures define the organization's boundaries, network types, common control implementations, processes, security protocols, enterprise security tools, and techniques are all developed in these models. An information system owner can gain great insight into the methods of implementing security controls in compliance with these architecture models and required tools, connectors and protocols. Designing and developing a system and the supporting security controls in line with the organization's architecture models and with the insight or enterprise and security architects.

Many of the organization common controls are implemented in the system and security architecture. System owners that consult with these architects prior to selecting hardware and software components can make these decisions with assurances that the selected components will be the best selection to be implemented into the organization's architecture. This will assist in ensuring that the monitoring of controls and output of metrics fits with the organizations overall ISCM strategy.

NIST SP 800-37 Text

ENTERPRISE ARCHITECTURE

TASK P-16 Determine the placement of the system within the enterprise architecture.

Potential Inputs: Security and privacy requirements; organization- and system-level risk assessment results; enterprise architecture information; security architecture information; privacy architecture information; asset information.

Expected Outputs: Updated enterprise architecture; updated security architecture; updated privacy architecture; plans to use cloud-based systems and shared systems, services, or applications.

Primary Responsibility: Mission or Business Owner; Enterprise Architect; Security Architect; Privacy Architect.

Supporting Roles: Chief Information Officer; Authorizing Official or Authorizing Official Designated Representative; Senior Agency Information Security Officer; Senior Agency Official for Privacy; System Owner; Information Owner or Steward.

System Development Life Cycle Phase: New – Initiation (concept/requirements definition). Existing – Operations/Maintenance.

Discussion: Enterprise architecture is a management practice used to maximize the effectiveness of mission/business processes and information resources and to achieve mission and business success. An enterprise architecture can provide greater understanding of information and operational technologies included in the initial design and development of information systems and is a prerequisite for achieving resilience and survivability of those systems in an environment of increasingly sophisticated threats. Enterprise architecture also provides an opportunity for organizations to consolidate, standardize, and optimize information and technology assets. An effectively implemented architecture produces systems that are more transparent and therefore, easier to understand and protect. Enterprise architecture also establishes an unambiguous connection from investments to measurable performance improvements. The placement of a system within the enterprise architecture is important as it provides greater visibility and understanding about the other systems (internal and external) that are connected to the system and can also be used to establish security domains for increased levels of protection for the system.
The security architecture and the privacy architecture are integral parts of the enterprise architecture. These architectures represent the parts of the enterprise architecture related to the implementation

of security and privacy requirements. The primary purpose of the security and privacy architectures is to ensure that security and privacy requirements are consistently and cost-effectively met in organizational systems and are aligned with the risk management strategy. The security and privacy architectures provide a roadmap that facilitates traceability from the strategic goals and objectives of organizations, through protection needs and security and privacy requirements, to specific security and privacy solutions provided by people, processes, and technologies.

References: [SP 800-39] (Mission/Business Process Level); [SP 800-64]; [SP 800-160 v1] (System Requirements Definition Process); [NIST CSF] (Core [Identify Function]; Profiles); [OMB FEA].

EXERCISE 5.9

Why is it important that the security or risk professional need to be aware of the enterprise architecture?

_____

_____

_____

_____

TASK P17 REQUIREMENTS ALLOCATION

Responsibilities	
Primary Responsibility	Supporting Roles
- Security Architect - Privacy Architect - System Security Officer - System Privacy Officer	- Chief Information Officer - Authorizing Official or Authorizing Official Designated Representative - Mission or Business Owner; Senior Agency Information Security Officer - Senior Agency Official for Privacy - System Owner

SDLC Alignment	
New Systems	Legacy Systems
- Initiation (concept/requirements definition)	- Operations/Maintenance

CSF Alignment	
CSF Number	CSF Task
	ID.GV

Task Flow	
Inputs	Outputs
- Organization- and system-level risk assessment results - Documented security and privacy requirements - Organization- and system-level risk assessment results - List of common control providers and common controls available for inheritance - System description - System element information - System component inventory - Relevant laws, executive orders, directives, regulations, and policies	- List of security and privacy requirements allocated to the system, system elements, and the environment of operation

The requirements allocation assists the information system owner in determining where in the system controls will be implemented. This helps to increase efficiency and reduce the cost and time of developing information systems with required controls. Effective requirements allocation takes advantage of common controls that are available for inheritance from organizational common control providers. Requirements allocation can also take place within an individual information system by implementing controls in a specific systems component if that component ca provide protection to the entire system, reducing the duplication of controls without increasing security or reducing risk. Finally requirements allocation can identify components of the system that do not require a control be fully implemented or implemented at all, for example a publicly available web page may not require identification and authentication of users, but the underlying web server would still be required to implement this control.

NIST SP 800-37 Text

REQUIREMENTS ALLOCATION

TASK P-17 Allocate security and privacy requirements to the system and to the environment of operation.

Potential Inputs: Organization- and system-level risk assessment results; documented security and privacy requirements; organization- and system-level risk assessment results; list of common control providers and common controls available for inheritance; system description; system element information; system component inventory; relevant laws, executive orders, directives, regulations, and policies.

Expected Outputs: List of security and privacy requirements allocated to the system, system elements, and the environment of operation.
Primary Responsibility: Security Architect; Privacy Architect; System Security Officer; System Privacy Officer.

Supporting Roles: Chief Information Officer; Authorizing Official or Authorizing Official Designated Representative; Mission or Business Owner; Senior Agency Information Security Officer; Senior Agency Official for Privacy; System Owner.

System Development Life Cycle Phase: New – Initiation (concept/requirements definition). Existing – Operations/Maintenance.

Discussion: Security and privacy requirements are allocated to guide and inform control selection and implementation for the organization, system, system elements, and/or environment of operation.73 Requirements allocation identifies where controls will be implemented. The allocation of requirements conserves resources and helps to streamline the risk management process by ensuring that requirements are not implemented on multiple systems or system elements when implementation of a common control or a system-level control on a specific system element provides the needed protection capability.

References: [SP 800-39] (Organization, Mission/Business Process, and System Levels); [SP 800-64]; [SP 800-160 v1] (System Requirements Definition Process); [NIST CSF] (Core [Identify Function]; Profiles); [OMB FEA].

EXERCISE 5.10

Why is it important to allocate resources?

_____

_____

_____

_____

TASK P18 SYSTEM REGISTRATION

Responsibilities	
Primary Responsibility	Supporting Roles

- System Owner	- Mission or Business Owner
	- Chief Information Officer
	- System Security Officer
	- System Privacy Officer

SDLC Alignment	
New Systems	Legacy Systems
- Initiation (concept/requirements definition)	- Operations/Maintenance

CSF Alignment	
CSF Number	CSF Task
	- ID.GV

Task Flow	
Inputs	Outputs
- Organizational policy on system registration - system information	- Registered system in accordance with organizational policy

The final task in this step of the RMF, Categorize the Information System, is to register the information system. In this task, specific information about system is documented and presented to the organizations program or project management office (PMO).

Each organization is free to develop its own registration forms as long as these forms capture the required information in a manner that this information can be processed by the PMO. This includes but is not limited to the following items.

- Defining the existence of the information system
- The information systems Name
- The information system description
- The Information types processed, stored or displayed on the information system
- The information systems categorization
- The information system owner
- Other key characteristics of the information system

Once received by the PMO the system information is evaluated to ensure the information system being developed is not duplicating another system in the organizations portfolio or currently under development. The PMO may also consult with organizational budget teams to ensure funding exists to successfully complete the project. In many cases the PMO office will assist the information systems Project Manager (PM) in ensuring organizational requirements, including those surrounding the system development lifecycle (SDLC), security and compliance are met.

The following is the system registration template from the Cyber-Recon RMF Lab. This document captures the key information from the system owner and the PMO. This document will be used in the lab but can be tailored to meet your organizational needs if required.

The top half of the form is completed by the system owner and the bottom half of the form is completed by the PMO.

DSM PMO System Registration Form

Use the following form to register a system with the program management office (PMO). Once completed and approved the PMO will complete the second half of this form and return to the requester.

System Name:	System Acronym:
Department:	System Owner:
Describe System:	

PMO Office will complete the following

System Registration Number:	Assignment Date:
PMO Portfolio:	Project Manager (PM):
PMO System Notes:	

NIST SP 800-37 Text
SYSTEM REGISTRATION
TASK P-18 Register the system with organizational program or management offices.
Potential Inputs: Organizational policy on system registration; system information.

Expected Outputs: Registered system in accordance with organizational policy.

Primary Responsibility: System Owner.

Supporting Role: Mission or Business Owner; Chief Information Officer; System Security Officer; System Privacy Officer.

System Development Life Cycle Phase: New – Initiation (concept/requirements definition). Existing – Operations/Maintenance.

Discussion: System registration, in accordance with organizational policy, serves to inform the governing organization of plans to develop the system or the existence of the system; the key characteristics of the system; and the expected security and privacy implications for the organization due to the operation and use of the system. System registration provides organizations with a management and tracking tool to facilitate bringing the system into the enterprise architecture, implementation of protections that are commensurate with risk, and security and privacy posture reporting in accordance with applicable laws, executive orders, directives, regulations, policies, or standards. As part of the system registration process, organizations add the system to the organization-wide system inventory. System registration information is updated with security categorization and system characterization information upon completion of the *Categorize* step.

References: None.

EXERCISE 5.11

What is one benefit of registering an information system?

_____

_____

_____

_____

NOTES:

5. THE CATEGORIZE STEP

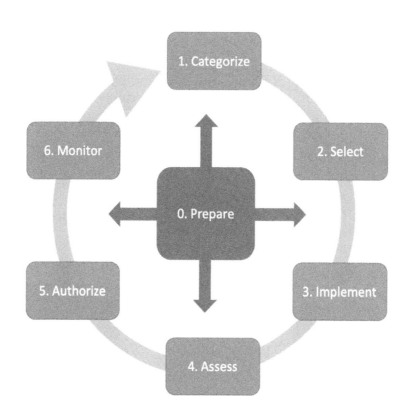

TASK C-1 SYSTEMS DESCRIPTION

Responsibilities	
Primary Responsibility	Supporting Roles
- System Owner	- Authorizing Official or Authorizing Official Designated Representative - Information Owner or Steward - System Security Officer - System Privacy Officer

SDLC Alignment	
New Systems	Legacy Systems
- Initiation (concept/requirements definition)	- Operations/Maintenance

CSF Alignment	
CSF Number	CSF Task
	- Profile

Task Flow	
Inputs	Outputs
System design and requirements documentation - Authorization boundary information - List of security and privacy requirements allocated to the system, system elements, and the environment of operation - Physical or other processes controlled by system elements - System element information - System component inventory - System element supply chain information, including inventory and supplier information; security categorization; data map of the information life cycle for information types processed, stored, and transmitted by the system; information on system use, users, and roles	- Documented system description

Describing the information system is generally the initial step in building the system security plan (SSP). The information documented in this task in the RMF develops the foundation for the full development of the SSP in future steps.

The following diagram details the six major areas of a basic SSP. The areas are

- General Information;
- Contact Information;
- Categorization Information;
- Diagrams;
- Hardware and Software Inventories, and;
- Control Implementation

Figure 6-1 SSP Development

Each step maps to one or more parts of the SSP template used in the Cyber-Recon RMF Lab. This template is like templates used in major organizations and the currently approved FedRAMP SSP template. Information from the first four areas should be available at this point in the systems development and may be discovered from various sources of RMF documentation. Some of the information required in the fifth area (Hardware and Software Inventory) may be available at this point but may be developed over time in the next two steps of the RMF. The final area will most likely not be available at this point but will be developed, updated and implemented in the next two steps.

Based on NIST SP 800-37 and SP 800-18 there are 28 key areas of information that can be documented to some level of detail at this point. These 28 areas as well as a general category of information that is required by individual organizations is detailed in the following list.

1. Full descriptive name of the information system including associated acronym;
2. Unique information system identifier (typically a number or code);
3. Information system owner and authorizing official including contact information;
4. Parent or governing organization that manages, owns, and/or controls the information system;
5. Location of the information system and environment in which the system operates;
6. Version or release number of the information system;
7. Purpose, functions, and capabilities of the information system and missions/business processes supported;
8. How the information system is integrated into the enterprise architecture and information security architecture;
9. Status of the information system with respect to acquisition and/or system development life cycle;
10. Results of the security categorization process for the information and information system;
11. Types of information processed, stored, and transmitted by the information system;
12. Boundary of the information system for risk management and security authorization purposes;
13. Applicable laws, directives, policies, regulations, or standards affecting the security of the information system;

14. Architectural description of the information system including network topology;
15. Hardware and firmware devices included within the information system;
16. System and applications software resident on the information system;
17. Hardware, software, and system interfaces (internal and external);
18. Subsystems (static and dynamic) associated with the information system;
19. Information flows and paths (including inputs and outputs) within the information system;
20. Cross domain devices/requirements;
21. Network connection rules for communicating with external information systems;
22. Interconnected information systems and identifiers for those systems;
23. Encryption techniques used for information processing, transmission, and storage;
24. Cryptographic key management information (public key infrastructures, certificate authorities, etc.);
25. Information system users (including organizational affiliations, access rights, privileges, citizenship, if applicable);
26. Ownership/operation of information system (e.g., government-owned, government-operated; government-owned, contractor-operated; contractor-owned, contractor-operated; nonfederal [state and local governments, grantees]);
27. Security authorization date and authorization termination date;
28. Incident response points of contact; and
29. Other information as required by the organization.

These requirements can be mapped to the following sections of the provided SSP template.

Cover Page
Full descriptive name of the information system including associated acronym;
Version or release number of the information system;

1. **Information System Name/Title**
- Full descriptive name of the information system including associated acronym;
- Unique information system identifier (typically a number or code);
- Location of the information system and environment in which the system operates;
- Other information as required by the organization.
2. **Information System Categorization**
- Results of the security categorization process for the information and information system;
- Other information as required by the organization.
2.1. **Information Types**
- Types of information processed, stored, and transmitted by the information system;
- Other information as required by the organization.
2.2. **Security Objectives Categorization (FIPS 199)**
- Results of the security categorization process for the information and information system
- Other information as required by the organization.

2.3. E-Authentication Determination

- Information system owner and
- Other information as required by the organization.

3. Information System Owner

- Information system owner and authorizing official including contact information;
- Parent or governing organization that manages, owns, and/or controls the information system;
- Ownership/operation of information system (e.g., government-owned, government-operated; government-owned, contractor-operated; contractor-owned, contractor-operated; nonfederal [state and local governments, grantees]);
- Other information as required by the organization.

4. Authorizing Official

- Information system owner and authorizing official including contact information;
- Other information as required by the organization.

4.1. Other Designated Contacts

- [Individuals with knowledge of the systems]
- Other information as required by the organization.

5. Assignment of Security Responsibility

- [ISSO, ISSE & contact info]
- Other information as required by the organization.

6. Information System Operational Status

- Security authorization date and authorization termination date;
- Other information as required by the organization.

7. General System Description

- - Status of the information system with respect to acquisition and/or system development life cycle;
- Applicable laws, directives, policies, regulations, or standards affecting the security of the information system;
- Subsystems (static and dynamic) associated with the information system;
- Encryption techniques used for information processing, transmission, and storage;
- Cryptographic key management information (public key infrastructures, certificate authorities, etc.);
- Incident response points of contact;
- Other information as required by the organization.

7.1. System Function or Purpose

- Purpose, functions, and capabilities of the information system and missions/business processes supported;
- Other information as required by the organization.

7.2. Information System Components and Boundaries

- Boundary of the information system for risk management and security authorization purposes;
- Other information as required by the organization.

7.3. Types of Users

- Information system users (including organizational affiliations, access rights, privileges, citizenship, if applicable);

- Other information as required by the organization.

7.4. Network Architecture

- Architectural description of the information system including network topology;
- How the information system is integrated into the enterprise architecture and information security architecture;
- Other information as required by the organization.

8. System Environment

- Other information as required by the organization.

8.1. Hardware Inventory

- Hardware and firmware devices included within the information system;
- Hardware, software, and system interfaces (internal and external);
- Other information as required by the organization.

8.2. Software Inventory

- Hardware and firmware devices included within the information system;
- System and applications software resident on the information system;
- Hardware, software, and system interfaces (internal and external);
- Other information as required by the organization.

8.3. Network Inventory

- Cross domain devices/requirements;
- Other information as required by the organization.

8.4. Data Flow

- Architectural description of the information system including network topology;
- Information flows and paths (including inputs and outputs) within the information system;
- Interconnected information systems and identifiers for those systems;
- Other information as required by the organization.

9.System Interconnections

- Network connection rules for communicating with external information systems;

Development of the initial draft of the SSP require reviewing available information system documentation including, but not limited to, system concepts of operations (CONOPS), system design documentation, kick off meeting notes and minutes, system diagrams, requirements documents, organization charts, email and other notes. This draft SSP will be used as the base for all future development of this document so correctness is important. The SSP is a living document that will be modified and updated over the information systems lifecycle.

NIST SP 800-37 Text

SYSTEM DESCRIPTION

TASK C-1 Document the characteristics of the system.

Potential Inputs: System design and requirements documentation; authorization boundary information; list of security and privacy requirements allocated to the system, system elements, and the environment of operation; physical or other processes controlled by system elements; system

---

element information; system component inventory; system element supply chain information, including inventory and supplier information; security categorization; data map of the information life cycle for information types processed, stored, and transmitted by the system; information on system use, users, and roles.

Expected Outputs: Documented system description.

Primary Responsibility: System Owner.

Supporting Roles: Authorizing Official or Authorizing Official Designated Representative; Information Owner or Steward; System Security Officer; System Privacy Officer.

System Development Life Cycle Phase: New – Initiation (concept/requirements definition). Existing – Operations/Maintenance.

Discussion: A description of the system characteristics is documented in the security and privacy plans, included in attachments to the plans, or referenced in other standard sources for the information generated as part of the SDLC. Duplication of information is avoided, whenever possible. The level of detail in the security and privacy plans is determined by the organization and is commensurate with the security categorization and the security and privacy risk assessments of the system. Information may be added to or updated in the system description as it becomes available during the system life cycle, during the execution of the RMF steps, and as any system characteristics change.

Examples of different types of descriptive information that organizations can include in security and privacy plans include: descriptive name of the system and system identifier; system version or release number; manufacturer and supplier information; individual responsible for the system; system contact information; organization that manages, owns, or controls the system; system location; purpose of the system and missions/business processes supported; how the system is integrated into the enterprise architecture; SDLC phase; results of the categorization process and privacy risk assessment; authorization boundary; laws, directives, policies, regulations, or standards affecting individuals' privacy and the security of the system; architectural description of the system including network topology; information types; hardware, firmware, and software components that are part of the system; hardware, software, and system interfaces (internal and external); information flows within the system; network connection rules for communicating with external systems; interconnected systems and identifiers for those systems; physical or other processes, components and equipment controlled by system elements; system users (including affiliations, access rights, privileges, citizenship); system provenance in the supply chain; maintenance or other relevant agreements; potential suppliers for replacement components for the system; alternative compatible system components; number and location in inventory of replacement system components; ownership or operation of the system (government-owned, government-operated; government-owned, contractor-operated; contractor-owned, contractor-operated; nonfederal [state and local governments, grantees]); incident response points of contact; authorization date and authorization termination date; and ongoing authorization status. System registration information is updated with the system characterization information (see Task P-18).

References: [SP 800-18]; [NIST CSF] (Core [Identify Function]).

EXERCISE #.#

The following is an excerpt from an information systems CONOPS document. Review this information and identify the areas of the SSP that can be developed based on this information. Document this information in the table that follows

Scope
The scope of this CONOPS covers the development and fielding of the Next Generation Workstation (NGW) information system. This includes acquisition, development, testing, security assessment and authorization (A&A) and operations and maintenance (O&M)

1.1 Identification
System Name: Next Generation Workstation
System Unique ID: FDT00564
System Version: 1

1.2 Document security
This document Unclassified but considered for official use only (FOUO) as it contains unique system information about a system developed for the United States Government.

1.3 System security
The system will not house classified information and has a tentative security classification of **Low**.

2. Current system or situation

2.1 Background, objectives, and scope
The system is currently under development and will be developed following DSM program management principles.
The NGW system is an enterprise end user compute workstation that will allow the DSM to standardize the end user computer hardware and software on a single maintainable platform. NGW will be based on a standard operating system (OS) with variations of the baseline build based on user roles, responsibilities and job title.
The system is not intended to interface with the general public or be accessed via the Internet, however users will have the ability to access Internet based resources.
The system is government developed, owned and operated by either government employees or government contractors.

2.2 Operational policies and constraints
The system will be developed, operated and maintained in accordance with applicable laws, DSM standards, policies and guidelines.

2.3 Description of current system or situation
- Currently the system is in development. Once complete NGW will replace existing desperate hardware and software solution currently in place in the DSW. The current state of end user computer systems is not maintainable, scalable or securable. NGW seeks to resolve these problems.

2.4 Users or affected personnel

The users impacted directly by this system are all computer end users in the DSM.

2.5 Support concept
The system will be supported directly by DSM system administrators and help desk analysts. Secondary support will be offered by the software development team and the software vendors.

SSP Information Area	CONOPS Information

TASK C-2 SECURITY CATEGORIZATION

Responsibilities	
Primary Responsibility	Supporting Roles
- System Owner - Information Owner or Steward	- Senior Accountable Official for Risk Management or Risk Executive (Function) - Chief Information Officer - Senior Agency Information Security Officer - Senior Agency Official for Privacy - Authorizing Official or Authorizing Official Designated Representative - System Security Officer - System Privacy Officer

SDLC Alignment	
New Systems	Legacy Systems
- Initiation (concept/requirements definition).	- Operations/Maintenance.

CSF Alignment	
CSF Number	CSF Task
	- ID.AM-1 - ID.AM-2 - ID.AM-3 - ID.AM-4 - ID.AM-5

Task Flow	
Inputs	Outputs
- Risk management strategy - Organizational risk tolerance - Authorization boundary (i.e., system) information - Organization- and system-level risk assessment results - Information types processed, stored, or transmitted by the system -List of security and privacy requirements allocated to the system, system elements, and environment of operation - Organizational authority or purpose for operating the system - Business impact analyses or criticality analyses - Information about missions, business functions, and mission/business processes supported by the	Impact levels determined for each information type and for each security objective (confidentiality, integrity, availability); security categorization based on high-water mark of information type impact levels.

system	

By evaluating each column, the highest impact level can be identified, and this becomes the impact level for the security objectives for the entire information system.

Information Type	Confidentiality	Integrity	Availability
Information Security	Low	Moderate	Low
Infrastructure Maintenance	Low	Low	Low
System and Network Monitoring	Moderate	Moderate	Low
Information System Impact Level	Moderate	Moderate	Low

Information systems that are managed by organizations that do not belong to the Intelligence Community (IC) or Department of Defense (DoD) use a process called the "High Water Mark". That is the highest of the impact levels for the security objectives becomes the impact level for the information system. This is illustrated in the following table.

Information System Impact Level	Moderate	Moderate	Low
High water Mark	Moderate		

For those systems supporting the IC or DoD this last step is omitted and the three individual impact levels for the security objectives is used. For example, this system would be categorized as Moderate, Moderate, Low in the IC or DoD.

This determination of the provisional impact level is just the beginning in determining the systems actual impact level. The final impact level is accomplished by reviewing and adjusting the impact levels based on appropriateness of the impact level to the organizational mission and the information system. Once adjusted this impact level is finalized and documented based on the organizations requirements for security documentation.

NIST SP 800-37 Text
TASK C-2 Categorize the system and document the security categorization results. **Potential Inputs:** Risk management strategy; organizational risk tolerance; authorization boundary (i.e., system) information; organization- and system-level risk assessment results; information types processed, stored, or transmitted by the system; list of security and privacy requirements allocated to

the system, system elements, and environment of operation; organizational authority or purpose for operating the system; business impact analyses or criticality analyses; information about missions, business functions, and mission/business processes supported by the system.

Expected Outputs: Impact levels determined for each information type and for each security objective (confidentiality, integrity, availability); security categorization based on high-water mark of information type impact levels.

Primary Responsibility: System Owner; Information Owner or Steward.

Supporting Roles: Senior Accountable Official for Risk Management or Risk Executive (Function); Chief Information Officer; Senior Agency Information Security Officer; Senior Agency Official for Privacy; Authorizing Official or Authorizing Official Designated Representative; System Security Officer; System Privacy Officer.

System Development Life Cycle Phase: New – Initiation (concept/requirements definition). Existing – Operations/Maintenance.

Discussion: Security categorization determinations consider potential adverse impacts to organizational operations, organizational assets, individuals, other organizations, and the Nation resulting from the loss of confidentiality, integrity, or availability of information. Organizations have flexibility in conducting a security categorization using either [FIPS 200] to establish a single impact level for a system based on the high-water mark concept (for other than national security systems), or [CNSSI 1253] to establish three impact values that may vary for each of the security objectives of confidentiality, integrity, and availability (for national security systems). The security categorization process is carried out by the system owner and the information owner or steward in cooperation and collaboration with senior leaders and executives with mission, business function, or risk management responsibilities. Cooperation and collaboration helps to ensure that individual systems are categorized based on the mission and business objectives of the organization. The system owner and information owner or steward consider the results from the security risk assessment (and the privacy risk assessment when the system processes PII) as a part of the security categorization decision. The decision is consistent with the risk management strategy. The results of the categorization process influence the selection of security controls for the system. Security categorization information is documented in the system security plan or included as an attachment to the plan and can be cross-referenced in a privacy plan when the system processes PII.

The security categorization results for the system can be further refined by the organization to facilitate an impact-level prioritization of systems with the same impact level (see Task P-6). Results from the impact-level prioritization conducted by the organization can be used to help system owners in control selection and tailoring decisions.

References: [FIPS 199]; [FIPS 200]; [SP 800-30]; [SP 800-39] (System Level); [SP 800-59]; [SP 800-60 v1]; [SP 800-60 v2]; [SP 800-160 v1] (Stakeholder Needs and Requirements Definition and System Requirements Definition Processes); [IR 8179]; [CNSSI 1253]; [NIST CSF] (Core [Identify Function]).

Using the following information complete the exercise using knowledge gained from this module.

You have been informed that the information system you have been assigned to will be processing the information types in the following tables. Using NIST SP 800-60 (Volumes I and II) complete each table.

1. **Information** Type: Policy and Guidance Development Information Type
Special Factors: None

Information Type	Confidentiality	Integrity	Availability

2. **Information Type:** Budget Formulation Information Type
Special Factors: None

Information Type	Confidentiality	Integrity	Availability

3. **Information Type:** International Development and Humanitarian Aid Information Type
Special Factors: None

Information Type	Confidentiality	Integrity	Availability

4. **Information Type:** Conservation, Marine and Land Management Information Type
Special Factors: This information is critical to fire-fighting operations

Information Type	Confidentiality	Integrity	Availability

5. Information Type: Community and Regional Development Information Type
Special Factors: In this case this information type does contain Privacy Act information

Information Type	Confidentiality	Integrity	Availability

6. The information types described in questions 1 through 5 are being implemented in an information system. Use the following table to determine the information systems impact levels and high-water mark.

Information Type	Confidentiality	Integrity	Availability
Information System Impact level			
High Water Mark			

TASK C-3 SECURITY CATEGORIZATION REVIEW AND APPROVAL

Responsibilities	
Primary Responsibility	Supporting Roles
- Authorizing Official or Authorizing Official Designated Representative - Senior Agency Official for Privacy	- Senior Accountable Official for Risk Management or Risk Executive (Function) - Chief Information Officer - Senior Agency Information Security Officer

SDLC Alignment	
New Systems	Legacy Systems
- Initiation (concept/requirements definition).	- Operations/Maintenance.

CSF Alignment	
CSF Number	CSF Task

Task Flow	
Inputs	Outputs
- Impact levels determined for each information type and for each security objective (confidentiality, integrity, availability) - Security categorization based on high-water mark of information type impact levels - List of high value assets for the organization	- Approval of security categorization for the system

The information system owner determines the initial information types, information categorization and the overall security categorization for the information system itself either using the high water mark to determine one overall categorization for the information system or separate categorizations for each of the security objectives (confidentiality, integrity, and availability). These categorizations are tentative until approved by the required organizational officials. For all systems the AO or AOs designated representative must approve the information types, information categorization, and the information systems categorization. For those systems that process personally identifiable information (PII) the senior agency official for privacy will review and approve the categorizations prior to these being approved by the AO or AODR.

To determine if the information system contains PII the system owner will complete the Privacy Threshold Assessment (PTA). Based on the results of the PTA a Privacy Impact Assessment (PIA) may be required.

Privacy Threshold Analysis and Privacy Impact Analysis
The Privacy Threshold Analysis (PTA) and Privacy Impact Analysis (PIA) are tools that are used by organizations to determine if Personally Identifiable Information (PII) is stored on, processed by or displayed on an information system. Determination of privacy information including PII is normally in the preview of an organizations Privacy office or the responsibility of the Privacy Officer.

It is important that information system owner and those tasked with security and privacy responsibilities should understand the basics of the PTA, the PIA and protection of PII. The following section introduces the PTA and PIA.

The Privacy Threshold Analysis (PTA)

The Privacy Threshold Analysis (PTA) is a tool that helps information system owners in determine if the system they are developing or are operating does or will contain Personally Identifiable Information (PII) as defined in OMB Memo M-07-16. This information can be used to use on its own or with other information to distinguish an individual's identity. Common information that could be tied to more than one person, such as date of birth, is generally not considered PII unless it is combined with other information that would make the set of information unique such as combining this information with the individual's home address. The following is a partial listing of information that can be considered PII. This list is not exhaustive and other information can be considered PII, this listing is provided as an illustration of PII.

- Social Security numbers
- Passport numbers
- Driver's license numbers
- Biometric information
- DNA information
- Bank account numbers

PII does not refer to business information or government information that cannot be traced back to an individual person.

The following PTA is based on a FedRAMP document that helps in identifying information systems that may contain PII. If there is a possibility that the system may contain PII based on the PTA a full Privacy Impact Assessment (PIA) will be conducted. This document is included in this manual to provide you with familiarization of this document.

<Information System Owner> performs a Privacy Threshold Analysis annually to determine if PII is collected by any of the **<Information System Name>** components. If PII is discovered, a Privacy Impact Assessment is performed. The Privacy Impact Assessment template used by **<Information System Owner>** can be found in the next section of this lab. This section constitutes the Privacy Threshold Analysis and findings.

Qualifying Questions

1) Does the **<Information System Name>** collect, maintain, or share PII in any identifiable form?

☐ No
☐ Yes

2) Does the **<Information System Name>** collect, maintain, or share PII information from or about the public?

☐ No
☐ Yes

3) Has a Privacy Impact Assessment ever been performed for the **<Information System Name>**?

☐ No

☐ Yes

4) Is there a Privacy Act System of Records Notice (SORN) for this system?
☐ No
☐ Yes, the SORN identifier and name is:

If answers to questions 1-4 are all "No" then a Privacy Impact Assessment may be omitted. If any of the answers to question 1-4 are "Yes" then complete a Privacy Impact Assessment

Designation
☐ A Privacy Sensitive System

☐ Not a Privacy Sensitive System (in its current version)

Privacy Impact Assessment (PIA)

The Privacy Impact Assessment (PIA) is an analysis of how personally identifiable information is collected, used, shared, and maintained. The purpose of a PIA is to demonstrate that program managers and system owners have consciously incorporated privacy protections throughout the development life cycle of a system or program. PIAs are required by the E-Government Act of 2002, which was enacted by Congress to improve the management and promotion of Federal electronic government services and processes. PIAs allow us to communicate more clearly with the public about how we handle information, including how we address privacy concerns and safeguard information.

The Privacy Impact Assessment (PIA) is a decision tool used to identify and mitigate privacy risks and if needed notifies the public:
- What Personally Identifiable Information (PII) a given information system or organization is collecting;
- Why the PII is being collected; and
- How the PII will be collected, used, accessed, shared, safeguarded and stored

The PIA should accomplish 3 main goals.
- Ensure conformance with applicable legal, regulatory, and policy requirements for privacy;
- Determine the risks and effects; and
- Evaluate protections and alternative processes to mitigate potential privacy risks.

The following is a modification of the FedRAMP PIA document that has been tailored to work with not only cloud-based systems but also non-cloud-based systems. This document is included in this manual to provide you with familiarization of this document.

1. **Privacy Impact Assessment**

A Privacy Impact Assessment has been conducted for the **<Information System Name>** on **<date>**.

PII Mapping of Components

<Information System Name> consists of <number> key components. Each component has been analyzed to determine if any elements of that component collect PII. The type of PII collected by <Information System Name> and the functions that collect it are recorded in Table 4-1.

Table 4-1. PII Mapped to Components

Components	Does this function collect or store PII? (Yes/No)	Type of PII	Reason for Collection of PII	Safeguards

PII In Use

1) What PII (name, social security number, date of birth, address, etc.) is contained in the CSP service offering? Explain.

2) Can individuals "opt-out" by declining to provide PII or by consenting only to a particular use (e.g., allowing basic use of their personal information, but not sharing with other government agencies)? Explain.

☐ Yes. Explain the issues and circumstances of being able to opt-out (either for specific data elements or specific uses of the data):

☐ No. Explain:

Sources of PII and Purpose

3) Does the CSP have knowledge of federal agencies that provide PII to the system? Explain.

4) Has any agency that is providing PII to the system provided a stated purpose for populating the system with PII? Explain.

5) Does the CSP populate the system with PII? If yes, what is the purpose? Explain.

6) What other third-party sources will be providing PII to the system? Explain the PII that will be provided and the purpose for it.

Access to PII and Sharing

7) What federal agencies have access to the PII, even if they are not the original provider? Who establishes the criteria for what PII can be shared? Explain.

8) What CSP personnel will have access to the system and the PII (e.g., users, managers, system administrators, developers, contractors, other)? Explain the need for CSP personnel to have access to the PII.

9) How is access to the PII determined? Are criteria, procedures, controls, and responsibilities regarding access documented? Does access require manager approval? Explain.

10) Do other systems share, transmit, or have access to the PII in the system? If yes, explain the purpose for system to system transmission, access, or sharing.

PII Safeguards and liabilities

11) What controls are in place to prevent the misuse (e.g., browsing) of data by those having access? Explain.

12) Who will be responsible for protecting the privacy rights of the individuals whose PII is collected, maintained, or shared on the system? Have policies and/or procedures been established for this responsibility and accountability? Explain.

13) Does the CSP annual security training include privacy training? Does the CSP require contractors to take the training? Explain.

14) Who is responsible for assuring safeguards for the PII? Explain.

15) What is the magnitude of harm if privacy related data is disclosed, intentionally or unintentionally? Would the reputation of the CSP or its customers be affected? Explain.

16) What is the magnitude of harm to the individuals if privacy related data is disclosed, intentionally or unintentionally? Explain.

17) What involvement will contractors have with the design and maintenance of the system? Has a contractor confidentiality agreement or a Non-Disclosure Agreement (NDA) been developed for contractors who work on the system? Explain.

18) Is the PII owner advised about what federal agencies or other organizations share or have access to the data? Explain.

Contracts, agreements, and ownership

19) NIST SP 800-144 states, "Organizations are ultimately accountable for the security and privacy of data held by a cloud provider on their behalf." Is this principle described in contracts with customers? Why or why not? Explain.

20) Do contracts with customers establish who has ownership rights over data including PII? Explain.

21) Do contracts with customers require that customers notify the CSP if the customer intends to populate the service platform with PII?   Why or why not?

22) Do CSP contracts with customers establish record retention responsibilities for both the customer and the CSP? Explain.

23) Is the degree to which the CSP will accept liability for expose of PII clearly defined in agreements with customers?

Attributes and accuracy of the PII
24) Is the PII collected verified for accuracy? Why or why not? Explain.

25) Is the PII current? How is this determined? Explain.

Maintenance and Administrative Controls
26) If the system is operated in more than one site, how is consistent use of the system and PII maintained in all sites? Are the same controls be used? Explain.

27) What are the retention periods of PII for this system? Under what guidelines are the retention periods determined? Who establishes the retention guidelines? Explain.

28) What are the procedures for disposition of the PII at the end of the retention period? How long will any reports that contain PII be maintained? How is the information disposed (e.g., shredding, degaussing, overwriting, etc.)? Who establishes the decommissioning procedures? Explain.

29) Is the system using technologies that contain PII in ways that have not previously deployed? (e.g., smart cards, caller-ID, biometrics, PIV cards, etc.)? Explain.

30) How does the use of this technology affect privacy? Does the use of this technology introduce compromise that did not exist prior to the deployment of this technology? Explain.

31) Is access to the PII being monitored, tracked, or recorded? Explain.

32) If the system is in the process of being modified and a SORN exists, will the SORN require amendment or revision? Explain.

Business Processes and Technology
33) Does the conduct of this PIA result in circumstances that requires changes to business processes? Explain.

34) Does the completion of this PIA potentially result in technology changes? Explain.

Privacy Policy
35) Is there a CSP privacy policy and is it provided to all individuals whose PII you collect, maintain or store? Explain.

36) Is the privacy policy publicly viewable?　　　　If yes, provide the URL:
Assessor and Signatures
This Privacy Impact Assessment has been conducted by **<name of organization>** and has been reviewed by the **<CSP>** Chief Privacy Officer for accuracy.

_____
Assessor Name (Please Print)

_____　　　_____
Assessor Signature　　　　　　　　　　　　　　Date

_____
Chief Privacy Officer Name (Please Print)

_____.　_____
Chief Privacy Officer Signature　　　　　　　　Date

NIST SP 800-37 Text

SECURITY CATEGORIZATION REVIEW AND APPROVAL

TASK C-3 Review and approve the security categorization results and decision.

Potential Inputs: Impact levels determined for each information type and for each security objective (confidentiality, integrity, availability); security categorization based on high-water mark of information type impact levels; list of high value assets for the organization.

Expected Outputs: Approval of security categorization for the system.

Primary Responsibility: Authorizing Official or Authorizing Official Designated Representative; Senior Agency Official for Privacy.

Supporting Roles: Senior Accountable Official for Risk Management or Risk Executive (Function); Chief Information Officer; Senior Agency Information Security Officer.

System Development Life Cycle Phase: New – Initiation (concept/requirements definition). Existing – Operations/Maintenance.

Discussion: For information systems that process PII, the senior agency official for privacy reviews and approves the security categorization results and decision prior to the authorizing official's review (Task S-2). If the security categorization decision is not approved, the system owner initiates steps to repeat the categorization process and resubmits the adjusted results to the authorizing official or designated representative. System registration information is subsequently updated with the approved security categorization information (see Task P-18). Security categorization results and decisions are reviewed by the authorizing official or a designated representative to ensure that the security category selected for the information system is consistent with the mission and business functions of the organization and the need to adequately protect those missions and functions. The authorizing official or designated representative reviews the categorization results and decision from an organization-wide perspective, including how the decision aligns with the categorization decisions for all other organizational systems. The authorizing official collaborates with the senior accountable official for risk management or the risk executive (function) to ensure that the categorization decision for the system is consistent with the organizational risk management strategy and satisfies requirements for high value assets. As part of the approval process, the authorizing official can provide specific guidance to the system owner with respect to any limitations on baseline tailoring activities for the system that occur at the RMF *Select* step (see

References: [FIPS 199]; [SP 800-30]; [SP 800-39] (Organization Level); [SP 800-160 v1] (Stakeholder Needs and Requirements Definition Process); [CNSSI 1253]; [NIST CSF] (Core [Identify Function]).

EXERCISE 6.2

Why is it important to determine if an information system contains protected privacy information?

_____

_____

_____

_____

7. THE SELECT STEP

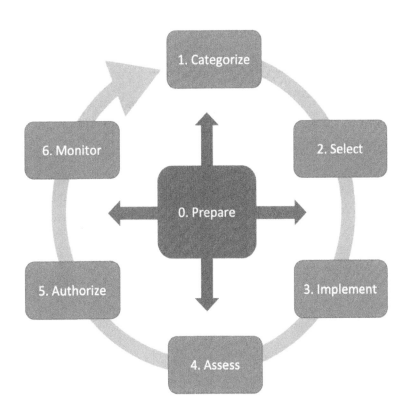

Task S-1 Control Selection

Responsibilities	
Primary Responsibility	Supporting Roles
- System Owner - Common Control Provider	- Authorizing Official or Authorizing Official Designated Representative - Information Owner or Steward - Systems Security Engineer; Privacy Engineer - System Security Officer - System Privacy Officer

SDLC Alignment	
New Systems	Legacy Systems
- Development/Acquisition.	- Operations/Maintenance

CSF Alignment	
CSF Number	CSF Task
	Profile

Task Flow	
Inputs	Outputs
- Security categorization - Organization- and system-level risk assessment results - System element information - System component inventory - List of security and privacy requirements allocated to the system, system elements, and environment of operation - List of contractual requirements allocated to external providers of the system or system element - Business impact analysis or criticality analysis - Risk management strategy - Organizational security and privacy policy - Federal or organization-approved or mandated baselines or overlays - Cybersecurity Framework Profiles.	- Controls selected for the system and the environment of operation.

Setting the information system high water mark is an essential input to this task and is critical in selecting the correct baseline security controls. Starting with the information systems security baseline the correct security baseline controls can be identified using NIST SP 800-53. This is done into different and distinct ways depending on your organization's approach to baseline security controls as set forth in the security controls traceability matrix (SCTM). The primary way of doing this is called the high watermark that is used by organizations that do not fall under the Intelligence Community (IC) for the Department of Defense (DoD).

Categorization using the high watermark begins by identifying be high water mark from step 1-1, this single categorization is either high, moderate, or low. Using table D-2 from NIST SP 800-53, the system owner can identify those controls that are applicable to the categorization high watermark that has been identified. An excerpt from table D-2 is illustrated in figure 7-1 and will be used to illustrate how to select the required baseline security controls using the high watermark process.

TABLE D-2: SECURITY CONTROL BASELINES[92]

CNTL NO.	CONTROL NAME	PRIORITY	INITIAL CONTROL BASELINES		
			LOW	MOD	HIGH
Access Control					
AC-1	Access Control Policy and Procedures	P1	AC-1	AC-1	AC-1
AC-2	Account Management	P1	AC-2	AC-2 (1) (2) (3) (4)	AC-2 (1) (2) (3) (4) (5) (11) (12) (13)
AC-3	Access Enforcement	P1	AC-3	AC-3	AC-3
AC-4	Information Flow Enforcement	P1	Not Selected	AC-4	AC-4
AC-5	Separation of Duties	P1	Not Selected	AC-5	AC-5

Figure 7-1 NIST SP 800-53, Table D-2

In this table, we can see five of the access control (AC) controls. In the column header on the right of the table, the initial control baselines are identified. Directly under the low moderate or high column headers Controls required for that baseline are identified. For example, control AC-1 is required for low, moderate, and high baselines. The control AC-2 is also required for all baselines (low, moderate, and high) however no enhancements are required for low baseline, enhancements 1, 2, 3, and 4 are required for the moderate base, and enhancements 1, 2,3, 4, 5, 11, 12, and 13 are required for the high base. Following this process throughout table D-2 a baseline SCTM appropriate for the systems high water mark can be developed.

Systems within the IC and DoD do not use the system high water mark categorization for their information systems. Instead, they use a high watermark for each of the security objectives (confidentiality, integrity, and availability) resulting in a more granular baseline SCTM. While this baseline is more granular there are a greater number out security baselines available for users in these communities. For example, there are only three different baselines identified using the system high water mark, there are 27 different baselines available two members of IC or DoD. In identifying a in A baseline using this process the high-water mark for each of the security objectives is listed, for example low, low, low where the confidentiality, integrity and availability are listed sequentially. Using this method confidentiality will have an individual high watermark of low, moderate, or high; integrity will have an individual high watermark of low, moderate, or high; and availability will have a high watermark of low, moderate, or high.

Selection of baseline controls for Intelligence Community and the Department of Defense is accomplished using CNSSI 1253, Table D-1. An excerpt of this table is illustrated in figure 8-4 and will be used for this example. In this example, we will assume our system has a security objective based high water mark of low, moderate, low (LML). Again, looking at AC-1 this control will apply to every baseline as an "X" appears in the column under each of the categorization levels for each of the objectives. Further, looking at AC-2(1) is slightly more complex. We know this systems confidentiality is low, the integrity is moderate, and the availability is low. AC-2(1) only applies to baselines with confidentiality levels of moderate or high so for the security objective of confidentiality this enhancement does not apply. The system has an integrity level of moderate and this enhancement applies to systems with an integrity level of moderate or high, therefore this enhancement will need to be added to the systems SCTM. Our final security objective is availability where the level is low, this enhancement is not required for low, moderate, or high availability. In this method, the enhancement will be added to the SCTM if any of the security objectives levels match that of the control or enhancement levels listed in the table. In the case of a system with an LML security objective baseline the controls and enhancements AC-1, AC2, AC-2(1), AC-2(2), AC-2(3), AC-2(4), AC-2(5), and AC-2(7) would be added to the baseline and the SCTM. Controls AC-2(6), and AC-2(8) would not apply as there are no "X" or "+" in the columns under the security objectives and levels for those enhancements.

In this table controls that are required in the system baselines are identifies with either an "X" or a "+". Those items that ate identified with an "X" are those controls or enhancements that are identified for the baseline by NIST SP 800-53. Those items that are indicated for inclusion with a "+" have been added by CNSSI 1253 and did not exist in the NIST security control baseline as defined by SP 800-53.

Table D-1: NSS Security Control Baselines

ID	TITLE	Confidentiality			Integrity			Availability		
		L	M	H	L	M	H	L	M	H
AC-1	Access Control Policy and Procedures	X	X	X	X	X	X	X	X	X
AC-2	Account Management	X	X	X	X	X	X			
AC-2(1)	Account Management | Automated System Account Management		X	X		X	X			
AC-2(2)	Account Management | Removal of Temporary / Emergency Accounts		X	X		X	X			
AC-2(3)	Account Management | Disable Inactive Accounts		X	X		X	X			
AC-2(4)	Account Management | Automated Audit Actions	+	X	X	+	X	X			
AC-2(5)	Account Management | Inactivity Logout	+	+	X	+	+	X	+	+	X
AC-2(6)	Account Management | Dynamic Privilege Management									
AC-2(7)	Account Management | Role-Based Schemes	+	+	+	+	+	+			
AC-2(8)	Account Management | Dynamic Account Creation									

Figure 7-2 CNSSI 1253

NIST SP 800-37 Text

CONTROL SELECTION

TASK S-1 Select the controls for the system and the environment of operation.

Potential Inputs: Security categorization; organization- and system-level risk assessment results; system element information; system component inventory; list of security and privacy requirements allocated to the system, system elements, and environment of operation; list of contractual requirements allocated to external providers of the system or system element; business impact analysis or criticality analysis; risk management strategy; organizational security and privacy policy; federal or organization-approved or mandated baselines or overlays; Cybersecurity Framework Profiles.

Expected Outputs: Controls selected for the system and the environment of operation.

Primary Responsibility: System Owner; Common Control Provider.

Supporting Roles: Authorizing Official or Authorizing Official Designated Representative; Information

Owner or Steward; Systems Security Engineer; Privacy Engineer; System Security Officer; System Privacy Officer.

System Development Life Cycle Phase: New – Development/Acquisition.
Existing – Operations/Maintenance.

Discussion: There are two approaches that can be used for the initial selection of controls: a *baseline* control selection approach, or an *organization-generated* control selection approach. The baseline control selection approach uses control baselines, which are pre-defined sets of controls specifically assembled to address the protection needs of a group, organization, or community of interest. Control baselines serve as a starting point for the protection of individuals' privacy, information, and information systems. Federal control baselines are provided in [SP 800-53B]. The system security categorization (see Task C-2) and the security requirements derived from stakeholder protection needs, laws, executive orders, regulations, policies, directives, instructions, and standards (see Task P-15) can help inform the selection of security control baselines. A privacy risk assessment (see Task P-14) and privacy requirements derived from stakeholder protection needs, laws, executive orders, regulations, policies, directives, instructions, and standards (see Task P-15) can help inform the selection of privacy control baselines. Privacy programs use security and privacy control baselines to manage the privacy risks arising from both unauthorized system activity or behavior, as well as from authorized activities. After the pre-defined control baseline is selected, organizations tailor the baseline in accordance with the guidance provided (see Task S-2). The baseline control selection approach can provide consistency across a broad community of interest.

The organization-generated control selection approach differs from the baseline selection approach because the organization does not start with a pre-defined set of controls. Rather, the organization uses its own selection process to select controls. This may be necessary when the system is highly specialized (e.g., a weapons system or a medical device) or has limited purpose or scope (e.g., a smart meter). In these situations, it may be more efficient and cost-effective for an organization to select a specific set of controls for the system (i.e., a bottom-up approach) instead of starting with a pre-defined set of controls from a broad-based control baseline and subsequently eliminating controls through the tailoring process (i.e., top-down approach).

In both the baseline control selection approach and organization-generated control selection approach, organizations develop a well-defined set of security and privacy requirements using a life cycle-based systems engineering process (e.g., [ISO 15288] and [SP 800-160 v1] as described in the RMF *Prepare-System Level* step, Task P-15. This process generates a set of requirements that can be used to guide and inform the selection of a set of controls to satisfy the requirements (whether the organization starts with a control baseline or generates the set of controls from its own selection process). Similarly, organizations can use the [NIST CSF] to develop Cybersecurity Framework *Profiles* representing a set of organization-specific security and privacy requirements—and thus, guiding and informing control selection from [SP 800-53]. Tailoring may also be required in the organization-generated control selection approach (see Task S-2). Organizations do not need to choose one approach for the selection of controls for each of their systems, but instead, may use different approaches as circumstances dictate.

References: [FIPS 199]; [FIPS 200]; [SP 800-30]; [SP 800-53]; [SP 800-53B]; [SP 800-160 v1] (System Requirements Definition, Architecture Definition, and Design Definition Processes); [SP 800-161] (Respond and Chapter 3); [IR 8062]; [IR 8179]; [CNSSI 1253]; [NIST CSF] (Core [Identify, Protect, Detect, Respond, Recover Functions]; Profiles).

EXERCISE 7.1

You have been asked by the system owner of a system that you support to determine the Awareness and Training (AT) controls that apply to the moderate high-water mark system that they are developing. You have not yet tailored the security controls and just need the required baseline AT controls. Using the excerpt from NIST SP 800-53 R4 in figure 7-3 (below) identify the required controls and enhancements and list them in table 7-1.

CNTL NO.	CONTROL NAME / Control Enhancement Name	WITHDRAWN	ASSURANCE	CONTROL BASELINES		
				LOW	MOD	HIGH
AT-1	Security Awareness and Training Policy and Procedures		X	X	X	X
AT-2	Security Awareness Training		X	X	X	X
AT-2(1)	SECURITY AWARENESS | PRACTICAL EXERCISES		X			
AT-2(2)	SECURITY AWARENESS | INSIDER THREAT		X		X	X
AT-3	Role-Based Security Training		X	X	X	X
AT-3(1)	ROLE-BASED SECURITY TRAINING | ENVIRONMENTAL CONTROLS		X			
AT-3(2)	ROLE-BASED SECURITY TRAINING | PHYSICAL SECURITY CONTROLS		X			
AT-3(3)	ROLE-BASED SECURITY TRAINING | PRACTICAL EXERCISES		X			
AT-3(4)	ROLE-BASED SECURITY TRAINING | SUSPICIOUS COMMUNICATIONS AND ANOMALOUS SYSTEM BEHAVIOR		X			
AT-4	Security Training Records		X	X	X	X
AT-5	Contacts with Security Groups and Associations	X	Incorporated into PM-15.			

Figure 7-0-3 AT Controls

Control Number	Control Name

Table 7-1

Task S-2 Control Tailoring

Responsibilities	
Primary Responsibility	Supporting Roles
- System Owner - Common Control Provider	- Authorizing Official or Authorizing Official Designated Representative - Information Owner or Steward - Systems Security Engineer - Privacy Engineer - System Security Officer - System Privacy Officer

SDLC Alignment	
New Systems	Legacy Systems
- Development/Acquisition	- Operations/Maintenance

CSF Alignment	
CSF Number	CSF Task
	- PR.IP

Task Flow	
Inputs	Outputs
- Initial control baselines - Organization- and system-level risk assessment results - System element information - System component inventory - List of security and privacy requirements allocated to the system, system elements, and environment of operation - Business impact analysis or criticality analysis	- List of tailored controls for the system and environment of operation (i.e., tailored control baselines).

- Risk management strategy - Organizational security and privacy policies - Federal or organization-approved or mandated overlays	

This baseline SCTM is the starting point for determining the controls that we'll be required for the information system. To develop the SCTM him into a document that can be used to identify the relevant security controls security control tailoring is implemented. In the tailoring process Controls are added and removed to develop a security control traceability matrix that is in line with the risk level of the information system that is being developed. Detailing process can also determine controls that are implemented only on a portion of the information system such as a dynamic or static subsystem, a protected enclave within the information system or a portion of the system that controls will either be applied more or less stringently. The tailoring process also replaces the organizational variable placeholders with the actual values that will be required by the organization, the business unit or the system he developed.

Organizationally Defined Variables

NIST designed the control catalog (NIST SP 800-53) to provide security controls that were generic enough to be relevant across many organizations regardless of business mission. To provide the flexibility needed for organizations of different sizes, with different budgets, and different missions it was imperative to in clued organizationally defined variables in the control catalog. These variables appear as square brackets in the control documentation and allow organizations to define these variables customizing the security controls for their business and mission needs. An example of organizationally defined variables as they appear in NIST Special Publication 800-53 appears in figure 7-4.

PE-8   VISITOR ACCESS RECORDS

Control: The organization:

a. Maintains visitor access records to the facility where the information system resides for [*Assignment: organization-defined time period*]; and

b. Reviews visitor access records [*Assignment: organization-defined frequency*].

Supplemental Guidance: Visitor access records include, for example, names and organizations of persons visiting, visitor signatures, forms of identification, dates of access, entry and departure times, purposes of visits, and names and organizations of persons visited. Visitor access records are not required for publicly accessible areas.

Control Enhancements:

(1) *VISITOR ACCESS RECORDS | AUTOMATED RECORDS MAINTENANCE / REVIEW*
     The organization employs automated mechanisms to facilitate the maintenance and review of visitor access records.

(2) *VISITOR ACCESS RECORDS | PHYSICAL ACCESS RECORDS*
     [Withdrawn: Incorporated into PE-2].

References: None.

Priority and Baseline Allocation:

P3	LOW PE-8	MOD PE-8	HIGH PE-8 (1)

Figure 7-4 NIST SP 800-53 Excerpt

The control PE-8 discusses the need for maintaining visitor access records. In the control statement, we can see there are two locations that are identified using square brackets where organizationally defined variables must be described by the organization. In this example part a requires the organization determine how long will the organization maintain visitor records and in part b how frequently will those records be reviewed. Doing this for one control can be time consuming when coordinating with different organizational components, but it needs to be completed at tier 1 and 2 within the organization.

In addition to those areas where the organization is required to make an assignment of a variable, the control catalog also contains Square bracket locations where organizational officials must select from available options. An example of this is illustrated in figure 8-7 where the organization must select if the information system Will require the authentication of users, devices, or both.

<u>Control Enhancements</u>:

(1) *WIRELESS ACCESS | AUTHENTICATION AND ENCRYPTION*

The information system protects wireless access to the system using authentication of [*Selection (one or more): users; devices*] and encryption.

<u>Supplemental Guidance</u>: Related controls: SC-8, SC-13.

Figure 7-5 NIST SP 800-53 Excerpt

In Defining variables that cover the entirety of the control catalog can be an arduous and daunting task for the organization. In total there are 799 locations where an organizational variable must be defined by the enterprise, and an additional 68 locations where a selection must be made.

If organizational variables are not defined at enterprise-level, System owners Will be required to define the variables at the system, for tier 3 level. This is not ideal for a solid implementation of a security program and the risk management framework as different Systems will define and select different organizational variables.   For this reason, it is critical that one of the initial tasks and enterprise accomplishes when moving to the RMF is define organizational variables in the control catalog.

In defining variables, it is important to review policies regulations and laws to ensure the correct variable is determined. Check list security guides and information from hardware and software vendors can be helpful in developing organizational variables.

Controls Not Required by policy, law or requirements
At some point in the ceiling process a control will be identified that is not required for the information system.   In these cases that control should be identified as not requiring implementation, but not removed from the SCTM.   An example of this type of tailoring would be if the system being developed does not require encryption, in those controls supporting encryption can be identified in the matrix as not requiring implementation.   Again, these controls should remain in the matrix and not be removed but instead should be identified as not requiring implementation and justification statement should be made.

Controls that only Apply to a Subsystem or Component

In today's complex systems it is possible that only a portion of a system may require enhanced security controls. One example of this would be if a subsystem is the only portion of the information system that processes personally identifiable information (PII).   If that portion of the system has protections that ensure the PII information cannot transfer to the entirety of the information system, it can be possible to implement those enhanced PII or privacy controls only at that component or subsystem.   It is critical to ensure that the protected information with in that component is not allowed to traverse to the main information systems.

It is also possible that a component or portion of the information system may be excluded from the requirements of a security control.   An example of when this would apply is the public portion of an organization's website. The information in this component (the public website) I May not require the protections of the security controls identify for the entire system.   In this example, we may not require that users of the public website implement identification and authentication, that is the public website may not require username and password.

In both cases, we identify in the SCTM how the control applies to the identified subsystem or component. It is important to fully document this in the justification for the explanation for that control.

Additional and Compensating Controls

At times, it may be that the baseline at CTM does not contain Controls that will be required to properly secure the information system, in these cases we add additional controls.   There may also be the case when Controls that are required cannot be implemented or cannot be fully implemented and require compensating controls to help mitigate the identified risk to the system and the organization.

Additional controls are those controls that the system owner determines should be added to the matrix to allow full protection or the information and the information system.   These controls normally are selected from the control catalog to meet a specific security requirement that is not addressed by the baseline SCTM.

Compensating controls on the other hand seek to reinforce and compensate for controls that are required in the matrix but cannot be fully implemented due to limitations in the system. In these cases, controls should be selected from the control catalog that help mitigate the risk that remains when the required control is not implemented or only partially implemented.

As with other steps in the tailoring process additional and compensating controls should be identified in the SCTM with documented justification, or explanation of the requirements for adding these controls.

NIST SP 800-37 Text

CONTROL TAILORING

TASK S-2 Tailor the controls selected for the system and the environment of operation.

Potential Inputs: Initial control baselines; organization- and system-level risk assessment results; system element information; system component inventory; list of security and privacy requirements allocated to the system, system elements, and environment of operation; business impact analysis or criticality analysis; risk management strategy; organizational security and privacy policies; federal or organization-approved or mandated overlays.

Expected Outputs: List of tailored controls for the system and environment of operation (i.e., tailored control baselines).

Primary Responsibility: System Owner; Common Control Provider.

Supporting Roles: Authorizing Official or Authorizing Official Designated Representative; Information Owner or Steward; Systems Security Engineer; Privacy Engineer; System Security Officer; System Privacy Officer.

System Development Life Cycle Phase: New – Development/Acquisition.
Existing – Operations/Maintenance.

Discussion: After selecting the applicable control baselines, organizations tailor the controls based on various factors (e.g., missions or business functions, threats, security and privacy risks (including supply chain risks), type of system, or risk tolerance). The tailoring process includes identifying and designating common controls in the control baselines (see Task P-5); applying scoping considerations to the remaining baseline controls; selecting compensating controls, if needed; assigning values to organization-defined control parameters using either assignment or selection statements; supplementing baselines with additional controls; and providing specification information for control implementation. Organizations determine the amount of detail to include in justifications or supporting rationale required for tailoring decisions. For example, the justification or supporting rationale for scoping decisions related to a high-impact system or high value asset may necessitate greater specificity than similar decisions for a low-impact system. Such determinations are consistent with the organization's missions and business functions; stakeholder needs; and any relevant laws, executive orders, regulations, directives, or policies. Controls related to the SDLC and SCRM provide the basis for determining whether an information system is fit-for-purpose79 and need to be tailored accordingly.
Organizations use risk assessments to inform and guide the tailoring process. Threat information from security risk assessments provides information on adversary capabilities, intent, and targeting that may affect organizational decisions regarding the selection of security controls, including the associated costs and benefits. Privacy risk assessments, including the contextual factors therein, will also influence tailoring when an information system processes PII.Task P-4). Risk assessment results are also leveraged when identifying common controls to determine if the controls available for inheritance meet the security and privacy requirements for the system and its environment of operation. When common controls provided by the organization do not provide adequate protection for the systems inheriting the controls, system owners can either supplement the common controls with system-specific or hybrid controls to achieve the required level of protection or recommend a greater acceptance of risk to the authorizing official. Organizations may also consider federally or organizationally directed or approved overlays, tailored baselines, or Cybersecurity Framework Profiles when tailoring controls (see

References: [FIPS 199]; [FIPS 200]; [SP 800-30]; [SP 800-53]; [SP 800-53B]; [SP 800-160 v1] (System Requirements Definition, Architecture Definition, and Design Definition Processes); [SP 800-161] (Respond and Chapter 3); [IR 8179]; [CNSSI 1253]; [NIST CSF] (Core [Identify, Protect, Detect, Respond, Recover Functions]; Profiles).

EXERCISE 7.2

What is a major benefit of tailoring the baseline control set required for an information system?

_____

_____

_____

_____

TASK S-3 CONTROL ALLOCATION

Responsibilities	
Primary Responsibility	Supporting Roles
- Security Architect - Privacy Architect - System Security Officer - System Privacy Officer	- Chief Information Officer - Authorizing Official or Authorizing Official Designated Representative - Mission or Business Owner - Senior Agency Information Security Officer - Senior Agency Official for Privacy - System Owner

SDLC Alignment	
New Systems	Legacy Systems
- Initiation (concept/requirements definition).	- Operations/Maintenance.

CSF Alignment	
CSF Number	CSF Task
	- Profile - PR.IP

Task Flow	
Inputs	Outputs
- Security categorization - Organization- and system-level risk assessment results - Organizational policy on system registration	- List of security and privacy controls allocated to the system, system elements, and the environment of operation

| Enterprise architecture
- Security and privacy architectures
- Security and privacy requirements
- List of security and privacy requirements allocated to the system, system elements, and the environment of operation
- List of common control providers and common controls available for inheritance
- System description
- System element information
- System component inventory; relevant laws, executive orders, directives, regulations, and policies. | |

Common Controls

Controls are those controls that are implemented by a common control provider (CCP) and made available to one or more information systems across the organization. It is important that a registry of common controls be maintained at the enterprise level so that system owners can reference this registry to determine which controls can be inherited by their system.

A major task in tailoring process is determining those controls on the SCTM that can be inherited from enterprise CCPs. In organizations with well-developed security program and stratified common control providers several controls can be moved from the system owner's responsibility that of common control providers across the organization. This will reduce the cost of developing individual system and speed the development process while not impacting security or compliance of these systems.

When a control is aerated from a common control provider it is important that the SCTM reflect that inheritance and the control does not get removed from the matrix. By doing this the control can be tracked through the system lifecycle and if the CCP stops offering the inheritance, at some point in the future, the Control can be identified and shifted to either of another CCP the system owner for implementation.

Hybrid Controls

Many times, common controls do not provide the level of security or compliance that is required by the system owner based on individual system risk or requirements you derived from information types that are present on that system. In these cases, the system owner can still inherit the base control and at the security level enhance the security for compliance of that control maintaining the inheritance but adding the needed for compliance at the system level. In this way, System owner can inherit many parts of the control and only enhance those portions needed to achieve the level of security needed at the system-level. In this case the control becomes hybrid, or a shared responsibility, between the common control provider and the system owner.

Hybrid controls are also common when a common folder provider offers training, guidance, templates and examples but it requires the system owner to complete documentation and implement the program at the system level. In this case the control is shared between the common control provider and system owner as well.

In both these cases the control should be identified as a hybrid control on SCTM regarding which portions of the control will be implemented by the common people provider and which portion will be implemented by this system owner. In this way authorizing official can't determine planned implementation of the control, and once implemented the security control assessor and test that portion of the control that is implemented by the system owner.

NIST SP 800-37 Text

CONTROL ALLOCATION

TASK S-3 Allocate security and privacy controls to the system and to the environment of operation.

Potential Inputs: Security categorization; organization- and system-level risk assessment results; organizational policy on system registration; enterprise architecture; security and privacy architectures; security and privacy requirements; list of security and privacy requirements allocated to the system, system elements, and the environment of operation; list of common control providers and common controls available for inheritance; system description; system element information; system component inventory; relevant laws, executive orders, directives, regulations, and policies.

Expected Outputs: List of security and privacy controls allocated to the system, system elements, and the environment of operation.

Primary Responsibility: Security Architect; Privacy Architect; System Security Officer; System Privacy Officer.

Supporting Roles: Chief Information Officer; Authorizing Official or Authorizing Official Designated Representative; Mission or Business Owner; Senior Agency Information Security Officer; Senior Agency Official for Privacy; System Owner.

System Development Life Cycle Phase: New – Initiation (concept/requirements definition). Existing – Operations/Maintenance.

Discussion: The organization designates controls as system-specific, hybrid, or common, and allocates the controls to the system elements (i.e, machine, physical, or human elements) responsible for providing a security or privacy capability. Controls are allocated to a system or an organization consistent with the organization's enterprise architecture and security or privacy architecture and the allocated security and privacy requirements. Not all controls need to be allocated to every system element. Controls providing a specific security or privacy capability are only allocated to system elements that require that capability. The security categorization, privacy risk assessment, security and privacy architectures, and the allocation of controls work together to help achieve a suitable balance between security and privacy protections and the mission-based function of the system. Security and privacy requirements allocated to the system, system elements, and the environment of operation (see Task P-17) guide and inform control allocation to system elements. Common controls that are made available by the organization during the RMF *Prepare-Organization Level* step (see Task P-5), are selected for inheritance; hybrid controls are also selected. Common controls satisfy security and privacy requirements allocated to the organization and provide a protection capability that is inherited by one or more systems. Hybrid controls satisfy security and privacy requirements allocated to the system and to the organization and provide a protection capability that is partially inherited by one or more systems. And finally, system-specific controls satisfy security and privacy requirements allocated to the system and provide a protection capability for that system. Controls can be allocated to specific system elements rather than to every element within a system. For example, system-specific controls associated with management of audit logs may be allocated to a log management server and need not be implemented on every system element.

References: [SP 800-39] (Organization, Mission/Business Process, and System Levels); [SP 800-64]; [SP 800-160 v1] (System Requirements Definition, Architecture Definition, and Design Definition Processes); [NIST CSF] (Core [Identify Function]; Profiles); [OMB FEA].

EXERCISE 7.3

What is a benefit of inheriting controls from a approved common control provider?

_____

_____

_____

_____

TASK S-4 DOCUMENTATION OF PLANNED CONTROL IMPLEMENTATIONS

Responsibilities	
Primary Responsibility	Supporting Roles
- System Owner - Common Control Provider	- Authorizing Official or Authorizing Official Designated Representative - Information Owner or Steward - Systems Security Engineer - Privacy Engineer - System Security Officer - System Privacy Officer

SDLC Alignment	
New Systems	Legacy Systems
- Development/Acquisition	- Operations/Maintenance

CSF Alignment	
CSF Number	CSF Task
	- Profile

Task Flow	
Inputs	Outputs
- Security categorization - Organization- and system-level risk assessment results (security, privacy, and/or supply chain) - System element information - System component inventory - Business impact or criticality analysis - List of security and privacy requirements allocated to the system, system elements, and environment of operation - Risk management strategy; list of selected controls for the system and environment of operation - Organizational security, privacy, and SCRM policies	- Security and privacy plans for the system

After the initial baseline controls are selected and tailored to meet the risk requirements of the system it is essential to document how each of the required controls is planned to be implemented. Documentation must include information on how the system level controls and the system portion of hybrid controls will be implemented to satisfy the requirements as defined in NIST SP 800-53 and specified by organizational requirements. This documentation will be used later to determine if the controls planned implementation will meet the requirements of the organizational leadership including the systems authorizing official. This documentation will also assist assessors in evaluating the effectiveness of the control.

The inputs and outputs for the controls should be includes as well as any expected behavior or metric values. All controls should be documented in the plan including system, hybrid and common controls. The documentation of common controls should define the common control provider as well as linkage to documentation about the implementation of the common control's implementation by that provider. Beyond defining the provider and providing the actual documentation of the common controls or linkage to this documentation the system owner is not required to further document the implementation of the common controls that are inherited. Common controls like policies may be consolidated into s single plan that is provided to the entire organization if determined to be more efficient.

The planned control documentation provides traceability for system staff and other stakeholders. This allows the authorizing official and supporting personnel to review the planned implementation to determine if it will meet the security, and privacy requirements of the information types identified by the system and the risk requirements of the organization. This traceability of controls implementation should extend to third party providers for outsourced controls as well.

When documenting control implementation, the system owner should maximize the reuse of existing documentation that may be cross referenced at the organizational level or even better yet through the use of an automated tracking system.

The implementation of the controls should follow the organizations architecture, and policy requirements and provide enough detail that the reader can understand how the control is to be implemented and even assessed.

NIST SP 800-37 Text

DOCUMENTATION OF PLANNED CONTROL IMPLEMENTATIONS

TASK S-4 Document the controls for the system and environment of operation in security and privacy plans.

Potential Inputs: Security categorization; organization- and system-level risk assessment results (security, privacy, and/or supply chain); system element information; system component inventory; business impact or criticality analysis; list of security and privacy requirements allocated to the system, system elements, and environment of operation; risk management strategy; list of selected controls for the system and environment of operation; organizational security, privacy, and SCRM policies.

Expected Outputs: Security and privacy plans for the system.

Primary Responsibility: System Owner; Common Control Provider.

Supporting Roles: Authorizing Official or Authorizing Official Designated Representative; Information Owner or Steward; Systems Security Engineer; Privacy Engineer; System Security Officer; System Privacy Officer.

System Development Life Cycle Phase: New – Development/Acquisition.
Existing – Operations/Maintenance.

Discussion: Security and privacy plans contain an overview of the security and privacy requirements for the system and the controls selected to satisfy the requirements. The plans describe the intended application of each selected control in the context of the system with a sufficient level of detail to correctly implement the control and to subsequently assess the effectiveness of the control. The control documentation describes how system-specific and hybrid controls are implemented and the

---

plans and expectations regarding the functionality of the system. The description includes planned inputs, expected behavior, and expected outputs where appropriate, typically for those controls implemented in the hardware, software, or firmware components of the system. Common controls are also identified in the plans. There is no requirement to provide implementation details for inherited common controls. Rather, those details are provided in the plans for common control providers and are made available to system owners. For hybrid controls, the organization specifies in the system-level plans the parts of the control that are provided by the common control provider and the parts of the control that are implemented at the system level.

Organizations may develop a consolidated plan that incorporates security and privacy plans or maintain separate plans. If developing a consolidated plan, privacy programs collaborate with security programs to ensure that the plan reflects the selection of controls that provide protections with respect to managing the confidentiality, integrity, and availability of PII; and delineates roles and responsibilities for control implementation, assessment, and monitoring. For separate system security plans and privacy plans, organizations cross-reference the controls in all plans to help maintain accountability and awareness. The senior agency official for privacy reviews and approves the privacy plan (or integrated plan) before the plan is provided to the authorizing official or designated representative for review (see Task S-6). Organizations may document the control selection and tailoring information in documents equivalent to security and privacy plans, for example, in systems engineering or system life cycle artifacts or documents.

Documentation of planned control implementations allows for traceability of decisions prior to and after the deployment of the system. To the extent possible, organizations reference existing documentation (either by vendors or other organizations that have employed the same or similar systems or system elements), use automated support tools, and coordinate across the organization to reduce redundancy and increase the efficiency and cost-effectiveness of control documentation. The documentation also addresses platform dependencies and includes any additional information necessary to describe how the capability required is to be achieved at the level of detail sufficient to support control implementation and assessment. Documentation for control implementations follows best practices for hardware and software development and for systems security and privacy engineering disciplines and is also consistent with established policies and procedures for documenting activities in the SDLC. In certain situations, security controls can be implemented in ways that create privacy risks. The privacy program supports documentation of privacy risk considerations and the implementations intended to mitigate them.

For controls that are mechanism-based, organizations take advantage of the functional specifications provided by or obtainable from manufacturers, vendors, and systems integrators. This includes any documentation that may assist the organization during the development, implementation, assessment, and monitoring of controls. For certain controls, organizations obtain control implementation information from the appropriate organizational entities (e.g., physical security offices, facilities offices, records management offices, and human resource offices). Since the enterprise architecture and the security and privacy architectures established by the organization guide and inform the organizational approach used to plan for and implement controls, documenting the process helps to ensure traceability in meeting the security and privacy requirements.

References: [FIPS 199]; [FIPS 200]; [SP 800-18]; [SP 800-30]; [SP 800-53]; [SP 800-64]; [SP 800-160 v1] (System Requirements Definition, Architecture Definition, and Design Definition Processes); [SP 800-161] (Respond and Chapter 3); [IR 8179]; [CNSSI 1253]; [NIST CSF] (Core [Identify, Protect, Detect, Respond, Recover Functions]; Profiles).

EXERCISE 7.4

Why is it important to document how controls are planned to be implemented?

_____

_____

_____

_____

TASK S-5 CONTINUOUS MONITORING STRATEGY - SYSTEM

Responsibilities	
Primary Responsibility	Supporting Roles
- System Owner - Common Control Provider	- Senior Accountable Official for Risk Management or Risk Executive (Function) - Chief Information Officer - Senior Agency Information Security Officer - Senior Agency Official for Privacy - Authorizing Official or Authorizing Official Designated Representative - Information Owner or Steward - Security Architect; Privacy Architect - Systems Security Engineer - Privacy Engineer- System Security Officer - System Privacy Officer

SDLC Alignment	
New Systems	Legacy Systems
- Development/Acquisition.	- Operations/Maintenance

CSF Alignment	
CSF Number	CSF Task
	- ID.GV - DE.CM

Task Flow	

Inputs	Outputs
- Organizational risk management strategy - Organizational continuous monitoring strategy - Organization- and system-level risk assessment results - Security and privacy plans - Organizational security and privacy policies	- Continuous monitoring strategy for the system including time-based trigger for ongoing authorization

A monitoring strategy establishes the proposed method and frequency of security control assessment through the systems lifecycle. This strategy should define how each of the security controls will be assessed to ensure that each control is working as designed, providing the correct level of protection, and providing the correct output. This assessment strategy should be detailed enough to assess each required portion of control fully resulting in a complete assessment finding. This finding should detail the portions of the controls working correctly, those that are not working as required and those that are not implemented. Assessment procedures should be documented in the continuous monitoring strategy, the security plan, or both.

The monitoring strategy should also detail the frequency, or how often a control will be assessed. This frequency should first be drawn from the organizational Information Security Continuous Monitoring Strategy, the organizations policy documentation, and all applicable laws, guidance and regulations. In those areas where this guidance cannot be found the system owner can look for community security guidelines, best business practices and vendor security implementation guides. The frequency of assessment of controls that are more perishable, provide organizational protections or those controls that are listed on a Plan of Actions and Milestones (POA&M) will be higher than those controls that do not fall into this category. The frequency of security control assessment should be documented in the continuous monitoring strategy, the security plan, or both.

The continuous monitoring strategy document should contain a table that allows easy reference to the frequency of assessment of each required control. These frequencies include, but are not limited to, continuous and ongoing, daily, weekly, monthly, quarterly, semiannual, annual and every 2 or more years. An example of what a portion of this document could look like is illustrated in table 8-2

Row #	Control	Control Name	Control Description
		Continuous & Ongoing	
1	SI-4	Information System Monitoring	The organization: a. Monitors the information system to detect: 1. Attacks and indicators of potential attacks in accordance with [Assignment: organization-defined monitoring objectives]; and

2. Unauthorized local, network, and remote connections;

b. Identifies unauthorized use of the information system through [Assignment: organization-defined techniques and methods];

c. Deploys monitoring devices: (i) strategically within the information system to collect organization-determined essential information; and (ii) at ad hoc locations within the system to track specific types of transactions of interest to the organization;

…

2	AU-6a	Weekly Audit Review, Analysis, & Reporting	System Owners must review and analyze information system audit records for indications of inappropriate or unusual activity.
3	RA-5d	Monthly Vulnerability Scanning	System Owners must mitigate all discovered high-risk vulnerabilities within 30 days and mitigate moderate vulnerability risks in 90 days. CSPs must send their ISSO updated artifacts every 30 days to show evidence that outstanding high-risk vulnerabilities have been mitigated.
4	CA-7g	Continuous Monitoring Security State	System Owners must report the security state of the system to their own organizational officials on a monthly basis.

Configuration Management and Control Processes

A sound configuration management program ensures that systems are configured, or built, within the approved standard. When a system is designed, and the initial security documentation is created, the configuration of the system including software installed, version, hardware make model and type and general settings of the system are noted in the system configuration management plan and possibly the security. As the system is developed any changes to this baseline are noted in the baseline configuration is updated. Configuration management begins no later than step two of the RMF and continues throughout entire lifecycle.

Strict configuration management control should be maintained route system lifecycle that have been implemented are not impact buy changes to the system. It should be possible anytime in the system lifecycle to track all changes through the configuration management plan back to the original baseline that was authorized during the RMF.

Change management boards or configuration control boards should be comprised of individuals throughout the organization that would be considered stakeholders any information system that is being monitored. This often includes security personnel, System administrators, network administrators, help desk personnel, finance professionals, and members of the organizational leadership. This group Will evaluate changes proposed by system owners to ensure destruction of the information system, the organizational network environment, other systems or business processes are not impacted by the proposed change.

When making the changes it is important that the system owner develop plans that would allow the system to be reverted to its previous state should something go wrong during or after the change is implemented.

Security Impact Analyses on Proposed or Actual Changes
Reviewing proposed changes to a system for security impact is accomplished by security personnel optimally before the proposed change is presented to the configuration management board or change control board, and before the change is actually made. If this is not possible the security member or members of those boards would review the proposed change during or after the meeting. No decision on the change should be made to the system until a full security impact analysis is completed on the requested change and determination is made that change will not cause an unacceptable increase risk to the system, the business unit or, the organization.

The impact analysis must be conducted by an individual or team that has technical and administrative experience to evaluate the changes to the system at the smallest detail. Changes to the system can impact configuration settings, ports and protocols, disable security configurations and change file systems just to name a few things that might be impacted by a change. The individual or team must be able to identify and document these changes and if necessary adjust organizational procedures or policies to ensure the system maintains its approval and the enterprise risk posture is not impacted beyond an acceptable state.

The results of this analysis must be documented and cataloged in the board meeting minutes as well as in the configuration management plan as well as the security plan.

Assessment of Security Controls Employed and Inherited
Approved changes to the system may require full assessment of the impacted controls. The impact assessment conducted in this step determines the amount of the impacted security controls that will need to be assessed up to and including the entirety of the impacted controls. This applies to controls implemented by the system, inherited controls and hybrid controls.

Those controls assessed in this step should be assessed by an independent control assessor to assist with ongoing authorization, however this is not required. If the system owner conducts the assessment the results may come under increased scrutiny during the ongoing authorization

Security Status Reporting

172

Changes made to the information system through the continuous monitoring process must be reported to organizational officials including the authorizing official. The reporting process, including the report format, report structure, report frequency and report audience should be set at the enterprise level in the organizations ISCM strategy and program. If the enterprise has not yet accomplished this task, the security status reporting process is the responsibility of the system owner.

Contents of the security status reports should inform leadership of significant changes to the systems security status. This should include changes to the Plan of Actions & Milestones (POA&M), results of changes requested, approved and implemented by the change management and configuration control process, and changes to the systems environment. Changes to the environment can be physical, logical or even changes to the threat landscape.

The main outcomes of the reporting process is informing organizational leadership of changes to systems and the environment the systems operate in. This helps leadership ensure security requirements are progressing as required including compliance with POA&M and ATO restrictions. Leaders will use this information to continue to authorize systems, update organizations policy, and provide funding and projects to meet organizational security deficiencies.

NIST SP 800-37 Text

CONTINUOUS MONITORING STRATEGY—SYSTEM

TASK S-5 Develop and implement a system-level strategy for monitoring control effectiveness that is consistent with and supplements the organizational continuous monitoring strategy.

Potential Inputs: Organizational risk management strategy; organizational continuous monitoring strategy; organization- and system-level risk assessment results; security and privacy plans; organizational security and privacy policies.

Expected Outputs: Continuous monitoring strategy for the system including time-based trigger for ongoing authorization.

Primary Responsibility: System Owner; Common Control Provider.

Supporting Roles: Senior Accountable Official for Risk Management or Risk Executive (Function); Chief Information Officer; Senior Agency Information Security Officer; Senior Agency Official for Privacy; Authorizing Official or Authorizing Official Designated Representative; Information Owner or Steward; Security Architect; Privacy Architect; Systems Security Engineer; Privacy Engineer; System Security Officer; System Privacy Officer.

System Development Life Cycle Phase: New – Development/Acquisition.
Existing – Operations/Maintenance.
Discussion: An important aspect of risk management is the ongoing monitoring of controls implemented within or inherited by an information system. An effective continuous monitoring

---

strategy at the system level is developed and implemented in coordination with the organizational continuous monitoring strategy early in the SDLC (i.e., during initial system design or procurement decision). The system-level continuous monitoring strategy is consistent with and supplements the continuous monitoring strategy for the organization. The system-level strategy addresses monitoring those controls for which monitoring is not provided as part of the continuous monitoring strategy and implementation for the organization. The system-level strategy identifies the frequency of monitoring for controls not addressed by the organization-level strategy and defines the approach to be used for assessing those controls. The system-level continuous monitoring strategy, consistent with the organizational monitoring strategy, defines how changes to the system and the environment of operation[81] are to be monitored; how risk assessments are to be conducted; and the security and privacy posture reporting requirements including recipients of the reports. The system-level continuous monitoring strategy can be included in security and privacy plans.[82]

For controls that are not addressed by the organizational continuous monitoring strategy, the system-level continuous monitoring strategy identifies the criteria for determining the frequency with which controls are monitored post-implementation and the plan for the ongoing assessment of those controls. The criteria are established by the system owner or common control provider in collaboration with other organizational officials (e.g., the authorizing official or designated representative; senior accountable official for risk management or risk executive [function]; senior agency information security officer; senior agency official for privacy; and chief information officer). The frequency criteria at the system level reflect organizational priorities and the importance of the system to the organization's operations and assets, individuals, other organizations, and the Nation. Controls that are volatile (i.e., where the control or the control implementation is most likely to change over time),[83] critical to certain aspects of the protection needs for the organization, or identified in plans of action and milestones, may require more frequent assessment. The approach to control assessments during continuous monitoring may include reuse of assessment procedures and results that supported the initial authorization decision; detection of the status of system elements; and analysis of historical and operational data.

The authorizing official or designated representative approves the continuous monitoring strategy and the minimum frequency with which each control is to be monitored. The approval of the strategy can be obtained in conjunction with the security and privacy plan approval. The monitoring of controls begins at the start of the operational phase of the SDLC and continues through the disposal phase.

References: [SP 800-30]; [SP 800-39] (Organization, Mission or Business Process, System Levels); [SP 800-53]; [SP 800-53A]; [SP 800-137]; [SP 800-161]; [IR 8011 v1]; [CNSSI 1253]; [NIST CSF] (Core [Detect Function]).

EXERCISE 7.5

Why is it important to determine the control continuous monitoring strategy at this point in the RMF?

TASK S-6 PLAN REVIEW AND APPROVAL

Responsibilities	
Primary Responsibility	Supporting Roles
- Authorizing Official or Authorizing Official Designated Representative	- Senior Accountable Official for Risk Management or Risk Executive (Function) - Chief Information Officer; Chief Acquisition Officer - Senior Agency Information Security Officer - Senior Agency Official for Privacy

SDLC Alignment	
New Systems	Legacy Systems
- Development/Acquisition	- Operations/Maintenance

CSF Alignment	
CSF Number	CSF Task

Task Flow	
Inputs	Outputs
- Security and privacy plans - Organization- and system-level risk assessment results	- Security and privacy plans approved by the authorizing official

The Authorizing Official (AO) or the Authorizing Officials Designated Representative (AODR) is responsible for reviewing the system or controls sets security plan to ensure the system being built will comply with security and compliance requirements. Normally the AO does not accomplish this task without the support from other senior organizational officials including the senior information security officer (or chief information security officer), the chief information officer, and the reis executive (function). These individuals will provide input on the review of the SSP and supporting documentation, helping to ensure these plans and documents meet the requirements of the organization, regulations and laws.

The AO or AODR will review the SSP to ensure the plan for implementing the controls in the SCTM will provide the level of protection required for the information types housed by the information system and within the organizations level of risk tolerance. These officials will also review the plan for implementing each control as described in the SSP, ensuring that each will meet the requirements of the security control requirements. Finally, the ISCM will be reviewed to ensure that the strategy and plan will meet the requirements of and enhance the organizations ISCM strategy and plan.

When the SSP is approved by the AO or AODR the system owner is given the approval to build the system with the described controls developed as the plan describes the planned implementation. By getting this approval the system owner is granted some level of assurance that if the system is built according to the approved plan with the approved controls, approval of the system in step 5 will occur more easily.

The ISCM helps the system owner and organizational leadership understand the cost that will be incurred in operating the system and maintaining the required security controls. If there are any problems with the cost of monitoring the controls, it can be identified prior to the system being developed. The AO can determine if the system should be built without being able to fully monitor the security controls, if additional funding is required so that the controls can be monitored correctly, or if the system must be delayed or canceled due to the lack of monitoring.

Approval of the SSP
Once the SSP and supporting documents have been reviewed by the AO or AODR an approval decision. This can be approving the documents sending the system into step 3 or requiring the information system owner or common control provider make corrections and resubmit the documentation. If the plan is not approved the system owner or CCP can make the required corrections and resubmit the documentation.

NIST SP 800-37 Text

PLAN REVIEW AND APPROVAL

TASK S-6 Review and approve the security and privacy plans for the system and the environment of operation.

Potential Inputs: Security and privacy plans; organization- and system-level risk assessment results.

Expected Outputs: Security and privacy plans approved by the authorizing official.
Primary Responsibility: Authorizing Official or Authorizing Official Designated Representative.

Supporting Roles: Senior Accountable Official for Risk Management or Risk Executive (Function); Chief Information Officer; Chief Acquisition Officer; Senior Agency Information Security Officer; Senior Agency Official for Privacy.

System Development Life Cycle Phase: New – Development/Acquisition.

Existing – Operations/Maintenance.

Discussion: The security and privacy plan review by the authorizing official or designated representative with support from the senior accountable official for risk management or risk executive (function), chief information officer, senior agency information security officer, and senior agency official for privacy, determines if the plans are complete, consistent, and satisfy the stated security and privacy requirements for the system. Based on the results from this review, the authorizing official or designated representative may recommend changes to the security and privacy plans. If the plans are unacceptable, the system owner or common control provider make appropriate changes to the plans. If the plans are acceptable, the authorizing official or designated representative approves the plans. The acceptance of the security and privacy plans represents an important milestone in the SDLC and risk management process. The authorizing official or designated representative, by approving the plans, agrees to the set of controls (i.e., system-specific, hybrid, or common controls) and the description of the proposed implementation of the controls to meet the security and privacy requirements for the system and the environment in which the system operates. *Implement* step. The approval of the plans also establishes the level of effort required to successfully complete the remainder of the RMF steps and provides the basis of the security and privacy specifications for the acquisition of the system or individual system elements. The approval of the plans allows the risk management process to proceed to the RMF

References: [SP 800-30]; [SP 800-53]; [SP 800-160 v1] (System Requirements Definition, Architecture Definition, and Design Definition Processes).

EXERCISE 7.6

Why is it important to have the security plan approved at this step of the RMF?

_____

_____

_____

_____

8- THE IMPLEMENT STEP

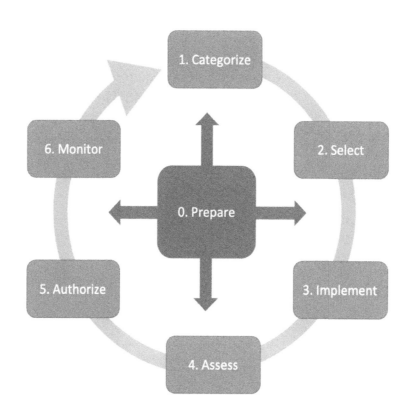

TASK I-1 CONTROL IMPLEMENTATION

Responsibilities	
Primary Responsibility	Supporting Roles
- System Owner - Common Control Provider	- Information Owner or Steward - Security Architect - Privacy Architect - Systems Security Engineer - Privacy Engineer - System Security Officer - System Privacy Officer - Enterprise Architect - System Administrator

SDLC Alignment	
New Systems	Legacy Systems
- Development/Acquisition - Implementation/Assessment	- Operations/Maintenance

CSF Alignment	
CSF Number	CSF Task
	- PR.IP-1 - PR.IP-2

Task Flow	
Inputs	Outputs
- Approved security and privacy plans - System design documents; organizational security and privacy policies and procedures - Business impact or criticality analyses - Enterprise architecture information - Security architecture information - Privacy architecture information - List of security and privacy requirements allocated to the system, system elements - Environment of operation - System element information - System component inventory - Organization- and system-level risk assessment results	- Implemented controls

179

Enterprise Architecture

It is important that the information system owner designs and implements the required security controls to integrate with the enterprise architecture including integration with organizational security systems. For example, if the enterprise uses a specific type of log collection, aggregation, and correlation it is important that the information system and its components are compliant with that enterprise log collection system. This helps to ensure that the system being developed will be able to provide the correct type of feed to the enterprise security systems and provide the security metrics that are required for the enterprise ISCM program can be provided. To successfully accomplish this the information owner should consult with the enterprise security architecture or enterprise architecture team.

Early Integration

Designing and implementing the required security controls early in the system development lifecycle eases this implementation and reduces the cost to development of the system. This is achieved through designing the system to be compliant with the specific control requirements up front so that the system will not be designed without fully implementing the controls and then redesigned later when it is determined that the system is not fully compliant with the security control requirements. Security control implementation is more effective and efficient when developed in parallel with the information system.

Mandatory Configuration Settings

Many organizations develop minimum configuration baselines for the systems that are common across the enterprise. In organizations with developed security programs the minimum required security controls integrated into these configuration baselines. For example, many organizations develop configuration baselines for servers, endpoints and network components. This way all systems will start from the same secure baseline and be developed securely from that point.

Common baselines can be developed by the organization or may be adopted from published government of civilian baselines. The most common baseline used by the government is the United States Government Core Configuration (USGCC) available at https://usgcb.nist.gov/. The USGCC was formerly known as the FDCC and has undergone some specific updates from that time. Organizations can use the USGCC is only available for endpoints like user workstations, but is available for many operating systems including Windows, and Linux. Commercially organizations like the Center for Internet Security (CIS) have developed security baselines for endpoints, servers and network components. CIS is a commercial organization therefore access to all its products requires a subscription, but they have made many products, including manual CIS Benchmarks are available for download if you register with the center.

Organizations can use these baselines and benchmarks as a starting point to develop enterprise specific baselines that meet the organizations requirements, risk profile and minimum-security baseline. These baselines can then be used as not only the starting point for systems being developed under the RMF but also as the starting point for the organizations configuration management plan and program.

Third Party Validation

There are products available that have been validated by third party organizations and programs. One of the most well-known programs is Common Criteria Evaluation (https://www.commoncriteriaportal.org/). Common Criteria uses independent laboratories to evaluate products and provides a report of the security posture of the product. While it is not the only third party available to validate security products, it is arguably the most well-known and widely accepted.

By using products that have been evaluated by an organizationally approved third party organization the system owner can be relatively confident that these products can be integrated into an organizations architecture securely. This can help the system owner implement the required security controls more confidently and with more ease than components that do not have these third-party assessments.

Integration of Common Controls

Most information system owners will take advantage of the benefits that come with the integration of common controls. Common control inheritance is one of the benefits of the RMF that decreases overall system development time, security control development time, and system development cost while not impacting the security and compliance requirements of the system. Common controls, sometimes called inherited controls, move the security controls implementation requirements from the system owners to common control providers.

When a system owner accepts common controls, they must be aware of the requirements made by that common control provider. These may be that the common control can only be inherited by specific hardware or software components. It may also be that the components developed by the system owner is configured in a specific way, allow a certain type of input, output or even require the ability to install specific software to function correctly.

In earlier steps the identification of common controls may have been deferred until later in the systems development. If that was the case these common controls must be identified and documented at this point.

Common Control – System Control Gap Analysis

When the system owner decides to inherit common control, it is often assumed that the common control provider will be able to implement the entirety of all the control requirements of the identified common controls. Many times, this is the case, however it is possible that the common control provider did not fully implement all the requirements of the control and either control requirements are placed on a plan of actions and milestones (POA&M), or it has been determined that the CCP would not be providing portions of the control for inheritance. In other cases, the system designed by the information system owner does not have the required hardware, software, or configuration needed for full common control inheritance.

In these cases, the system owner will need to evaluate this common control inheritance to ensure that the control is fully in place for the system inheriting the control. This evaluation, or gap analysis, is conducted by evaluating the authorization package of the CCP, including the SSP, the POA&M, the security assessment report (SAR), and the authorization to operate (ATO) memo. The assessment will also include evaluation of how the control is inherited by the system owner's system. Any gaps identified will need to be resolved and implemented by the system owner or common control provider.

Concurrent Security Control Implementation and Assessment
Dramatic savings on systems and security development costs can be realized without compromising the security or compliance and increasing the speed of development of an information system if control assessment can be accomplished in parallel with system development. This is done by having an independent security control assessor available to assess the security controls as the system is developed and the control implementation is completed. The results of the assessment will be documented during development and the results will be brought forward to step 4 and the assessment of the system. It important that the security controls implementation is not changed after the control is assessed.

Many organizations do not have the ability to realize these benefits as independent security control assessors are often not available to complete assessments during development. It is a great benefit to the enterprise security and project management program if this method of assessment is possible.

NIST SP 800-37 Text

CONTROL IMPLEMENTATION

TASK I-1 Implement the controls in the security and privacy plans.

Potential Inputs: Approved security and privacy plans; system design documents; organizational security and privacy policies and procedures; business impact or criticality analyses; enterprise architecture information; security architecture information; privacy architecture information; list of security and privacy requirements allocated to the system, system elements; and environment of operation; system element information; system component inventory; organization- and system-level risk assessment results.

Expected Outputs: Implemented controls.

Primary Responsibility: System Owner; Common Control Provider.

Supporting Roles: Information Owner or Steward; Security Architect; Privacy Architect; Systems Security Engineer; Privacy Engineer; System Security Officer; System Privacy Officer; Enterprise Architect; System Administrator.

System Development Life Cycle Phase: New – Development/Acquisition; Implementation/Assessment. Existing – Operations/Maintenance.

Discussion: Organizations implement the controls as described in the security and privacy plans. The control implementation is consistent with the organization's enterprise architecture and associated security and privacy architectures. Organizations use best practices when implementing controls, including systems security and privacy engineering methodologies, concepts, and principles. Risk assessments guide and inform decisions regarding the cost, benefit, and risk trade-offs in using different technologies or policies for control implementation. Organizations also ensure that mandatory configuration settings are established and implemented on system elements in accordance with federal and organizational policies. When organizations have no direct control over what controls are implemented in a system element, for example, in commercial off-the-shelf products, organizations consider the use of system elements that have been tested, evaluated, or validated by approved, independent, third-party assessment facilities (e.g., NIST Cryptographic Module Validation Program Testing Laboratories, National Information Assurance Partnership Common Criteria Testing Laboratories). The tests, evaluations, and validations consider products in specific configurations and in isolation; control implementation addresses how the product is integrated into the system while preserving security functionality and assurance.

Organizations also address, where applicable, assurance requirements when implementing controls. Assurance requirements are directed at the activities that control developers and implementers carry out to increase the level of confidence that the controls are implemented correctly, operating as intended, and producing the desired outcome with respect to meeting the security and privacy requirements for the system. The assurance requirements address quality of the design, development, and implementation of the controls.85

For the common controls inherited by the system, systems security and privacy engineers with support from system security and privacy officers, coordinate with the common control provider to determine the most appropriate way to implement common controls. System owners can refer to the authorization packages prepared by common control providers when making determinations regarding the adequacy of common controls inherited by their systems. During implementation, it may be determined that common controls previously selected to be inherited by the system do not meet the specified security or privacy requirements for the system. For common controls that do not meet the requirements for the system inheriting the controls or when common controls have unacceptable deficiencies, the system owners identify compensating or supplementary controls to be implemented. System owners can supplement the common controls with system-specific or hybrid controls to achieve the required protection for their systems or they can accept greater risk with the acknowledgement and approval of the organization. Risk assessments may determine how gaps in security or privacy requirements between systems and common controls affect the risk associated with the system, and how to prioritize the need for compensating or supplementary controls to mitigate specific risks.

Consistent with the flexibility allowed in applying the tasks in the RMF, organizations conduct initial control assessments during system development and implementation. Conducting such assessments in parallel with the development and implementation phases of the SDLC facilitates early identification of deficiencies and provides a cost-effective method for initiating corrective actions. Issues discovered during these assessments can be referred to authorizing officials for resolution. The results of the initial control assessments can also be used during the authorize step to avoid delays or costly repetition of assessments. Assessment results that are subsequently reused in other phases of the SDLC meet the reuse requirements established by the organization.

References: [FIPS 200]; [SP 800-30]; [SP 800-53]; [SP 800-53A]; [SP 800-160 v1] (Implementation, Integration, Verification, and Transition Processes); [SP 800-161]; [IR 8062]; [IR 8179].

EXERCISE 7.1

Why is it important to implement controls as early as possible in the SDLC?

_____

_____

_____

_____

TASK I-2 UPDATE CONTROL IMPLEMENTATION INFORMATION

Responsibilities	
Primary Responsibility	Supporting Roles
- System Owner - Common Control Provider	- Information Owner or Steward - Security Architect - Privacy Architect - Systems Security Engineer - Privacy Engineer - System Security Officer - System Privacy Officer - Enterprise Architect - System Administrator

SDLC Alignment	
New Systems	Legacy Systems
- Development/Acquisition - Implementation/Assessment.	- Operations/Maintenance

CSF Alignment	
CSF Number	CSF Task
	- Profile
	- PR.IP-1

Task Flow	
Inputs	Outputs
- Security and privacy plans - Information from control implementation efforts	- Security and privacy plans updated with implementation detail sufficient for use by assessors - System configuration baseline

Many times, the implementation of controls cannot be implemented as planned. Control implementation is changed due to configuration requirements of the hardware of software, requirements of the information technology or security architecture, or even lack of the skills required. There are numerous ways to successfully implement controls, therefore when the planned implementation of a control changes it is important to update the implementation documentation in the security plan. The security plan should always contain the most accurate information on either the planned, or actual implementation of the controls that protect the system and the information.

Any changes to the controls planned implementation must be updated in the security plan to reflect how the control is actually implemented. The plan should detail the inputs, outputs, and behavior of the controls, in sufficient details so that the controls implementation can be understood by the reader and assessed by auditors and assessors.

All changes to the implementation of controls must be approved as required by organizational leadership. The changed implementation must also be evaluated to determine if the risk the control is implemented to reduce the risk to an acceptable level.

NIST SP 800-37 Text
UPDATE CONTROL IMPLEMENTATION INFORMATION **TASK I-2** Document changes to planned control implementations based on the "as-implemented" state of controls. **Potential Inputs:** Security and privacy plans; information from control implementation efforts. **Expected Outputs:** Security and privacy plans updated with implementation detail sufficient for use by assessors; system configuration baseline.

Primary Responsibility: System Owner; Common Control Provider.

Supporting Roles: Information Owner or Steward; Security Architect; Privacy Architect; Systems Security Engineer; Privacy Engineer; System Security Officer; System Privacy Officer; Enterprise Architect; System Administrator.

System Development Life Cycle Phase: New – Development/Acquisition; Implementation/Assessment. Existing – Operations/Maintenance.

Discussion: Despite the control implementation details in the security and privacy plans and the system design documents, it is not always feasible to implement controls as planned. Therefore, as control implementations are carried out, the security and privacy plans are updated with as-implemented control implementation details. The updates include revised descriptions of implemented controls including changes to planned inputs, expected behavior, and expected outputs with sufficient detail to support control assessments. Documenting the "as implemented" control information is essential to providing the capability to determine when there are changes to the controls, whether those changes are authorized, and the impact of the changes on the security and privacy posture of the system and the organization.

References: [SP 800-53]; [SP 800-128]; [SP 800-160 v1] (Implementation, Integration, Verification, and Transition, Configuration Management Processes).

EXERCISE 7.2

Why is it important to update the planned control implementation in the security plan at this point in the RMF?

_____

_____

_____

_____

NOTES:

9- THE ASSESS STEP

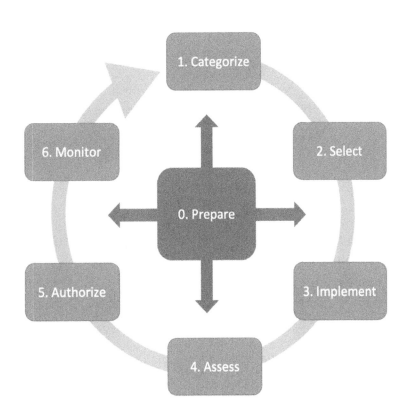

TASK A-1 ASSESSOR SELECTION

Responsibilities	
Primary Responsibility	Supporting Roles
- Authorizing Official - Authorizing Official Designated Representative	- Chief Information Officer - Senior Agency Information Security Officer - Senior Agency Official for Privacy

SDLC Alignment	
New Systems	Legacy Systems
- Development/Acquisition - Implementation/Assessment	- Operations/Maintenance

CSF Alignment	
CSF Number	CSF Task

Task Flow	
Inputs	Outputs
- Security, privacy, and SCRM plans - Program management control information - Common control documentation - Organizational security and privacy program plans - SCRM strategy - System design documentation - Enterprise, security, and privacy architecture information - Security, privacy, and SCRM policies and procedures applicable to the system	- Selection of assessor or assessment team responsible for conducting the control assessment

It is important for an organization to identify and select qualified and independent assessors to evaluate the functionality of controls. Assessors skills must be appropriate for the technologies being used and understand the hardware and software components they are evaluating. In addition, the assessor must be independent to ensure the assessment results are not biased.

Assessors can be individuals or a team that evaluate the systems controls and determine their effectiveness and that they are operating as required and producing the desired results and output. Assessors can be members of the organization, can be from another organization or outsourced or contractor staff.

The skillset of the assessor is a critical factor when the organization is selecting personnel for this role. They must we skilled in the assessment of all three types of controls, system, hybrid and common. They must also have a solid understanding of the hardware and software that they will be responsible for assessing. It is common for an assessment team to be made up of professional assessors that focus on one specific technology, for example server operating systems, or networking. A highly successful team can be created by combining people with the correct skill sets for the system being assessed. Matching the assessment team's skillset with the system being assessed is central to successful assessments of controls.

The independence of the assessor is also important. The RMF assigns responsibility for determining the independence of the assessor with the authorizing official (AO) or authorizing officials designated representative. The organizations senior agency official for privacy is responsible for the correct assessment and documentation of privacy controls, for this reason the senior agency official for privacy should consult with the AO on the assessors. The AO will also consult with Office of the Inspector General, chief information officer, and senior agency information security officer when selecting qualified and independent assessors. The assessor should be free of actual or even perceived conflicts of interest with the system being developed to be seen as fully independent.

The senior agency official for privacy is responsible for conducting assessments of privacy controls and documenting the results of the assessments

System owners may conduct self-assessments to ensure that the systems controls are in place and functioning as required before official independent assessment, however independent assessment is required for a system to submit a complete authorization package. These self-assessments can also take place during the continuous monitoring step; however, the system owner should verify with the AO on the requirements on assessments by the independent assessors and self-assessments.

NIST SP 800-37 Text

ASSESSOR SELECTION

TASK A-1 Select the appropriate assessor or assessment team for the type of control assessment to be conducted.

Potential Inputs: Security, privacy, and SCRM plans; program management control information; common control documentation; organizational security and privacy program plans; SCRM strategy; system design documentation; enterprise, security, and privacy architecture information; security, privacy, and SCRM policies and procedures applicable to the system.

Expected Outputs: Selection of assessor or assessment team responsible for conducting the control assessment.

Primary Responsibility: Authorizing Official or Authorizing Official Designated Representative.

Supporting Roles: Chief Information Officer; Senior Agency Information Security Officer; Senior Agency Official for Privacy.

System Development Life Cycle Phase: New – Development/Acquisition;
Implementation/Assessment.
Existing – Operations/Maintenance.

Discussion: Organizations consider both the technical expertise and level of independence required in selecting control assessors. Organizations ensure that control assessors possess the required skills and technical expertise to develop effective assessment plans and to conduct assessments of program management, system-specific, hybrid, and common controls, as appropriate. This includes general knowledge of risk management concepts and approaches as well as comprehensive knowledge of and experience with the hardware, software, and firmware components implemented. In organizations where the assessment capability is centrally managed, the senior agency information security officer may have the responsibility of selecting and managing the security control assessors or assessment teams for organizational systems. As controls may be implemented to achieve security and privacy objectives, organizations consider the degree of collaboration between security control and privacy control assessors that is necessary.

Organizations can conduct self-assessments of controls or obtain the services of an independent control assessor. An independent assessor is an individual or group that can conduct an impartial assessment. Impartiality means that assessors are free from perceived or actual conflicts of interest with respect to the determination of control effectiveness or the development, operation, or management of the system, common controls, or program management controls. The authorizing official determines the level of assessor independence based on applicable laws, executive orders, directives, regulations, policies, or standards. The authorizing official consults with the Office of the Inspector General, chief information officer, senior agency official for privacy, and senior agency information security officer to help guide and inform decisions regarding assessor independence. The system privacy officer is responsible for identifying assessment methodologies and metrics to determine if privacy controls are implemented correctly, operating as intended, and sufficient to ensure compliance with applicable privacy requirements and manage privacy risks. The senior agency official for privacy is responsible for conducting assessments of privacy controls and documenting the results of the assessments. At the discretion of the organization, privacy controls may be assessed by an independent assessor. However, in all cases, the senior agency official for privacy is responsible and accountable for The senior agency official for privacy is responsible for providing privacy information to the authorizing official.

References: [FIPS 199]; [SP 800-30]; [SP 800-53A]; [SP 800-55].

EXERCISE 8.1

Why is it important that the control assessor is independent of the system being assessed?

_____
_____
_____
_____
_____

TASK A-2 ASSESSMENT PLAN

Responsibilities	
Primary Responsibility	Supporting Roles
- Authorizing Official - Authorizing Official Designated Representative - Control Assessor	- Senior Agency Information Security Officer - Senior Agency Official for Privacy - System Owner - Common Control Provider - Information Owner or Steward - System Security Officer - System Privacy Officer

SDLC Alignment	
New Systems	Legacy Systems
- Development/Acquisition - Implementation/Assessment	- Operations/Maintenance

CSF Alignment	
CSF Number	CSF Task

Task Flow	
Inputs	Outputs
- Security, privacy, and SCRM plans; program management control information - Common control documentation - Organizational security and privacy program plans - SCRM strategy - System design documentation - Supply chain information - Enterprise, security, and privacy architecture information; security, privacy, and SCRM policies and procedures applicable to the system	- Security and privacy assessment plans approved by the authorizing official

The Security Assessment Plan (SAP) schedules and roadmaps the process that will be used to effectively conduct the assessment of the systems required controls. In the initial task of this step you will compile available reference materials and evidence provided by the system owner that will be used to evaluate the effectiveness of the security controls implementation.

These plans reflect the type of assessment that is being conducted including the most common types
- Developmental Testing and Evaluation
- Independent Verification and Validation
- Assessments Supporting Authorizations or Reauthorizations
- Audits
- Continuous Monitoring
- Assessments Subsequent to Remediation Actions

When security control assessments are conducted in parallel with the development of the system the organization and system owner can benefit from the most cost effective and efficient testing and remediation cycle as the system developers are available and correct identified deficiencies almost immediately.

The assessment plan, once complete, are approved by the appropriate organizational officials to ensure it meets with
- The organizations security objectives
- State-of-the practice tools, techniques, and procedures
- Effective use of automation

It is important to understand the two objectives of the security assessment plan.
- To establish the appropriate expectations for the security control assessment
- To bound the level of effort for the security control assessment

A. Prepare for Security Control Assessment

A.1 Establish objectives and scope
Establishing the objectives and scope to the assessment should be directly tied to the risk assessment and impact of the information system or common control set being assessed. Higher risk systems should warrant more detailed and thorough objectives and more detailed scoping statements than those systems with lower risk impacts to the organization.

A.2 Establish points of contact, provide notifications and timelines
Conducting a security control assessment can impact several groups and individuals supporting an information system or common control set. This could include those directly supporting the system, those using the system or even organizational stakeholders.

The security assessment plan (SAP) should contain contact information from those that are directly supporting the system and those impacted by the system or the assessment effort. Point of contact listings should include the relevant information that would facilitate effective communications through the SAP development, the assessment itself and the security assessment report generation, this generally includes relevant phone numbers as well as relevant physical and email addresses. This listing should include the following personnel, at a minimum.

- System Owner
- ISSO
- System Administrator
- Security Control Assessor(s)
- AO
- Security or Network Operations Center

The provided timeline should cover the major milestones of the assessment that would impact the organization or the information system. Important milestones include

- Assessment kick off meeting
- SAP completion date
- Assessment window (start and completion)
- Final report due date
- Out briefing date

A.3 Select security control assessor (e.g., independence, competency)
It is important that the security control assessor, or assessment team is both skilled in the required technology and determined to be independent. This ensures that the assessment results are as complete as possible and at the same tome free of any actual or perceived bias. This ensures the assessor or assessors can evaluate the effectiveness of system, inherited and hybrid controls.

The assessor or assessment team should have specific familiarity with the information systems specific

- Hardware
- Software
- Firmware

The impartiality of the assessor ensures the control assessment results are free of actual or perceived bias to the system. This can be accomplished by using internal or external assessors that have been determined to be independent by appropriate organizational personnel, normally this includes the organizations authorizing official or officials as they will be the individuals relying on the completeness of the assessment report when making an authorization decision. Therefore, the independence of the assessor or assessment team must be consistent and impartial enough to provide the information that will allow the AO to make an informed risk based decision on the authorization of the system or common control set.

When using an outside assessment team, it is important that the system owner is not directly involved in the selection of the outside vendor providing the services, to ensure the team is deemed to be independent.

To ensure independence of the assessment the AO often consults with the Office of the Inspector General, Senior Information Security Officer, Chief Information Officer and others to determine the implications of the assessor independence determination.

A.4 Collect and review artifacts (e.g., previous assessments, system documentation, policies)

The speed and efficiency of the assessment can be increased by ensuring that the assessor has all relevant documentation supporting the information system ahead of the actual assessment. This includes contacting the information system owner and relevant stakeholders, including common control providers to collect and assemble the documentation that will support the event. This documentation includes previous assessment results or SARs, relevant system documentation, applicable policies and common control provider documentation.

Previous assessment results and evidence from past assessments, audits and reviews (generically called assessments in this paragraph) should be made available to the assessor. This allows the assessor to have a full picture of the information system including those items that were discovered as findings in the past. Previous findings that have been corrected can be validated as corrected, and those finding that have not been corrected can be brought forward to the new SAR. The status of previous findings can prove valuable to the authorizing official as they can provide insight into the system owners track record of correcting deficiencies. Relevant documentation from previous assessments should be included as evidence in the current assessment and be available to the authorizing official as part of the authorization package developed in step 5.

Documentation from common control providers provides the evidence needed that the common controls that are being inherited by the information system are in place and functioning as designed and required. Documentation should include, at a minimum, the common control set Authorization to Operate (ATO) and the Plan of Actions & Milestones (POA&M). Some organizations require the CCP to provide the security plan and assessment results as part of the documentation that is provided to the information system that is inheriting the controls.

Organization, department and system level policies should be available to the assessor. These documents often support the validation of controls, especially when assessing security controls using the examine method. These documents may also define specific variables that would need to be evaluated during the assessment, for example higher level policies may require a password length of 8 characters, the department policy may require 10 characters and the system policy may require 14. In this case, the password length assessment should be evaluated to ensure the minimum password length is 14 characters, the most stringent requirement spelled out in the three policies.

B. Develop Security Control Assessment Plan

B.1 Determine security assessment methods and level of effort
Assessment methods focus the assessor on one facet of the controls implementation. Use of these methods individually or in combination, as required, ensure the control is fully and correctly implemented. NIST has determined three methods, examine, interview and test will provide the necessary level of assessment to ensure the control is implemented and functioning as required. While there are three assessment methods available, each security controls will be specific in the methods appropriate for that specific control.

Each assessment method focuses on an assessment object that will be the focus of the assessment. These objects will often serve as the evidence that the security control is implemented correctly.

The assessment methods also have attributes that help the assessor tailor the level of effort to the information system or common control set being assessed. This ensures that resources are allocated correctly and the security controls are assessed to the level required for the risk level of the system being assessed. These attributes are depth and coverage.

Depth
The depth of the assessment describes the level of rigor or detail the assessor uses when reviewing the assessment object. In basic terms this is the level of detail that the assessor will require to ensure the control is in place and working as required.

There are three levels of depth the assessor can use when developing the assessment plan and conducting the assessment basic, focused and comprehensive. These three levels apply to each of the assessment methods.

Basic Level of Depth
When using the basic level of assessment, the assessor focuses on high-level reviews of the assessment object. For depth, this could be a basic review of a document such as a policy, or the basic review of the configuration of a computers operating system.

Focused Level of Depth
When using the focused level of assessment, the assessor implements as more in-depth review of the assessment of the assessment object. For depth, this could be a review of the policy as well as other documents supporting the policy, for a computer system this could include the basic testing and could include reviews of the systems design.

Comprehensive Level of Depth

When using the comprehensive level of examination, the assessor implements the most in depth review of the assessment object. For depth, this could be a detailed and thorough review of the policy, the supporting documentation and other factors that impact the policy, for a computer system this level requires the system to undergo a detailed and focused review of how the operating system is configured to ensure the security controls are implemented correctly.

Coverage

The coverage of the assessment describes how many assessment objects will be inspected during the assessment, this is often described as the breadth of the assessment. In basic terms coverage describes the number of things that the assessor will examine to determine if the security control is in place for the system.

There are three levels of depth the assessor can use when developing the assessment plan and conducting the assessment basic, focused and comprehensive. These three levels apply to each of the assessment methods.

Basic Level of Coverage

When using the basic level of coverage, the assessor selects a representative sampling of the assessment objects to examine. For example, an assessor implementing a basic test of a system may select 10% of the computer systems to inspect for the assessment.

Focused Level of Coverage

When the assessor selects the focused level of assessment they select a representative sample as in basic coverage, but may also focus on assessing more systems that support unique functions. For example, the assessor may test 10% of all computer systems, but also test 100% of all administrator systems.

Comprehensive Level of Coverage

When selecting the comprehensive coverage level the assessor will inspect all the assessment objects in the system. For example, the assessor would test all the computer systems in the system being tested when they select the comprehensive level of coverage.

Examine

When using the examine method the assessor will generally review documentation that supports the implementation of the security control in the information system or common control set.

NIST provides the following guidance about the examine method

ASSESSMENT METHOD: Examine

ASSESSMENT OBJECTS:
- Specifications (e.g., policies, plans, procedures, system requirements, designs)
- Mechanisms (e.g., functionality implemented in hardware, software, firmware)
- Activities (e.g., system operations, administration, management; exercises)

DEFINITION: The process of checking, inspecting, reviewing, observing, studying, or analyzing one or more assessment objects to facilitate understanding, achieve clarification, or obtain evidence, the results of which are used to support the determination of security and privacy control existence, functionality, correctness, completeness, and potential for improvement over time.

SUPPLEMENTAL GUIDANCE : Typical assessor actions may include, for example: reviewing information security policies, plans, and procedures; analyzing system design documentation and interface specifications; observing system backup operations; reviewing the results of contingency plan exercises; observing incident response activities; studying technical manuals and user/administrator guides; checking, studying, or observing the operation of an information technology mechanism in the information system hardware/software; or checking, studying, or observing physical security measures related to the operation of an information system.

SCAP-validated tools that support the OCIL component specification may be used to automate the collection of assessment objects from specific, responsible individuals within an organization. The resulting information can then be examined by assessors during the security and privacy control assessments.

ATTRIBUTES: Depth, Coverage
- The depth attribute addresses the rigor of and level of detail in the examination process. There are three possible values for the depth attribute: (i) basic; (ii) focused; and (iii) comprehensive.

- **Basic examination**: Examination that consists of high-level reviews, checks, observations, or inspections of the assessment object. This type of examination is conducted using a limited body of evidence or documentation (e.g., functional-level descriptions for mechanisms; high level process descriptions for activities; actual documents for specifications). Basic examinations provide a level of understanding of the security and privacy controls necessary for determining whether the controls are implemented and free of obvious errors.

- Focused examination: Examination that consists of high-level reviews, checks, observations, or inspections and more in-depth studies/analyses of the assessment object. This type of examination is conducted using a substantial body of evidence or documentation (e.g., functional-level descriptions and where appropriate and available, high-level design information for mechanisms; high-level process descriptions and implementation procedures for activities; the actual documents and related documents for specifications). Focused examinations provide a level of understanding of the security and privacy controls necessary for determining whether the controls are implemented and free of obvious errors and whether there are increased grounds for confidence that the controls are implemented correctly and operating as intended.

- Comprehensive examination: Examination that consists of high-level reviews, checks, observations, or inspections and more in-depth, detailed, and thorough studies/analyses of the assessment object. This type of examination is conducted using an extensive body of evidence or documentation (e.g., functional-level descriptions and where appropriate and available, high-level design information, low-level design information, and implementation information for mechanisms; high-level process descriptions and detailed implementation procedures for activities; the actual documents and related documents for specifications. Comprehensive examinations provide a level of understanding of the security and privacy controls necessary for determining whether the controls are implemented and free of obvious errors and whether there are further increased grounds for confidence that the controls are implemented correctly and operating as intended on an ongoing and consistent basis, and that there is support for continuous improvement in the effectiveness of the controls.

Interview

The interview method focuses on asking questions to individuals or groups of people about the security control being assessed.

NIST provides the following guidance about the interview method

ASSESSMENT METHOD: Interview
ASSESSMENT OBJECTS:
- Individuals or groups of individuals.

DEFINITION: The process of conducting discussions with individuals or groups within an organization to facilitate understanding, achieve clarification, or lead to the location of evidence, the results of which are used to support the determination of security and privacy control existence, functionality, correctness, completeness, and potential for improvement over time.

SUPPLEMENTAL GUIDANCE : Typical assessor actions may include, for example, interviewing agency heads, chief information officers, senior agency information security officers, authorizing officials, information owners, information system and mission owners, information system security officers, information system security managers, personnel officers, human resource managers, facilities managers, training officers, information system operators, network and system administrators, site managers, physical security officers, and users.

SCAP-validated tools that support the OCIL component specification may be used to automate the interview process for specific individuals or groups of individuals. The resulting information can then be examined by assessors during the security and privacy control assessments.

    ATTRIBUTES: Depth, Coverage
    • The depth attribute addresses the rigor of and level of detail in the interview process. There are three possible values for the depth attribute: (i) basic; (ii) focused; and (iii) comprehensive.

    - **Basic interview**: Interview that consists of broad-based, high-level discussions with individuals or groups of individuals. This type of interview is conducted using a set of generalized, high-level questions. Basic interviews provide a level of understanding of the security and privacy controls necessary for determining whether the controls are implemented and free of obvious errors.

    - **Focused interview**: Interview that consists of broad-based, high-level discussions and more in depth discussions in specific areas with individuals or groups of individuals. This type of interview is conducted using a set of generalized, high-level questions and more in-depth questions in specific areas where responses indicate a need for more in-depth investigation. Focused interviews provide a level of understanding of the security and privacy controls necessary for determining whether the controls are implemented and free of obvious errors and whether there are increased grounds for confidence that the controls are implemented correctly and operating as intended.

    - **Comprehensive interview**: Interview that consists of broad-based, high-level discussions and more in-depth, probing discussions in specific areas with individuals or groups of individuals. This type of interview is conducted using a set of generalized, high-level questions and more in depth, probing questions in specific areas where responses indicate a need for more in-depth investigation. Comprehensive interviews provide a level of understanding of the security and privacy controls necessary for determining whether the controls are implemented and free of obvious errors and whether there are further increased grounds for confidence that the controls are implemented correctly and operating as intended on an ongoing and consistent basis, and that there is support for continuous improvement in the effectiveness of the controls.

• The coverage attribute addresses the scope or breadth of the interview process and includes the types of individuals to be interviewed (by organizational role and associated responsibility), the number of individuals to be interviewed (by type), and specific individuals to be interviewed. There are three possible values for the coverage attribute: (i) basic; (ii) focused; and (iii) comprehensive.

- **Basic interview**: Interview that uses a representative sample of individuals in key organizational roles to provide a level of coverage necessary for determining whether the security and privacy controls are implemented and free of obvious errors.

- **Focused interview**: Interview that uses a representative sample of individuals in key organizational roles and other specific individuals deemed particularly important to achieving the assessment objective to provide a level of coverage necessary for determining whether the security and privacy controls are implemented and free of obvious errors and whether there are increased grounds for confidence that the controls are implemented correctly and operating as intended.

- **Comprehensive interview**: Interview that uses a sufficiently large sample of individuals in key organizational roles and other specific individuals deemed particularly important to achieving the assessment objective to provide a level of coverage necessary for determining whether the security and privacy controls are implemented and free of obvious errors and whether there are further increased grounds for confidence that the controls are implemented correctly and operating as intended on an ongoing and consistent basis, and that there is support for continuous improvement in the effectiveness of the controls.

Test

The test method generally is a technical examination of the various components of the information system or common control set.

NIST provides the following guidance about the test method

ASSESSMENT METHOD: Test

ASSESSMENT OBJECTS:
- Mechanisms (e.g., hardware, software, firmware)
- Activities (e.g., system operations, administration, management; exercises)

DEFINITION: The process of exercising one or more assessment objects under specified conditions to compare actual with expected behavior, the results of which are used to support the determination of security and privacy control existence, functionality, correctness, completeness, and potential for improvement over time.

SUPPLEMENTAL GUIDANCE: Typical assessor actions may include, for example: testing access control, identification and authentication, and audit mechanisms; testing security configuration settings; testing physical access control devices; conducting penetration testing of key information system components; testing information system backup operations; testing incident response capability; and exercising contingency planning capability.

SCAP-validated tools can be used to automate the collection of assessment objects and evaluate these objects against expected behavior. The use of SCAP is specifically relevant to the testing of mechanisms that involve assessment of actual machine state. The National Checklist Program catalogs a number of SCAP-enabled checklists that are suitable for assessing the configuration posture of specific operating systems and applications. SCAP-validated tools can use these checklists to determine the aggregate compliance of a system against all of the configuration settings in the checklist (e.g., CM-6) or specific configurations that are relevant to a security or privacy control that pertains to one or more configuration settings. SCAP-validated tools can also determine the absence of a patch or the presence of a vulnerable condition. The results produced by the SCAP tools can then be examined by assessors as part of the security and privacy control assessments.

ATTRIBUTES: Depth, Coverage
  • The depth attribute addresses the types of testing to be conducted. There are three possible values for the depth attribute: (i) basic testing; (ii) focused testing; and (iii) comprehensive testing.
  - **Basic testing**: Test methodology (also known as black box testing) that assumes no knowledge of the internal structure and implementation detail of the assessment object. This type of testing is conducted using a functional specification for mechanisms and a high-level process description for activities. Basic testing provides a level of understanding of the security and privacy controls necessary for determining whether the controls are implemented and free of obvious errors.

  - **Focused testing**: Test methodology (also known as gray box testing) that assumes some knowledge of the internal structure and implementation detail of the assessment object. This type of testing is conducted using a functional specification and limited system architectural information (e.g., high-level design) for mechanisms and a high-level process description and high-level description of integration into the operational environment for activities. Focused testing provides a level of understanding of the security and privacy controls necessary for determining whether the controls are implemented and free of obvious errors and whether there are increased grounds for confidence that the controls are implemented correctly and operating as intended.

- **Comprehensive testing**: Test methodology (also known as white box testing) that assumes explicit and substantial knowledge of the internal structure and implementation detail of the assessment object. This type of testing is conducted using a functional specification, extensive system architectural information (e.g., high-level design, low-level design) and implementation representation (e.g., source code, schematics) for mechanisms and a high-level process description and detailed description of integration into the operational environment for activities. Comprehensive testing provides a level of understanding of the security and privacy controls necessary for determining whether the controls are implemented and free of obvious errors and whether there are further increased grounds for confidence that the controls are implemented correctly and operating as intended on an ongoing and consistent basis, and that there is support for continuous improvement in the effectiveness of the controls.

- The coverage attribute addresses the scope or breadth of the testing process and includes the types of assessment objects to be tested, the number of objects to be tested (by type), and specific objects to be tested. There are three possible values for the coverage attribute: (i) basic; (ii) focused; and (iii) comprehensive.

- **Basic testing**: Testing that uses a representative sample of assessment objects (by type and number within type) to provide a level of coverage necessary for determining whether the security and privacy controls are implemented and free of obvious errors.

- **Focused testing**: Testing that uses a representative sample of assessment objects (by type and number within type) and other specific assessment objects deemed particularly important to achieving the assessment objective to provide a level of coverage necessary for determining whether the security and privacy controls are implemented and free of obvious errors and whether there are increased grounds for confidence that the controls are implemented correctly and operating as intended.

- **Comprehensive testing**: Testing that uses a sufficiently large sample of assessment objects (by type and number within type) and other specific assessment objects deemed particularly important to achieving the assessment objective to provide a level of coverage necessary for determining whether the security and privacy controls are implemented and free of obvious errors and whether there are further increased grounds for confidence that the controls are implemented correctly and operating as intended on an ongoing and consistent basis, and that there is support for continuous improvement in the effectiveness of the controls.

B.2 Develop the Security Assessment Plan
The security assessment plan serves as a roadmap that will be used by the assessor during the assessment. It sets the scope of what will be tested, the levels of rigor and depth for the assessment as well as the rules that will be followed by all participants for the assessment. Approval of the SAP is normally completed by the authorizing official (AO) or designated representative as the assessor serves as the eyes and ears for the AO.

Most organizations develop their own template that will be used for all assessments. The DSM has developed a SAP that will be used in this lab and is located at http://www.cyber-recon.com/wp-content/uploads/2015/11/SAP_Template_DSM-blank3.docx. (you will need to be registered for the labs to access this document) By using this template the assessor will ensure that all of the portions of the template required by the organization are completed. Completing the SAP is best achieved by focusing on one section at a time.

Angle Brackets
Templates often contain placeholders with text and special characters that facilitate easy replacement of key words and phrases. For example, the SAP template has the term <Information System Name> in several places. The characters "<" and ">" are referred to as angle brackets and are placed around words that should be replaced to assist with the find and replace function in most word processing systems. Using this process the template author will indicate every place that the document should contain the systems actual name with the phrase <Information System>. When using the template the word processors find and replace function can be used to find the term <Information System> and replace it with the actual name you supply in the find and replace dialog. This ensures that only those areas a placeholder is used are updated with the system name and areas where the term "information system" (without the angle brackets) remain unchanged. The following is a good example of this feature.

Template sentence:
The information system being assessed is named <Information System>.

When completing a find and replace the term <Information System> is replaced with the systems actual name "albatross" resulting in the updated sentence.'

The information system being assessed is named albatross.

This assists the person using the template as hundreds or even thousands of placeholders can be updated almost immediately using this process.

EXERCISE 8.2
Review the DSM SAP template for placeholders, list at least 5 placeholders you find.

1._____

2._____

3._____

4._____

5._____

Cover Page

The cover page provides basic details about the security assessment plan. It is similar to the cover of a book providing basic information about the plan that follows. There are many placeholders in the cover page and if the placeholder exercise was completed this page should be updated to describe the system being assessed.

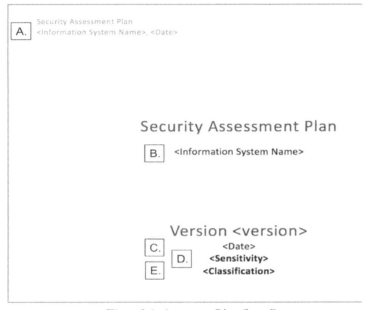

Figure 9-1 Assessment Plan Cover Page

    A. The information System Name and Date the plan was written
    B. The Information System Name
    C. The Date the plan was written
    D. The Sensitivity of the document
    E. The Classification of the document

Prepared By Block

The Prepared by block describes the organization that developed the SAP. This is normally the same organization that the SCA or SCA team is from but could be a different organization. In the blank cells on the right of the table update the block with the organizations name, street address, suite/room/building, and city, state, zip code. The table has a cell on the left where an image of the organizations logo can be pasted.

Security Control Assessor / Team that Prepared this Document		
	Organization Name	

Security Control Assessor / Team that Prepared this Document		
	Street Address	
	Suite/Room/Building	
	City, State Zip	

Table 9-1 Control Assessor Information

Prepared for Block

The Prepared for block is like the Prepared by block but describes the organization that the SAP is being prepared for. This is normally the same organization that owns the system being assessed but could be a different organization. In the blank cells on the right of the table update the block with the organizations name, street address, suite/room/building, and city, state, zip code. The table has a cell on the left where an image of the organizations logo can be pasted.

Identification of Information System Owner		
<insert logo>	Organization Name	
	Street Address	
	Suite/Room/Building	
	City, State Zip	

Table 9-2 Information Owner Information

Executive Summary

The Executive Summary provides an overview of the plan and is normally completed after the plan is fully complete. This section should be between one and five paragraphs and should provide a high-level overview of the SAP that follows. Some boilerplate text is provided but this section should be updated to reflect the completed SAP.

Document Revision History

The document revision history table tracks changes to the document from the time it is first created through its lifecycle. This table is updated every time the document is updated. The date should reflect the date of the change. The description cell should define a high-level view of the updates or changes that have been made to the document. As the document changes the version should be updated. This update could be major (the number to the left of the decimal point increases), or minor (the number to the right of the decimal point increases. The author should be the person, organization or team that made the update.

Date	Description	Version	Author
<Date>	Draft Document	0.1	

Table 9-3 Revision History

Table of Contents
The table of contents provides a quick reference to the locations of the sections and topics of the SAP.

About this Document
The about this document section contains two major sections, how this document is organized and conventions used in this document. It is recommended that the conventions used in this document section is deleted once the document is completed.

The how this document is organized provides a roadmap of the sections of the SAP. This is less detailed than the table of contents and omits the page numbers. This portion of the document details the six sections of the plan.
- Section 1 describes an overview of the testing process.
- Section 2 describes the scope of the security testing.
- Section 3 describes assumptions related to the security testing.
- Section 4 describes the security testing methodology.
- Section 5 describes the test plan and schedule.
- Section 6 describes the Rules of Engagement and signatures for security testing.

The conventions used in this document portion describes various editing features that are present in the template that assist the writer in using the template. As stated earlier it is recommended that this section is deleted after the plan is complete.

The document uses the following typographical conventions:

Italic
Italics are used for email addresses, security control assignments parameters, and formal document names.

Bold

    Bold text indicates a parameter or an additional requirement.

Constant width

    Constant width text is used for text that is representative of characters that would show up on a computer screen.

\<Brackets\>

Bold blue text in brackets indicates text that should be replaced with user-defined values. Once the text has been replaced, the brackets should be removed.

Notes

    Notes are found between parallel lines and include additional information that may be helpful to the users of this template.

Note: This is a note.

Sans Serif

    Sans Serif text is used for tables, table captions, figure captions, and table of contents.

Section 1. Overview

The overview section contains 3 parts that provide basic information about the assessment. These parts are Purpose, Applicable Laws and Regulations, and Applicable Standards and Guidance. Each of these parts has been preloaded with some boilerplate information that should be supplemented with specific information about the system being assessed.

Purpose describes why we are conducting the assessment. There is also a excerpt from NIST SP 800-39 that further explains why assessments are conducted. There is often no need to modify this part of the plan.

Applicable Laws and Regulations provides a listing of the laws and regulations that apply to the information system being assessed. A basic listing of laws and regulations is provided in the template; however, this listing should be modified by adding additional laws or regulations that apply to the information system and removing those that do not apply.

Applicable Standards and Guidance provides a listing of the standards and guidance that apply to the information system being assessed. A basic listing of standards and guidance is provided in the template; however, this listing should be modified by adding additional standards or guidance that apply to the information system and removing those that do not apply.

SCOPE

The section of the SAR titles Scope identifies the system that will be assessed by unique identifier, name and abbreviation. This section also identifies the documents that will be inspected and analyzed during the assessment.

In table 9-4 the system identification is document, including the unique identifier, information system name and information system abbreviation.

Unique Identifier	Information System Name	Information System Abbreviation

Table 9-4 System Identification

Following table 1.1 a listing of the basic documents that may be used in the assessment of the security controls and the system. In many cases these documents required to be assessed, at a minimum, to determine the systems security control state. Additional documents can be reviewed so that the assessor can get a full understanding of how the required security controls are assessed, these additional documents will be listed in appendix H, Auxiliary Documents.

These minimum documents should be inspected in the assessment to assist in determining the state of the implementation of the security controls. If the find and replace technique was used when starting the SAP, the system name will be inserted into this listing.

- Information System- *Control Tailoring Workbook*
- Information System- Control *Information Summary*
- Information System- *FIPS-199 Categorization*
- Information System- *E-Authentication Plan*
- Information System- *System Security Plan*
- Information System- *IT Contingency Plan & Test Results*
- Information System- *Business Impact Analysis*
- Information System- *Configuration Management Plan*
- Information System- *Incident Response Plan*
- Information System- *Privacy Threshold Analysis/Privacy Threshold Assessment*
- Information System- *Security Assessment Plan*

The physical locations of the system and all its components are listed in table 1.2. This should include every system inside the authorization boundary. This table should be completed with enough detail so that the system components can be located. This could be as simple as building and room number but could also be full address, room number, and server cabinet location. The point of this table is to ensure the assessor can find and identify each component that makes up the information system.

The site name is the general location of those components, for example Fox Lane Complex or Jefferson Data Center. The site name should match those names listed in the contingency plan.

Site Name	Address

Table 9-5 Location Information

B.3 Obtain necessary approvals (e.g., security assessment plan, rules of engagement, resources)
Under development

Once the security assessment plan is complete and has been peer reviewed and approved by the assessment lead, it is forwarded to the authorizing official or the authorizing officials designated representative for review and approval. The AO or AODR will review the SAP to ensure the scope and coverage requirements are met and the plan details the assessment to a level that ensures the AO will receive an accurate representation of the state of the security controls implementation

C.1 SAR

D.3 Propose remediation actions
Under development

E. Review Interim SAR and Perform Initial Remediation Actions
Under development

E.1 Determine initial risk responses
Under development

E.2 Apply initial remediations
Under development

E.3 Reassess and validate the remediated controls
Under development

F. Develop Final SAR and Optional Addendum
Under development

NIST SP 800-37 Text
ASSESSMENT PLAN

TASK A-2 Develop, review, and approve plans to assess implemented controls.

Potential Inputs: Security, privacy, and SCRM plans; program management control information; common control documentation; organizational security and privacy program plans; SCRM strategy; system design documentation; supply chain information; enterprise, security, and privacy architecture information; security, privacy, and SCRM policies and procedures applicable to the system.

Expected Outputs: Security and privacy assessment plans approved by the authorizing official.

Primary Responsibility: Authorizing Official or Authorizing Official Designated Representative; Control Assessor.

Supporting Roles: Senior Agency Information Security Officer; Senior Agency Official for Privacy; System Owner; Common Control Provider; Information Owner or Steward; System Security Officer; System Privacy Officer.

System Development Life Cycle Phase: New – Development/Acquisition; Implementation/Assessment.
Existing – Operations/Maintenance.

Discussion: Security and privacy assessment plans are developed by control assessors based on the implementation information contained in security and privacy plans, program management control documentation, and common control documentation. Organizations may choose to develop a single, integrated security and privacy assessment plan for the system or the organization. An integrated assessment plan delineates roles and responsibilities for control assessment. Assessment plans also provide the objectives for control assessments and specific assessment procedures for each control. Assessment plans reflect the type of assessment the organization is conducting, including for example: developmental testing and evaluation; independent verification and validation; audits, including supply chain; assessments supporting system and common control authorization or reauthorization; program management control assessments; continuous monitoring; and assessments conducted after remediation actions.
Assessment plans are reviewed and approved by the authorizing official or the designated representative of the authorizing official to help ensure that the plans are consistent with the security and privacy objectives of the organization; employ procedures, methods, techniques, tools, and automation to support continuous monitoring and near real-time risk management; and are cost-effective. Approved assessment plans establish expectations for the control assessments and the level of effort for the assessment. Approved assessment plans help to ensure that appropriate resources are applied toward determining control effectiveness while providing the necessary level of assurance in making such determinations. When controls are provided by an external provider through contracts, interagency agreements, lines of business arrangements, licensing agreements, or supply chain arrangements, the organization can request security and privacy assessment plans and assessments results or evidence from the provider.

References: [SP 800-53A]; [SP 800-160 v1] (Verification and Validation Processes); [SP 800-161]; [IR 8011 v1].

EXERCISE 9.2

Why would it be important for the system owner to be given a copy of the assessment plan?

_____

_____

_____

_____

TASK A-3 CONTROL ASSESSMENTS

Responsibilities	
Primary Responsibility	Supporting Roles
- Control Assessor	- Authorizing Official or Authorizing Official Designated Representative - System Owner; Common Control Provider - Information Owner or Steward; Senior Agency Information Security Officer - Senior Agency Official for Privacy - System Security Officer - System Privacy Officer

SDLC Alignment	
New Systems	Legacy Systems
- Development/Acquisition - Implementation/Assessment	- Operations/Maintenance

CSF Alignment	
CSF Number	CSF Task

Task Flow	
Inputs	Outputs
- Security and privacy assessment plans - Security and privacy plans - External assessment or audit results (if applicable)	- Completed control assessments and associated assessment evidence

The control assessment is conducted using the assessment plan to determine the effectiveness of the controls that are in place, functioning as expected and producing the desired outcomes in the system to meet the requirements for the control in providing security, reducing risk and protecting privacy. The assessor may assess privacy y controls; however, it is the responsibility of the senior agency official for privacy to conduct those assessments so they may conduct the assessment or delegate that to the independent assessor during the initial assessment or during continuous monitoring. The findings of the assessor are based in facts that are discovered during the assessment and serve as a view independent of the system owner on the controls implementation and effectiveness.

These assessments should take place as early as possible in the systems development to reduce the cost of correcting any deficiencies uncovered during the assessment of the controls. If possible, this should be in the development phase of the SDLC, where it is called developmental testing and evaluation.   In developmental testing and evaluation, the assessor may review the software code being developed, conduct automated vulnerability scans and other testing to ensure the controls are working correctly, again deficiencies are corrected more quickly and effectively in the development phase. These assessments can be used during the authorization of the system for maximum efficiency if conducted by an independent assessor.

Developmental testing and evaluation are especially effective when the system is being developed using agile development including Scrum. In these situations, the assessor will evaluate the controls that support the current version of the system and may not initially assess all of the controls. By the time the system reaches its full operational functionality all of the required controls will be implemented and assessed. When conducting agile development all controls required for the functionality of the system at that time must be in place. For example, before wireless capabilities can be implemented in the system undergoing the agile process, all of the required controls must be in place and assessed.

Assessors are responsible for assessing all of the controls required by the system, including reviewing hybrid and common controls, however the assessment of inherited controls is not necessary as long as those controls have been assessed, are compliant and the common control provider has a valid authorization to operate.

Reuse of previous assessments and audits is encouraged to reduce the cost of evaluating the system and its required controls as long as those evaluations are deemed independent.

NIST SP 800-37 Text
CONTROL ASSESSMENTS
TASK A-3 Assess the controls in accordance with the assessment procedures described in assessment

plans.

Potential Inputs: Security and privacy assessment plans; security and privacy plans; external assessment or audit results (if applicable).

Expected Outputs: Completed control assessments and associated assessment evidence.

Primary Responsibility: Control Assessor.

Supporting Roles: Authorizing Official or Authorizing Official Designated Representative; System Owner; Common Control Provider; Information Owner or Steward; Senior Agency Information Security Officer; Senior Agency Official for Privacy; System Security Officer; System Privacy Officer.

System Development Life Cycle Phase: New – Development/Acquisition; Implementation/Assessment. Existing – Operations/Maintenance.

Discussion: Control assessments determine the extent to which the selected controls are implemented correctly, operating as intended, and producing the desired outcome with respect to meeting security and privacy requirements for the system and the organization. The system owner, common control provider, and/or organization rely on the technical skills and expertise of assessors to assess implemented controls using the assessment procedures specified in assessment plans and provide recommendations on how to respond to control deficiencies to reduce or eliminate identified vulnerabilities or unacceptable risks. The senior agency official for privacy serves as the control assessor for the privacy controls and is responsible for conducting an initial assessment of the privacy controls prior to system operation, and for assessing the controls periodically thereafter at a frequency sufficient to ensure compliance with privacy requirements and to manage privacy risks.89 Controls implemented to achieve both security and privacy objectives may require a degree of collaboration between security and privacy control assessors. The assessor findings are a factual reporting of whether the controls are operating as intended and whether any deficiencies in the controls are discovered during the assessment.

Control assessments occur as early as practicable in the SDLC, preferably during the development phase. These types of assessments are referred to as developmental testing and evaluation, and validate that the controls are implemented correctly and are consistent with the established information security and privacy architectures. Developmental testing and evaluation activities include, for example, design and code reviews, regression testing, and application scanning. Deficiencies identified early in the SDLC can be resolved in a more cost-effective manner. Assessments may be needed prior to source selection during the procurement process to assess potential suppliers or providers before the organization enters into agreements or contracts to begin the development phase. The results of control assessments conducted during the SDLC can also be used (consistent with reuse criteria established by the organization) during the authorization process to avoid unnecessary delays or costly repetition of assessments. Organizations can maximize the use of automation to conduct control assessments to increase the speed, effectiveness, and efficiency of the assessments, and to support continuous monitoring of the security and privacy posture of organizational systems. Applying and assessing controls throughout the development process may be appropriate for iterative development processes. When iterative development processes (e.g., agile development) are employed, an iterative assessment may be conducted as each cycle is completed. A similar process is employed for assessing controls in commercial IT products that are used in the system. Organizations may choose to begin assessing controls prior to the complete implementation of all controls in the security and privacy plans. This type of incremental assessment is appropriate if it is more efficient or cost-effective to do so. Common controls (i.e., controls that are inherited by the system) are assessed separately (by assessors chosen by common control providers or the organization) and need not be assessed as part of a system-level assessment.

Organizations ensure that assessors have access to the information system and environment of operation where the controls are implemented and to the documentation, records, artifacts, test results, and other materials needed to assess the controls. This includes the controls implemented by external providers through contracts, interagency agreements, lines of business arrangements, licensing agreements, or supply chain arrangements. Assessors have the required degree of independence as determined by the authorizing official.91 Assessor independence during the continuous monitoring process facilitates reuse of assessment results to support ongoing authorization and reauthorization.

To make the risk management process more efficient and cost-effective, organizations may choose to establish reasonable and appropriate criteria for reusing assessment results as part of organization-wide assessment policy or in the security and privacy program plans. For example, a recent audit of a system may have produced information about the effectiveness of selected controls. Another opportunity to reuse previous assessment results may come from external programs that test and evaluate security and privacy features of commercial information technology products (e.g., Common Criteria Evaluation and Validation Program and NIST Cryptographic Module Validation Program,). If prior assessment results from the system developer or vendor are available, the control assessor, under appropriate circumstances, may incorporate those results into the assessment. In addition, if a control implementation was assessed during other forms of assessment at previous stages of the SDLC (e.g., unit testing, functional testing, acceptance testing), organizations may consider potential reuse of those results to reduce duplication of efforts. And finally, assessment results can be reused to support reciprocity, for example, assessment results supporting an authorization to use (see Appendix F). Additional information on assessment result reuse is available in [SP 800-53A].

References: [SP 800-53A]; [SP 800-160 v1] (Verification and Validation Processes); [IR 8011 v1].

EXERCISE 9.3

What is a benefit of using developmental testing and evaluation?

_____

_____

_____

_____

TASK A-4 ASSESSMENT REPORTS

Responsibilities	
Primary Responsibility	Supporting Roles
- Control Assessor	- System Owner
	- Common Control Provider
	- System Security Officer
	- System Privacy Officer

SDLC Alignment	
New Systems	Legacy Systems
- Development/Acquisition	- Operations/Maintenance
- Implementation/Assessment	

CSF Alignment	
CSF Number	CSF Task

Task Flow	
Inputs	Outputs
- Completed control assessments and associated assessment evidence	- Completed security and privacy assessment reports detailing the assessor findings and recommendations

The assessment report is developed based on the evidence gathered throughout the assessment. This report is one of the required documents for the authorization package – along with the security plan and the plan of actions and milestones. The assessment report contains all of the deficiencies that were discovered during the assessment including recommendations from the assessor on how to correct the weakness. The assessment of privacy and security controls can be independent reports or can be combined into a single report based on the requirements of the organization. The report the document that the authorizing official will use when determining the effectiveness of the required controls versus the risk appetite of the organization. The format and audience of the report can vary based on the type of assessment conducted, for example developmental testing and evaluation; independent verification and validation; independent assessments supporting information system or common control authorizations or reauthorizations; self-assessments; assessments after remediation actions; independent evaluations or audits; and assessments during continuous monitoring.

Assessments conducted early in the systems development may be reported in interim reports and updated as the system is developed, with these reports serving as an input to the final assessment report.

The use of an executive summary in the assessment report can help in summarizing the key facts of the assessment for organizational officials including the authorizing official.

The system owner cannot influence or change the content of the report but can develop an addendum to the report explaining or even disputing findings in the reports. This addendum will be evaluated when making a risk determination for the system.

NIST SP 800-37 Text
ASSESSMENT REPORTS **TASK A-4** Prepare the assessment reports documenting the findings and recommendations from the control assessments. **Potential Inputs:** Completed control assessments and associated assessment evidence. **Expected Outputs:** Completed security and privacy assessment reports detailing the assessor findings and recommendations. **Primary Responsibility:** Control Assessor. **Supporting Roles:** System Owner; Common Control Provider; System Security Officer; System Privacy Officer. **System Development Life Cycle Phase:** New – Development/Acquisition; Implementation/Assessment. Existing – Operations/Maintenance. **Discussion:** The results of the security and privacy control assessments, including recommendations for correcting deficiencies in the implemented controls, are documented in the assessment reports by control assessors. Organizations may develop a single, integrated security and privacy assessment report. Assessment reports are key documents in the system or common control authorization package that is developed for authorizing officials. The assessment reports include information based on assessor findings, necessary to determine the effectiveness of the controls implemented within or inherited by the information system. Assessment reports are an important factor in a determining risk to organizational operations and assets, individuals, other organizations, and the Nation by the authorizing official. The format and the level of detail provided in assessment reports are appropriate for the type of control assessment conducted, for example, developmental testing and evaluation; independent verification and validation; independent assessments supporting information system or common control authorizations or reauthorizations; self-assessments; assessments after remediation actions; independent evaluations or audits; and assessments during continuous monitoring. The reporting format may also be prescribed by the organization. Control assessment results obtained during the system development lifecycle are documented in an interim report and included in the final security and privacy assessment reports. Development of interim reports that document assessment results from relevant phases of the SDLC reinforces the concept that assessment reports are evolving documents. Interim reports are used, as appropriate, to inform the final assessment report. Organizations may choose to develop an executive summary from the control assessment findings. The executive summary provides authorizing officials and other interested individuals in the organization with an abbreviated version of the assessment reports that includes a synopsis of the assessment, findings, and the recommendations for addressing deficiencies in the controls. **References:** [SP 800-53A]; [SP 800-160 v1] (Verification and Validation Processes).

EXERCISE 9.4

How can the system owner dispute findings in the assessment report?

_____

_____

_____

_____

TASK A-5 REMEDIATION ACTIONS

Responsibilities	
Primary Responsibility	Supporting Roles
- System Owner - Common Control Provider - Control Assessor	- Authorizing Official - Authorizing Official Designated Representative - Senior Agency Information Security Officer - Senior Agency Official for Privacy - Senior Accountable Official for Risk Management or Risk Executive (Function) - Information Owner or Steward - Systems Security Engineer - Privacy Engineer - System Security Officer - System Privacy Officer

SDLC Alignment	
New Systems	Legacy Systems
- Development/Acquisition - Implementation/Assessment	- Operations/Maintenance

CSF Alignment	
CSF Number	CSF Task
	- Profile

Task Flow	
Inputs	Outputs
- Completed security and privacy assessment reports with findings and recommendations - Security and privacy plans - Security and privacy assessment plans - Organization- and system-level risk assessment results	- Completed initial remediation actions based on the security and privacy assessment reports; changes to implementations reassessed by the assessment team - Updated security and privacy assessment reports - Updated security and privacy plans including changes to the control implementations

The assessment of the systems controls may discover findings that create an unacceptable level of risk for the organization and will need to be corrected before the system can continue in the RMF. Remediation of critical findings is important in maintaining acceptable levels of risk for the organization. It is also possible that some findings from the assessment of the system are simple to correct and should be corrected during this task.

Remediated controls must be reassessed by the independent assessor and must appear on the assessment report, but the remediation and assessment validation must be updated. Once corrected they will not need to be included on the systems plan of actions and milestones if the control is determined to be compliant with requirements after remediation.

Changes in the controls implementation to become compliant must be updated in the systems security plan so that document reflect the actual configuration and implementation of the systems controls.

Controls that cannot be remediated in this task will be added to the system plan of actions and milestones, to provide information on when and how the control deficiency will be corrected.

NIST SP 800-37 Text

REMEDIATION ACTIONS

TASK A-5 Conduct initial remediation actions on the controls and reassess remediated controls.

Potential Inputs: Completed security and privacy assessment reports with findings and recommendations; security and privacy plans; security and privacy assessment plans; organization- and system-level risk assessment results.

Expected Outputs: Completed initial remediation actions based on the security and privacy assessment reports; changes to implementations reassessed by the assessment team; updated security and privacy assessment reports; updated security and privacy plans including changes to the control implementations.

Primary Responsibility: System Owner; Common Control Provider; Control Assessor.

Supporting Roles: Authorizing Official or Authorizing Official Designated Representative; Senior Agency Information Security Officer; Senior Agency Official for Privacy; Senior Accountable Official for Risk Management or Risk Executive (Function); Information Owner or Steward; Systems Security Engineer; Privacy Engineer; System Security Officer; System Privacy Officer.

System Development Life Cycle Phase: New – Development/Acquisition; Implementation/Assessment. Existing – Operations/Maintenance.

Discussion: The security and privacy assessment reports describe deficiencies in the controls that could

---

not be resolved during the development of the system or that are discovered post-development. Such control deficiencies may result in security and privacy risks (including supply chain risks). The findings generated during control assessments, provide information that facilitates risk responses based on organizational risk tolerance and priorities. The authorizing official, in consultation and coordination with system owners and other organizational officials, may decide that certain findings represent significant, unacceptable risk and require immediate remediation actions. Additionally, it may be possible and practical to conduct initial remediation actions for assessment findings that can be quickly and easily remediated with existing resources.

If initial remediation actions are taken, assessors reassess the controls. The control reassessments determine the extent to which remediated controls are implemented correctly, operating as intended, and producing the desired outcome with respect to meeting the security and privacy requirements for the system and the organization. The assessors update the assessment reports with the findings from the reassessment, but do not change the original assessment results. The security and privacy plans are updated based on the findings of the control assessments and any remediation actions taken. The updated plans reflect the state of the controls after the initial assessment and any modifications by the system owner or common control provider in addressing recommendations for corrective actions. At the completion of the control assessments, security and privacy plans contain an accurate description of implemented controls, including compensating controls.

Organizations can prepare an addendum to the security and privacy assessment reports that provides an opportunity for system owners and common control providers to respond to initial assessment findings. The addendum may include, for example, information regarding initial remediation actions taken by system owners or common control providers in response to assessor findings. The addendum can also provide the system owner or common control provider perspective on the findings. This may include providing additional explanatory material, rebutting certain findings, and correcting the record. The addendum does not change or influence the initial assessor findings provided in the reports. Information provided in the addendum is considered by authorizing officials when making risk-based authorization decisions. Organizations implement a process to determine the initial actions to take regarding the control deficiencies identified during the assessment. This process can address vulnerabilities and risks, false positives, and other factors that provide useful information to authorizing officials regarding the security and privacy posture of the system and organization including the ongoing effectiveness of system-specific, hybrid, and common controls. The issue resolution process can also ensure that only substantive items are identified and transferred to the plan of actions and milestones.

Findings from a system-level control assessment may necessitate an update to the system risk assessment and the organizational risk assessment. The updated risk assessments and any inputs from the senior accountable official for risk management or risk executive (function) determines the initial remediation actions and the prioritization of those actions. System owners and common control providers may decide, based on a system or organizational risk assessment, that certain findings are inconsequential and present no significant security or privacy risk. Such findings are retained in the security and privacy assessment reports and monitored during the monitoring step. The authorizing official is responsible for reviewing and understanding the assessor findings and for accepting the security and privacy risks (including any supply chain risks) that result from the operation the system or the use of common controls.

In all cases, organizations review assessor findings to determine the significance of the findings and whether the findings warrant any further investigation or remediation. Senior leadership involvement in the mitigation process is necessary to ensure that the organization's resources are effectively allocated in accordance with organizational priorities—providing resources to the systems that are supporting the most critical missions and business functions or correcting the deficiencies that pose the greatest risk.

References: [SP 800-53A]; [SP 800-160 v1] (Verification and Validation Processes).

EXERCISE 9.5

What would be a reason a system owner would remediate controls at this step of the RMF?

_____

_____

_____

_____

TASK A-6 PLAN OF ACTIONS AND MILESTONES

Responsibilities	
Primary Responsibility	Supporting Roles
- System Owner - Common Control Provider	- Information Owner or Steward - System Security Officer - System Privacy Officer - Senior Agency Information Security Officer - Senior Agency Official for Privacy - Control Assessor - Chief Acquisition Officer

SDLC Alignment	
New Systems	Legacy Systems
- Implementation/Assessment	- Operations/Maintenance

CSF Alignment	
CSF Number	CSF Task
	- ID.RA-6

Task Flow	
Inputs	Outputs
- Updated security and privacy assessment reports - Updated security and privacy plans - Organization- and system-level risk assessment results - Organizational risk management strategy and	- A plan of action and milestones detailing the findings from the security and privacy assessment reports that are to be remediated

risk tolerance	

The plan of actions and milestones is one of the key documents of the authorization package, along with the security plan and the assessment report. The plan of actions and milestones, or POAM, details the plan that will be followed to correct each of the findings listed on the assessment report, based on initial assessments, audits or continuous monitoring activities. The POAM should detail the specific resources required to correct the deficiency, the responsible party for correcting the weakness, the dated milestones that will need to be accomplished to correct the deficiency, how the finding was discovered and the status of the correction.

Items on the POAM will be periodically reported to officials in the organization, including the authorizing official who will use the progress of the POAM to determine if the system maintains its approval to operate. The authorizing official will determine if the plan will be sufficient to maintain the required level of organizational and system risk based on the individual controls listed and being noncompliant and the timelines defined to correct the deficiencies. The risk executive (function) and other roles in the organization will assist the authorizing official in determining if the POAM would be effective in maintaining the correct level of risk.

NIST SP 800-37 Text

PLAN OF ACTION AND MILESTONES

TASK A-6 Prepare the plan of action and milestones based on the findings and recommendations of the assessment reports.

Potential Inputs: Updated security and privacy assessment reports; updated security and privacy plans; organization- and system-level risk assessment results; organizational risk management strategy and risk tolerance.

Expected Outputs: A plan of action and milestones detailing the findings from the security and privacy assessment reports that are to be remediated.

Primary Responsibility: System Owner; Common Control Provider.

Supporting Roles: Information Owner or Steward; System Security Officer; System Privacy Officer; Senior Agency Information Security Officer; Senior Agency Official for Privacy; Control Assessor; Chief Acquisition Officer.

System Development Life Cycle Phase: New – Implementation/Assessment.
Existing – Operations/Maintenance.

Discussion: The plan of action and milestones is included as part of the authorization package. The plan of action and milestones describes the actions that are planned to correct deficiencies in the controls identified during the assessment of the controls and during continuous monitoring. The plan of action and milestones includes tasks to be accomplished with a recommendation for completion before or after system authorization; resources required to accomplish the tasks; milestones established to meet the tasks; and the scheduled completion dates for the milestones and tasks. The plan of action and milestones is reviewed by the authorizing official to ensure there is agreement with the remediation actions planned to correct the identified deficiencies. It is subsequently used to monitor progress in completing the actions. Deficiencies are accepted by the authorizing official as residual risk or are remediated during the assessment or prior to submission of the authorization package to the authorizing official. Plan of action and milestones entries are not necessary when deficiencies are accepted by the authorizing official as residual risk. However, deficiencies identified during assessment and monitoring are documented in the assessment reports, which can be retained within an automated security/privacy management and reporting tool to maintain an effective audit trail. Organizations develop plans of action and milestones based on assessment results obtained from control assessments, audits, and continuous monitoring and in accordance with applicable laws, executive orders, directives, policies, regulations, standards, or guidance.

Organizations implement a consistent process for developing plans of action and milestones that uses a prioritized approach to risk mitigation that is uniform across the organization. A risk assessment guides the prioritization process for items included in the plan of action and milestones. The process ensures that plans of action and milestones are informed by the security categorization of the system and security, privacy, and supply chain risk assessments; the specific deficiencies in the controls; the criticality of the identified control deficiencies (i.e., the direct or indirect effect that the deficiencies may have on the security and privacy posture of the system, and therefore, on the risk exposure of the organization; or the ability of the organization to perform its mission or business functions); and the proposed risk mitigation approach to address the identified deficiencies in the controls (e.g., prioritization of risk mitigation actions and allocation of risk mitigation resources). Risk mitigation resources include, for example, personnel, new hardware or software, and tools.

References: [SP 800-30]; [SP 800-53A]; [SP 800-160 v1] (Verification and Validation Processes); [IR 8062].

EXERCISE 9.6

What is the main purpose of the plan of actions and milestones?

_____

_____

_____

_____

10- THE AUTHORIZE STEP

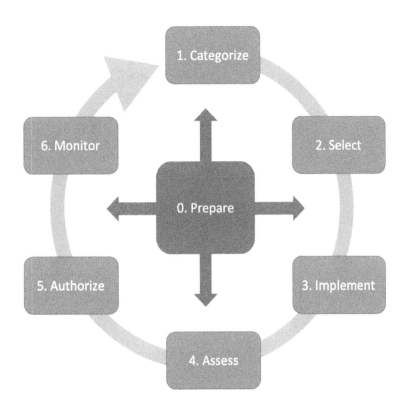

TASK R-1 AUTHORIZATION PACKAGE

Responsibilities	
Primary Responsibility	Supporting Roles
System Owner; Common Control Provider; Senior Agency Official for Privacy	System Security Officer; System Privacy Officer; Senior Agency Information Security Officer; Control Assessor

SDLC Alignment	
New Systems	Legacy Systems
Implementation/Assessment	Operations/Maintenance

CSF Alignment	
CSF Number	CSF Task

Task Flow	
Inputs	Outputs
Security and privacy plans; security and privacy assessment reports; plan of action and milestones; supporting assessment evidence or other documentation, as required	Authorization package (with an executive summary), which may be generated from a security or privacy management tool94 for submission to the authorizing official

The RMF requires only a few documents that must be included in the authorization package. These are the security and privacy plans, the assessment report and the plan of actions and milestones. The security and privacy plan may be combined into one document or may be two separate documents depending on the requirements of the organization. Individual organizations can require additional documents be included in the authorization package.

Documents in the authorization package are considered living documents, therefore they are updated frequently requiring strict version control. Timely updates to documents in the authorization package help in achieving near real-time risk management and the concept of ongoing authorization. In organizations that have not adopted ongoing authorization the maintenance and continual updating of documents in the authorization package will assist the system owner in the re-authorization process if that is required.

The authorization package is reviewed by senior organizational officials including the senior agency official for privacy who will review the package to ensure privacy concerns are addressed prior to forwarding the package to the authorizing official.

The authorization package contains sensitive information about both the system as well as the organization, therefore the documents must be marked and protected accordingly. Organizations should define how sensitive documents are marked, stored, and transported.

Once complete the authorization package is forwarded to the authorizing official either electronically or in hardcopy. To be most efficient organizations can use automated systems for development of documentation in the authorization package as well as transmittal two organizational officials including the authorizing official. Once in the monitoring step the package is presented to the authorizing official through designated reports and updates providing the most current information.

NIST SP 800-37 Text

AUTHORIZATION PACKAGE

TASK R-1 Assemble the authorization package and submit the package to the authorizing official for an authorization decision.

Potential Inputs: Security and privacy plans; security and privacy assessment reports; plan of action and milestones; supporting assessment evidence or other documentation, as required.

Expected Outputs: Authorization package (with an executive summary), which may be generated from a security or privacy management tool94 for submission to the authorizing official.

Primary Responsibility: System Owner; Common Control Provider; Senior Agency Official for Privacy.

Supporting Roles: System Security Officer; System Privacy Officer; Senior Agency Information Security Officer; Control Assessor.

System Development Life Cycle Phase: New – Implementation/Assessment.
Existing – Operations/Maintenance.

Discussion: Authorization packages include security and privacy plans, security and privacy assessment reports, plans of action and milestones, and an executive summary. Additional information can be included in the authorization package at the request of the authorizing official. Organizations maintain version and change control as the information in the authorization package is updated. Providing timely updates to the plans, assessment reports, and plans of action and milestones on an ongoing basis supports the concept of near real-time risk management and ongoing authorization, and can be used for reauthorization actions, if required.
The senior agency official for privacy reviews the authorization package for systems that process PII to ensure compliance with applicable privacy requirements and to manage privacy risks, prior to authorizing officials making risk determination and acceptance decisions.
The information in the authorization package is used by authorizing officials to make informed, risk-based decisions. When controls are implemented by an external provider through contracts, interagency agreements, lines of business arrangements, licensing agreements, or supply chain arrangements, the organization ensures that the information needed to make risk-based decisions is made available by the provider.
The authorization package may be provided to the authorizing official in hard copy or electronically or may be generated using an automated security/privacy management and reporting tool.

Organizations can use automated support tools in preparing and managing the content of the authorization package. Automated support tools provide an effective vehicle for maintaining and updating information for authorizing officials regarding the ongoing security and privacy posture of information systems within the organization.

When an information system is under ongoing authorization, the authorization package is presented to the authorizing official via automated reports to provide information in the most efficient and timely manner possible. Information to be presented to the authorizing official in assessment reports is generated in the format and with the frequency determined by the organization using information from the information security and privacy continuous monitoring programs.

The assessment reports presented to the authorizing official include information about deficiencies in system-specific, hybrid, and common controls (i.e., other than satisfied findings determined by assessors). The authorizing official uses automated security/privacy management and reporting tools or other automated methods, whenever practicable, to access the security and privacy plans and the plans of action and milestones. The authorization documents are updated at an organization-defined frequency using automated or manual processes in accordance with the risk management objectives of the organization.

References: [OMB A-130]; [SP 800-18]; [SP 800-160 v1] (Risk Management Process); [SP 800-161] (SCRM Plans).

EXERCISE 10.1

According to NIST, what documents must be included in the authorization package?

_____

_____

_____

_____

TASK R-2 RISK ANALYSIS AND DETERMINATION

Responsibilities	
Primary Responsibility	Supporting Roles
Authorizing Official or Authorizing Official Designated Representative	Senior Accountable Official for Risk Management or Risk Executive (Function); Senior Agency Information Security Officer; Senior Agency Official for Privacy

SDLC Alignment	
New Systems	Legacy Systems
Implementation/Assessment	Operations/Maintenance

CSF Alignment	
CSF Number	CSF Task

Task Flow	
Inputs	Outputs
Authorization package; supporting assessment evidence or other documentation as required; information provided by the senior accountable official for risk management or risk executive (function); organizational risk management strategy and risk tolerance; organization- and system-level risk assessment results	Risk determination

Organizational officials, including the authorizing official or authorizing officials designated representative analyze the information contained in the authorization package to determine the level of risk that would be added to the organization should the receive an authorization to operate and be put into operation. The senior agency information security officer, senior Agency officials for privacy, and the risk executive function assist in the determination of the change in risk level that will occur if the system is authorized. These individuals evaluate documents contained in the authorization package provided by the system owner including documentation from the common control provider. Documentation provided by the risk of executive function Will become part of the authorization package, additionally documentation provided by other organizational individuals can be included based on requirements of the enterprise.

The authorizing official may need information from the system owner, common control provider, control assessor to assist in understanding the controls implementation and vulnerabilities or threats that could impact the organizations risk posture should the System be authorized.

Systems that are in the monitoring step will continue to have this risk determination assessed based on changes to the system that may impact vulnerabilities threats that result in increased or reduced risk to the organization. After reviewing the documentation provided in the authorization package, and consulting with other organizational officials the authorizing official finalizes the determination of risk.

NIST SP 800-37 Text
RISK ANALYSIS AND DETERMINATION **TASK R-2** Analyze and determine the risk from the operation or use of the system or the provision of common controls.

Potential Inputs: Authorization package; supporting assessment evidence or other documentation as required; information provided by the senior accountable official for risk management or risk executive (function); organizational risk management strategy and risk tolerance; organization- and system-level risk assessment results.

Expected Outputs: Risk determination.

Primary Responsibility: Authorizing Official or Authorizing Official Designated Representative.

Supporting Roles: Senior Accountable Official for Risk Management or Risk Executive (Function); Senior Agency Information Security Officer; Senior Agency Official for Privacy.

System Development Life Cycle Phase: New – Implementation/Assessment.
Existing – Operations/Maintenance.

Discussion: The authorizing official or designated representative, in collaboration with the senior agency information security officer and the senior agency official for privacy (for information systems processing PII), analyzes the information in the authorization package provided by the control assessor, system owner, or common control provider, and finalizes the determination of risk. Further discussion with the control assessor, system owner, or common control provider may be necessary to help ensure a thorough understanding of risk by the authorizing official.
Risk assessments are employed to provide information99 that may influence the risk analysis and determination. The senior accountable official for risk management or risk executive (function) may provide additional information to the authorizing official that is considered in the final determination of risk to organizational operations and assets, individuals, other organizations, and the Nation resulting from either the operation or use of the system or the provision of common controls. The additional information may include, for example, organizational risk tolerance, dependencies among systems and controls, mission and business requirements, the criticality of the missions or business functions supported by the system, or the risk management strategy.
The authorizing official analyzes the information provided by the senior accountable official for risk management or risk executive (function) and information provided by the system owner or common control provider in the authorization package when making a risk determination. Any additional information provided by the senior accountable official for risk management or risk executive (function) is documented and included, to the extent it is relevant, as part of the authorization decision (see Task R-4). The authorizing official may also use an automated security/privacy management and reporting tool to annotate senior accountable official for risk management or risk executive (function) input.
When the system is operating under an ongoing authorization, the risk determination task is effectively unchanged. The authorizing official analyzes the relevant security and privacy information provided by the automated security/privacy management and reporting tool to determine the current security and privacy posture of the system.

References: [OMB A-130]; [SP 800-30]; [SP 800-39] (Organization, Mission/Business Process, and System Levels); [SP 800-137]; [SP 800-160 v1] (Risk Management Process); [IR 8062].

EXERCISE 10.2

What role(s) are responsible for this task?

_____

_____

_____

_____

TASK R-3 RISK RESPONSE

Responsibilities	
Primary Responsibility	Supporting Roles
Authorizing Official or Authorizing Official Designated Representative	Senior Accountable Official for Risk Management or Risk Executive (Function); Senior Agency Information Security Officer; Senior Agency Official for Privacy; System Owner or Common Control Provider; Information Owner or Steward; Systems Security Engineer; Privacy Engineer; System Security Officer; System Privacy Officer

SDLC Alignment	
New Systems	Legacy Systems
Implementation/Assessment	Operations/Maintenance

CSF Alignment	
CSF Number	CSF Task
	ID.RA-6

Task Flow	
Inputs	Outputs
Authorization package; risk determination; organization- and system-level risk assessment results	Risk responses for determined risks

The authorizing official or authorizing officials designated representative have evaluated the risk of the system receiving an authorization to operate the organization Will select a risk response. Generally, there are four accepted risk responses these are risk acceptance, risk avoidance, risk transference, or risk mitigation. In risk acceptance the authorizing official accepts the risk of the information system as a developed including the plan of actions and milestones. In risk avoidance the authorizing unofficial determines that the information system as it's been built Will present and an acceptable level of risk to the organization. In the risk transference the organizational official transfers some or all of the risk to another entity or organization. Finally, in risk mitigation the risks identified in the information system are reduced by compensating or mitigating controls or by corrections to the controls identified as deficient in the assessment report. Mitigated controls must be re-assessed by an independent assessor to validate that they have been implemented correctly and reduce the level of risk.

The authorizing official is the only role that can accept the risk for the system receiving an authorization to operate, they are responsible for reviewing the assessment reports plans of actions and milestones and security/privacy plans to understand the level of risk that would be introduced should the system go live, allowing that individual to make a risk-based authorization decision. This decision may include prioritization of the mitigation of deficient controls on the plan of action and milestones, addressing higher risk deficiencies before lower risk deficiencies. The authorizing official can inshore that the organizational resources are levied against those deficient controls that introduced the most risk to the organization when making a risk response determination.

NIST SP 800-37 Text

RISK RESPONSE

TASK R-3 Identify and implement a preferred course of action in response to the risk determined.
Potential Inputs: Authorization package; risk determination; organization- and system-level risk assessment results.

Expected Outputs: Risk responses for determined risks.

Primary Responsibility: Authorizing Official or Authorizing Official Designated Representative.

Supporting Roles: Senior Accountable Official for Risk Management or Risk Executive (Function); Senior Agency Information Security Officer; Senior Agency Official for Privacy; System Owner or Common Control Provider; Information Owner or Steward; Systems Security Engineer; Privacy Engineer; System Security Officer; System Privacy Officer.

System Development Life Cycle Phase: New – Implementation/Assessment.
Existing – Operations/Maintenance.

Discussion: After risk is analyzed and determined, organizations can respond to risk in a variety of ways, including acceptance of risk and mitigation of risk. Existing risk assessment results and risk assessment techniques may be used to help determine the preferred course of action for the risk response.100 When the response to risk is mitigation, the planned mitigation actions are included in and tracked using the plan of action and milestones. Once mitigated, assessors reassess the controls. Control reassessments determine the extent to which remediated controls are implemented correctly, operating as intended, and producing the desired outcome with respect to meeting the security and privacy requirements for the system and the organization. The assessors update the assessment reports with the findings from the reassessment, but do not change the original assessment results. The security and privacy plans are updated based on the findings of the control assessments and any remediation actions taken. The updated plans reflect the state of the controls after the initial assessment and any modifications by the system owner or common control provider in addressing recommendations for corrective actions.

At the completion of the control reassessments, security and privacy plans contain an accurate description of implemented controls, including compensating controls. When the response to risk is acceptance, the deficiencies found during the assessment process remain documented in the security and privacy assessment reports and are monitored for changes to the risk factors.101 Because the authorizing official is the only person who can accept risk, the authorizing official is responsible for reviewing the assessment reports and plans of action and milestones and determining whether the identified risks need to be mitigated prior to authorization. Decisions on the most appropriate course of action for responding to risk may include some form of prioritization. Some risks may be of greater concern to organizations than other risks. In that case, more resources may need to be directed at addressing higher-priority risks versus lower-priority risks. Prioritizing risk response does not necessarily mean that the lower-priority risks are ignored. Rather, it could mean that fewer resources are directed at addressing the lower-priority risks, or that the lower-priority risks are addressed later. A key part of the risk-based decision process is the recognition that regardless of the risk response, there remains a degree of residual risk. Organizations determine acceptable degrees of residual risk based on organizational risk tolerance.

References: [SP 800-30]; [SP 800-39] (Organization, Mission/Business Process, and System Levels); [SP 800-160 v1] (Risk Management Process); [IR 8062]; [IR 8179]; [NIST CSF] (Core [Identify Function]).

EXERCISE 10.3

What are the generally accepted risk responses as defined in this section?

_____
_____
_____
_____

TASK R-4 AUTHORIZATION DECISION

Responsibilities	
Primary Responsibility	Supporting Roles
Authorizing Official	Senior Accountable Official for Risk Management or Risk Executive (Function); Chief Information Officer; Senior Agency Information Security Officer; Senior Agency Official for Privacy; Authorizing Official Designated Representative

SDLC Alignment	
New Systems	Legacy Systems
Implementation/Assessment	Operations/Maintenance

CSF Alignment	
CSF Number	CSF Task

Task Flow	
Inputs	Outputs
Risk responses for determined risks	Authorization to operate, authorization to use, common control authorization; denial of authorization to operate, denial of authorization to use, denial of common control authorization

Making an authorization decision is the explicit responsibility of the authorizing official and cannot be delegated to anyone. The authorized official must evaluate information presented by the system owner in the authorization package as well as the risk determination made it in an earlier task when making the authorization decision. This documentation must be as current as possible to provide the authorizing a official with the most accurate risk picture available to make a risk-based authorization decision. Input from other officials in the organization including the senior accountable official for risk management or the risk executive function as well as the senior agency official for risk is evaluated when making this decision. The authorization decision must include evaluation of how the proposed system will interact with existing systems in the organization, and how this interaction will impact the organizational risk picture.

The authorizing the official informs the system owner, or common control provider, and other organizational officials on the authorization decision. The RMF identifies three separate authorization decisions that the authorizing official can make. These are the authorization to operate, the authorization to use, or denial of authorization to operate, common control providers must achieve an authorization to operate with indication on which controls can be inherited. This communication will include restrictions on system operation, caveats that must be followed to maintain the authorization, authorization termination date, and other information as determined by the organization.

Organizations that have a sufficient change management and continuous monitoring program may elect to eliminate the authorization termination date in favor of ongoing authorizations. Organizations using the ongoing authorization process continually evaluate the risk picture of the organization through the reporting process established in the monitoring step. Systems in the ongoing authorization process may be required to complete three authorization if there are significant changes to the risk picture or security status of the information system or organization.

When is the system owner or common control provider receive the authorization decision they will respond to the authorized official acknowledging they understand the limitations and restrictions imposed by the authorization decision. It is up to the organization to determine how the authorization decision is conveyed to the system owner or common control provider.

NIST SP 800-37 Text

AUTHORIZATION DECISION

TASK R-4 Determine if the risk from the operation or use of the information system or the provision or use of common controls is acceptable.

Potential Inputs: Risk responses for determined risks.

Expected Outputs: Authorization to operate, authorization to use, common control authorization; denial of authorization to operate, denial of authorization to use, denial of common control authorization.
Primary Responsibility: Authorizing Official.

Supporting Roles: Senior Accountable Official for Risk Management or Risk Executive (Function); Chief Information Officer; Senior Agency Information Security Officer; Senior Agency Official for Privacy; Authorizing Official Designated Representative.

System Development Life Cycle Phase: New – Implementation/Assessment.
Existing – Operations/Maintenance.

Discussion: The explicit acceptance of risk is the responsibility of the authorizing official and cannot be delegated to other officials within the organization. The authorizing official considers many factors when deciding if the risk to the organization's operations (including mission, functions, image, and reputation) and assets, individuals, other organizations, or the Nation, is acceptable. Balancing security and privacy considerations with mission and business needs is paramount to achieving an acceptable risk-based authorization decision. (Task R-2), and other relevant information that may affect the authorization decision. The authorization package provides the most current information on the security and privacy posture of the system or the common controls. The authorizing official issues an authorization decision for the system or for organization-designated common controls after reviewing the information in the authorization package, input from other organizational officials (see The authorizing official consults with the Senior Accountable Official for Risk Management or the Risk Executive (Function) prior to making the final authorization decision for the information system or the common controls. Because there are potentially significant dependencies among organizational systems and with external systems, the authorization decisions for individual systems consider the current residual risk, organizational plans of action and milestones, and the risk tolerance of the organization.

The authorization decision is conveyed by the authorizing official to the system owner or common control provider, and other organizational officials, as appropriate.103 The authorization decision also conveys the terms and conditions for the authorization to operate; the authorization termination date or time-driven authorization frequency; input from the senior accountable official for risk management or risk executive (function), if provided; and for common control authorizations, the system impact level supported by the common controls.

For systems, the authorization decision indicates to the system owner whether the system is authorized to operate or authorized to use, or not authorized to operate or not authorized to use.

For common controls, the authorization decision indicates to the common control provider and to the system owners of inheriting systems, whether the common controls are authorized to be provided or not authorized to be provided. The terms and conditions for the common control authorization provide a description of any specific limitations or restrictions placed on the operation of the system or the controls that must be followed by the system owner or common control provider.

The authorization termination date is established by the authorizing official and indicates when the authorization expires. Organizations may eliminate the authorization termination date if the system is operating under an ongoing authorization—that is, the continuous monitoring program is sufficiently robust and mature to provide the authorizing official with the needed information to conduct ongoing risk determination and risk acceptance activities regarding the security and privacy posture of the system and the ongoing effectiveness of the controls employed within and inherited by the system.

The authorization decision is included with the authorization package and is transmitted to the system owner or common control provider. Upon receipt of the authorization decision and the authorization package, the system owner or common control provider acknowledges and implements the terms and conditions of the authorization. The organization ensures that the authorization package, including the authorization decision for systems and common controls, is made available to organizational officials (e.g., system owners inheriting common controls; chief information officers; senior accountable officials for risk management or risk executive [function]; senior agency information security officers; senior agency officials for privacy; and system security and privacy officers). The authorizing official verifies on an ongoing basis as part of continuous monitoring (see Task M-2) that the established terms and conditions for authorization are being followed by the system owner or common control provider.

When the system is operating under ongoing authorization, the authorizing official continues to be responsible and accountable for explicitly understanding and accepting the risk of continuing to operate or use the system or continuing to provide common controls for inheritance. For ongoing authorization, the authorization frequency is specified in lieu of an authorization termination date. The authorizing official reviews the information with the specific time-driven authorization frequency defined by the organization as part of the continuous monitoring strategy and determines if the risk of continued system operation or the provision of common controls remains acceptable. If the risk remains acceptable, the authorizing official acknowledges the acceptance in accordance with organizational processes. If not, the authorizing official indicates that the risk is no longer acceptable and requires further risk response or a full denial of the authorization.

The organization determines the level of formality for the process of communicating and acknowledging continued risk acceptance by the authorizing official. The authorizing official may continue to establish and convey the specific terms and conditions to be followed by the system owner or common control provider for continued authorization to operate, continued common control authorization, or continued authorization to use. The terms and conditions of the authorization may be conveyed through an automated management and reporting tool as part of an automated authorization decision.

If control assessments are conducted by qualified assessors with the level of independence104 required, the assessment results support ongoing authorization and may be applied to a reauthorization. Organizational policies regarding ongoing authorization and reauthorization are consistent with laws, executive orders, directives, regulations, and policies.

Appendix F provides additional guidance on authorization decisions, the types of authorizations, and the preparation of the authorization packages.

References: [SP 800-39] (Organization, Mission/Business Process, and System Levels); [SP 800-160 v1] (Risk Management Process).

EXERCISE 10.4

According to NIST, what are the authorization decisions the authorizing official can make?

_____

_____

_____

_____

TASK R-5 AUTHORIZATION REPORTING

Responsibilities	
Primary Responsibility	Supporting Roles
Authorizing Official or Authorizing Official Designated Representative	System Owner or Common Control Provider; Information Owner or Steward; System Security Officer; System Privacy Officer; Senior Agency Information Security Officer; Senior Agency Official for Privacy

SDLC Alignment	
New Systems	Legacy Systems
Implementation/Assessment	Operations/Maintenance

CSF Alignment	
CSF Number	CSF Task

Task Flow	
Inputs	Outputs
Authorization decision	A report indicating the authorization decision for a system or set of common controls; annotation of authorization status in the organizational system registry

In organizations that have delegated the authorization function to rolls other than the head of the agency, authorization reporting must occur. In these cases be authorizing official reports their authorization decisions two organizational officials so that those decisions can be viewed in the context of the enterprise risk management program. The operation official must identify to these organizational officials anything that would introduce significant risk to the organization including unmitigated vulnerabilities, incorrectly implemented controls, or other deficiencies.

NIST SP 800-37 Text

AUTHORIZATION REPORTING

TASK R-5 Report the authorization decision and any deficiencies in controls that represent significant security or privacy risk.

Potential Inputs: Authorization decision.

Expected Outputs: A report indicating the authorization decision for a system or set of common controls; annotation of authorization status in the organizational system registry.

Primary Responsibility: Authorizing Official or Authorizing Official Designated Representative.

Supporting Roles: System Owner or Common Control Provider; Information Owner or Steward; System Security Officer; System Privacy Officer; Senior Agency Information Security Officer; Senior Agency Official for Privacy.

System Development Life Cycle Phase: New – Implementation/Assessment.
Existing – Operations/Maintenance.

Discussion: Authorizing officials report authorization decisions for systems and common controls to designated organizational officials so the individual risk decisions can be viewed in the context of organization-wide security and privacy risk to organizational operations and assets, individuals, other organizations, and the Nation. Reporting occurs only in situations where organizations have delegated the authorization functions to levels of the organization below the head of agency.

Authorizing officials also report exploitable deficiencies (i.e., vulnerabilities) in the system or controls noted during the assessment and continuous monitoring that represent significant security or privacy risk. Organizations determine, and the organizational policy reflects, what constitutes a significant security or privacy risk for reporting. Deficiencies that represent significant vulnerabilities and risk can be reported using the Subcategories, Categories, and Functions in the [NIST CSF]. Authorization decisions may be tracked and reflected as part of the organization-wide system registration process at the organization's discretion (see Task P-18).

References: [SP 800-39] (Organization, Mission/Business Process, and System Levels); [SP 800-160 v1] (Decision Management and Project Assessment and Control Processes); [NIST CSF] (Core [Identify, Protect, Detect, Respond, Recover Functions]).

EXERCISE 10.5

What would be a reason that authorization reporting is conducted?

_____

_____

_____

_____

NOTES:

11- THE MONITOR STEP

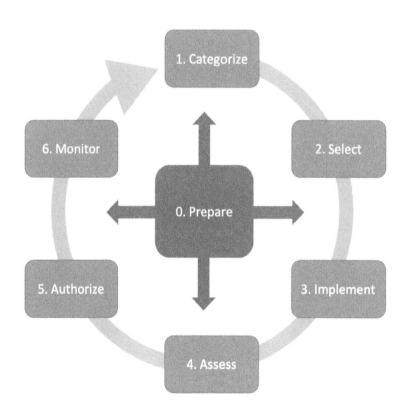

TASK M-1 SYSTEM AND ENVIRONMENT CHANGES

Responsibilities	
Primary Responsibility	Supporting Roles
- System Owner or Common Control Provider - Senior Agency Information Security Officer - Senior Agency Official for Privacy	- Senior Accountable Official for Risk Management or Risk Executive (Function) - Authorizing Official or Authorizing Official Designated Representative - Information Owner or Steward; System Security Officer - System Privacy Officer.

SDLC Alignment	
New Systems	Legacy Systems
- Operations/Maintenance	- Operations/Maintenance

CSF Alignment	
CSF Number	CSF Task
	- DE.CM - ID.GV

Task Flow	
Inputs	Outputs
- Organizational continuous monitoring strategy - Organizational configuration management policy and procedures; organizational policy and procedures for handling unauthorized system changes - Security and privacy plans - Configuration change requests/approvals - System design Documentation - Security and privacy assessment reports; plans of action and milestones - Information from automated and manual monitoring tools	- Updated security and privacy plans; updated plans of action and milestones - Updated security and privacy assessment reports

Once a system receives its authorization to operate, or authorization for use it is in a state of almost continual change. Change is to the configuration of the hardware or software including updates and patches, as well the operating environment, or modifications based on user requests must be strictly monitored by security and risk professionals. Changes can sometimes be difficult to detect, therefore a strict change management or change control process must be implemented by the organization. It is essential that security or risk professionals evaluate changes prior to them being made on the live system to ensure the changes do not impact the risk level or the security status of the system.

Changes in the logical or physical environment the system operates in can also introduce undesired risk, or changes in the security status of the system, therefore environmental changes must be monitors and reported as well.

Organizations should strive to have risk and security reviews of proposed changes before they are presented to change control or change management boards. This allows the full review of the change and the impact it would have on the system security or risk status before being presented to the larger board.

Organization should strive to detect unauthorized changes and create policies and enforcement protocols that discourage any change outside the approved change management program.

NIST SP 800-37 Text

SYSTEM AND ENVIRONMENT CHANGES

TASK M-1 Monitor the information system and its environment of operation for changes that impact the security and privacy posture of the system.

Potential Inputs: Organizational continuous monitoring strategy; organizational configuration management policy and procedures; organizational policy and procedures for handling unauthorized system changes; security and privacy plans; configuration change requests/approvals; system design documentation; security and privacy assessment reports; plans of action and milestones; information from automated and manual monitoring tools.

Expected Outputs: Updated security and privacy plans; updated plans of action and milestones; updated security and privacy assessment reports.

Primary Responsibility: System Owner or Common Control Provider; Senior Agency Information Security Officer; Senior Agency Official for Privacy.

Supporting Roles: Senior Accountable Official for Risk Management or Risk Executive (Function); Authorizing Official or Authorizing Official Designated Representative; Information Owner or Steward; System Security Officer; System Privacy Officer.

System Development Life Cycle Phase: New – Operations/Maintenance.
Existing – Operations/Maintenance.

Discussion: Systems and environments of operation are in a constant state of change with changes occurring in the technology or machine elements, human elements, and physical or environmental elements. Changes to the technology or machine elements include for example, upgrades to hardware, software, or firmware; changes to the human elements include for example, staff turnover or a reduction in force; and modifications to the surrounding physical and environmental elements include for example, changes in the location of the facility or the physical access controls protecting the facility. Changes made by external providers can be difficult to detect. A disciplined and structured approach to managing, controlling, and documenting changes to systems and environments of operation, and adherence with terms and conditions of the authorization, is an essential element of security and privacy programs. Organizations establish configuration management and control processes to support configuration and change management.105

Common activities within organizations can cause changes to systems or the environments of operation and can have a significant impact on the security and privacy posture of systems. Examples include installing or disposing of hardware, making changes to configurations, and installing patches outside of the established configuration change control process. Unauthorized changes may occur because of purposeful attacks by adversaries or inadvertent errors by authorized personnel. In addition to adhering to the established configuration management process, organizations monitor for unauthorized changes to systems and analyze information about unauthorized changes that have occurred to determine the root cause of the unauthorized change. In addition to monitoring for unauthorized changes, organizations continuously monitor systems and environments of operation for any authorized changes that impact the privacy posture of systems.106

Once the root cause of an unauthorized change (or an authorized change that impacts the privacy posture of the system) has been determined, organizations respond accordingly (see Task M-3). For example, if the root cause of an unauthorized change is determined to be an adversarial attack, multiple actions could be taken such as invoking incident response processes, adjusting intrusion detection and prevention tools and firewall configurations, or implementing additional or stronger controls to reduce the risk of future attacks. If the root cause of an unauthorized change is determined to be a failure of staff to adhere to established configuration management processes, remedial training for certain individuals may be warranted.

References: [SP 800-30]; [SP 800-128]; [SP 800-137]; [IR 8062].

EXERCISE 11.1

How could changes to the physical environment impact the system?

_____

_____

_____

_____

TASK M-2 ONGOING ASSESSMENTS

Responsibilities	
Primary Responsibility	Supporting Roles
- Control Assessor	- Authorizing Official or Authorizing Official Designated Representative - System Owner or Common Control Provider - Information Owner or Steward - System Security Officer - System Privacy Officer - Senior Agency Information Security Officer - Senior Agency Official for Privacy

SDLC Alignment	
New Systems	Legacy Systems
- Operations/Maintenance	- Operations/Maintenance

CSF Alignment	
CSF Number	CSF Task
	ID.SC-4

Task Flow	
Inputs	Outputs
- Organizational continuous monitoring strategy and system level continuous monitoring strategy (if applicable) - Security and privacy plans - Security and privacy assessment plans - Security and privacy assessment reports - Plans of action and milestones - Information from automated and manual monitoring tools Organization- and system-level risk assessment results - External assessment or audit results (if applicable).	- Updated security and privacy assessment reports.

Ongoing assessments are a critical part of the continuous monitoring activities that ensure that the system maintains its status with in risk tolerance and security levels required by the organization. The information security continuous monitoring program defines the required frequency for assessment of controls during ongoing assessment. Self-assessments can be conducted as part of ongoing assessments however it is recommended that an independent assessor be included in the ongoing assessment program to ensure the assessment results can be used to maintain the authorization or conduct reauthorization of the system. Ongoing assessment ensures that the system is compliant with the requirements levied by the authorized official when issuing an approval to operate, or approval to use determination.

During the step assessment procedures developed during the assessment step can be reused to increase efficiency and effectiveness of these assessments.

Assessment results from ongoing assessments can be used to fulfill the requirements of other audits and assessment programs, reducing duplication of effort introduced by different programs.

The use of automation in the step increases the frequency of assessments and introduces the ability to monitor a crater number of controls and systems.

NIST SP 800-37 Text
ONGOING ASSESSMENTS **Task M-2** Assess the controls implemented within and inherited by the system in accordance with the continuous monitoring strategy. **Potential Inputs:** Organizational continuous monitoring strategy and system level continuous monitoring strategy (if applicable); security and privacy plans; security and privacy assessment plans; security and privacy assessment reports; plans of action and milestones; information from automated and manual monitoring tools; organization- and system-level risk assessment results; external assessment or audit results (if applicable). **Expected Outputs:** Updated security and privacy assessment reports. **Primary Responsibility:** Control Assessor. **Supporting Roles:** Authorizing Official or Authorizing Official Designated Representative; System Owner or Common Control Provider; Information Owner or Steward; System Security Officer; System Privacy Officer; Senior Agency Information Security Officer; Senior Agency Official for Privacy. **System Development Life Cycle Phase:** New – Operations/Maintenance. Existing – Operations/Maintenance. **Discussion:** After an initial system or common control authorization, the organization assesses all

controls on an ongoing basis. Ongoing assessment of the control effectiveness is part of the continuous monitoring activities of the organization. The monitoring frequency for each control is based on the organizational continuous monitoring strategy (see Task P-7) and can be supplemented by the system-level continuous monitoring strategy (see Task S-5). Adherence to the terms and conditions specified by the authorizing official as part of the authorization decision are also monitored (see Task M-1). Ongoing control assessment continues as the information generated as part of continuous monitoring is correlated, analyzed, and reported to senior leaders.

For ongoing control assessments, assessors have the required degree of independence as determined by the authorizing official. Assessor independence during continuous monitoring introduces efficiencies into the process and may allow for reuse of assessment results in support of ongoing authorization and when reauthorization is required.

To satisfy the annual FISMA security assessment requirement, organizations can use assessment results from control assessments that occurred during authorization, ongoing authorization, or reauthorization; during continuous monitoring; or the during testing and evaluation of systems as part of the SDLC or an audit (provided the assessment results are current, relevant to the determination of control effectiveness, and obtained by assessors with the required degree of independence). Existing assessment results are reused consistent with the reuse policy established by the organization and are supplemented with additional assessments as needed. The reuse of assessment results is helpful in achieving a cost-effective, security program capable of producing the evidence necessary to determine the security posture of information systems and the organization. Finally, the use of automation to support control assessments facilitates a greater frequency, volume, and coverage of assessments.

References: [SP 800-53A]; [SP 800-137]; [SP 800-160 v1] (Verification, Validation, Operation, and Maintenance Processes); [IR 8011 v1].

EXERCISE 11.2

Why are ongoing assessments important to the security of the system?

_____

_____

_____

_____

TASK M-3 ONGOING RISK RESPONSE

Responsibilities	
Primary Responsibility	Supporting Roles
- Authorizing Official - System Owner - Common Control Provider	- Senior Accountable Official for Risk Management or Risk Executive (Function) - Senior Agency Official for Privacy

	- Authorizing Official Designated Representative
	- Information Owner or Steward
	- System Security Officer
	- System Privacy Officer
	- Systems Security Engineer
	- Privacy Engineer
	- Security Architect
	- Privacy Architect

SDLC Alignment	
New Systems	Legacy Systems
- Operations/Maintenance	- Operations/Maintenance

CSF Alignment	
CSF Number	CSF Task
	RS.AN

Task Flow	
Inputs	Outputs
- Security and privacy assessment reports	- Mitigation actions or risk acceptance decisions
- Organization- and system-level risk assessment results	- Updated security and privacy assessment reports
- Security and privacy plans	
- Plans of action and milestones	

Assessments connected during the monitoring step often resulting reports being created that either define new findings or established that the system has not changed since its authorization. This information is provided by the system owner or common control provider to the authorizing official to evaluate if any changes to the risk response need to be made based on information provided by the assessment.

The authorizing official will determine the appropriate risk response based on evaluation of the continuous monitoring reports with the help of other organizational officials including the risk and executive function. If a change is needed in the risk response the system owner or a common control provider are responsible to implement the required risk response. Changes to the risk response must be documented in the system or common control documentation. If new mitigations are required these must be added to the plan of action and milestones. Assessors maybe required to provide information or recommendation on remediation actions.

The result of ongoing assessments and continuous monitoring drive the need to continually update the risk response to provide a near real-time risk picture for the authorizing officials continued approval to operate or approval to use.

ONGOING RISK RESPONSE

Task M-3 Respond to risk based on the results of ongoing monitoring activities, risk assessments, and outstanding items in plans of action and milestones.

Potential Inputs: Security and privacy assessment reports; organization- and system-level risk assessment results; security and privacy plans; plans of action and milestones.

Expected Outputs: Mitigation actions or risk acceptance decisions; updated security and privacy assessment reports.

Primary Responsibility: Authorizing Official; System Owner; Common Control Provider.

Supporting Roles: Senior Accountable Official for Risk Management or Risk Executive (Function); Senior Agency Official for Privacy; Authorizing Official Designated Representative; Information Owner or Steward; System Security Officer; System Privacy Officer; Systems Security Engineer; Privacy Engineer; Security Architect; Privacy Architect.

System Development Life Cycle Phase: New – Operations/Maintenance.
Existing – Operations/Maintenance.

Discussion: Assessment information produced by an assessor during continuous monitoring is provided to the system owner and the common control provider in updated assessment reports or via reports from automated security/privacy management and reporting tools. The authorizing official determines the appropriate risk response to the assessment findings or approves responses proposed by the system owner and common control provider. The system owner and common control provider subsequently implement the appropriate risk response. When the risk response is acceptance, the findings remain documented in the security and privacy assessment reports and are monitored for changes to risk factors. When the risk response is mitigation, the planned mitigation actions are included in and tracked using the plans of action and milestones. If requested by the authorizing official, control assessors may provide recommendations for remediation actions. Recommendations for remediation actions may also be provided by an automated security/privacy management and reporting tool. An organizational assessment of risk (Task P-3) and system-level risk assessment results (Task P-14) guide and inform the decisions regarding ongoing risk response. Controls that are modified, enhanced, or added as part of ongoing risk response are reassessed by assessors to ensure that the new, modified, or enhanced controls have been implemented correctly, are operating as intended, and producing the desired outcome with respect to meeting the security and privacy requirements of the system.

References: [SP 800-30]; [SP 800-53]; [SP 800-53A]; [SP 800-137]; [SP 800-160 v1] (Risk Management Process); [IR 8011 v1]; [IR 8062]; [NIST CSF] (Core [Respond Function]).

EXERCISE 11.3

When new findings are discovered during the ongoing assessment, how can they impact the risk response?

_____

_____

_____

_____

TASK M-4 AUTHORIZATION PACKAGE UPDATES

Responsibilities	
Primary Responsibility	Supporting Roles
- System Owner - Common Control Provider	- Information Owner or Steward - System Security Officer - System Privacy Officer - Senior Agency Official for Privacy - Senior Agency Information Security Officer

SDLC Alignment	
New Systems	Legacy Systems
- Operations/Maintenance	- Operations/Maintenance

CSF Alignment	
CSF Number	CSF Task
	RS.IM

Task Flow	
Inputs	Outputs
- Security and privacy assessment reports - Organization- and system-level risk assessment results - Security and privacy plans - Plans of action and milestones	- Updated security and privacy assessment reports - Updated plans of action and milestones - Updated risk assessment results - Updated security and privacy plans

Documents in the authorization package are considered living documents and should be continually updated based on new information discovered about the information system, common control provider, or risk picture. And The main documents of the authorization package include the security/ privacy plan, assessment report, and plan of action and milestones. The system owner is responsible for insuring these documents remaining updated and reflect the current state of the system throughout lifecycle.

Milestones completed on the plan of action and milestones, new findings discovered during ongoing monitoring, and changes to the threat landscape should be updated in the appropriate document. New findings can be uncovered through other sources including audits, or incidents discovered by the organization. This supports the objective of near real-time monitoring and updating of the information system and IT support documentation.

The organization will determine the format of reporting as well as the frequency. The use of automated tools is highly encouraged to increase efficiency and effectiveness.

Updated documentation provides organizational officials including the authorizing official with the most current state of the security controls, and the risk posture of the information system. This allows for near real-time monitoring of the systems impact on the organizational risk picture and ensures that requirements levied by the authorizing official in the approval task are being followed.

NIST SP 800-37 Text
AUTHORIZATION PACKAGE UPDATES **Task M-4** Update plans, assessment reports, and plans of action and milestones based on the results of the continuous monitoring process. **Potential Inputs:** Security and privacy assessment reports; organization- and system-level risk assessment results; security and privacy plans; plans of action and milestones. **Expected Outputs:** Updated security and privacy assessment reports;108 updated plans of action and milestones; updated risk assessment results; updated security and privacy plans. **Primary Responsibility:** System Owner; Common Control Provider. **Supporting Roles:** Information Owner or Steward; System Security Officer; System Privacy Officer; Senior Agency Official for Privacy; Senior Agency Information Security Officer. **System Development Life Cycle Phase:** New – Operations/Maintenance. Existing – Operations/Maintenance **Discussion:** To achieve near real-time risk management, the organization updates security and privacy plans, security and privacy assessment reports, and plans of action and milestones on an ongoing basis. Updates to the plans reflect modifications to controls based on risk mitigation activities carried out by system owners or common control providers. Updates to control assessment reports reflect additional assessment activities carried out to determine control effectiveness based on implementation details in the plans. Plans of action and milestones are updated based on progress made on the current outstanding items; address security and privacy risks discovered as part of control effectiveness monitoring; and describe how the system owner or common control provider intends to address those risks. The updated information raises awareness of the security and privacy posture of the system and

the common controls inherited by the system, thereby, supporting near real-time risk management and the ongoing authorization process.

The frequency of updates to risk management information is at the discretion of the system owner, common control provider, and authorizing officials in accordance with federal and organizational policies and is consistent with the organizational and system-level continuous monitoring strategies. The updates to information regarding the security and privacy posture of the system and the common controls inherited by the system are accurate and timely since the information provided influences ongoing actions and decisions by authorizing officials and other senior leaders within the organization. The use of automated support tools and organization-wide security and privacy program management practices ensure that authorizing officials can readily access the current security and privacy posture of the system. Ready access to the current security and privacy posture supports continuous monitoring and ongoing authorization and promotes the near real-time management of risk to organizational operations and assets, individuals, other organizations, and the Nation.

Organizations ensure that information needed for oversight, management, and auditing purposes is not modified or destroyed when updating security and privacy plans, assessment reports, and plans of action and milestones. Providing an effective method to track changes to systems through configuration management procedures is necessary to achieve transparency and traceability in the security and privacy activities of the organization; to obtain individual accountability for any security or privacy actions; and to understand emerging trends in the security and privacy programs of the organization.

References: [SP 800-30]; [SP 800-53A].

EXERCISE 11.4

Why is it important to keep the systems security documentation updated?

_____

_____

_____

_____

TASK M-5 SECURITY AND PRIVACY REPORTING

Responsibilities	
Primary Responsibility	Supporting Roles
- System Owner - Common Control Provider - Senior Agency Information Security Officer - Senior Agency Official for Privacy.	- System Security Officer - System Privacy Officer

SDLC Alignment	
New Systems	Legacy Systems
- Operations/Maintenance	- Operations/Maintenance

CSF Alignment	
CSF Number	CSF Task

Task Flow	
Inputs	Outputs
- Security and privacy assessment reports - Plans of action and milestones - Organization- and system-level risk assessment results; organization- and system-level continuous monitoring strategy - Security and privacy plans - Cybersecurity Framework Profile	- Security and privacy posture reports

The results of the ongoing monitoring, ongoing assessment and ongoing remediation actions of the information system are reported to the officials defined by the organization. The organization should define primary and secondary officials that should receive reports on the risk and security status of specific information systems based on need to know.

The reporting format, frequency, method of presentation, and information provided in the reports is at the discretion of the organization. Organizations have Great flexibility in determining how reporting is conducted and who should receive the reports, however it is important to consider a Content of these reports when determining how widely they will be distributed based on the security and risk information contained in the reports.

While the organizations have great flexibility in determining form and content of reports, it is important that the information contained in these reports Will give the authorizing official and those rolls supporting him or her a picture of the ongoing risk assessment and security posture of the information system or common control set.

Reporting can be time driven for example monthly, event driven for example based on any event or incident, or a combination of the two. Organizational leadership should determine the correct reporting frequency method of reporting and format of reporting to inshore consistency of reporting buy different information systems and common control providers.

NIST SP 800-37 Text

SECURITY AND PRIVACY REPORTING

Task M-5 Report the security and privacy posture of the system to the authorizing official and other organizational officials on an ongoing basis in accordance with the organizational continuous monitoring strategy.

Potential Inputs: Security and privacy assessment reports; plans of action and milestones; organization- and system-level risk assessment results; organization- and system-level continuous monitoring strategy; security and privacy plans; Cybersecurity Framework Profile.

Expected Outputs: Security and privacy posture reports.

Primary Responsibility: System Owner; Common Control Provider; Senior Agency Information Security Officer; Senior Agency Official for Privacy.

Supporting Roles: System Security Officer; System Privacy Officer.

System Development Life Cycle Phase: New – Operations/Maintenance.
Existing – Operations/Maintenance.

Discussion: The results of monitoring activities are documented and reported to the authorizing official and other selected organizational officials on an ongoing basis in accordance with the organizational continuous monitoring strategy. Other organizational officials who may receive security and privacy posture reports include, for example, chief information officer, senior agency information security officer, senior agency official for privacy, senior accountable official for risk management or risk executive (function), information owner or steward, incident response roles, and contingency planning roles. Security and privacy posture reporting can be event-driven, time-driven, or event- and time-driven.110 The reports provide the authorizing official and other organizational officials with information regarding the security and privacy posture of the systems including the effectiveness of implemented controls. Security and privacy posture reports describe the ongoing monitoring activities employed by system owners or common control providers. The reports also include information about security and privacy risks in the systems and environments of operation discovered during control assessments, auditing, and continuous monitoring and how system owners or common control providers plan to address those risks.
Organizations have flexibility in the breadth, depth, formality, form, and format of security and privacy posture reports. The goal is efficient ongoing communication with the authorizing official and other organizational officials as necessary, conveying the current security and privacy posture of systems and environments of operation and how the current posture affects individuals, organizational missions, and business functions. At a minimum, security and privacy posture reports summarize changes to the security and privacy plans, security and privacy assessment reports, and plans of action and milestones that have occurred since the last report. The use of automated security and privacy management and reporting tools (e.g., a dashboard) by the organization facilitates the effectiveness and timeliness of security and privacy posture reporting.
The frequency of security and privacy posture reports is at the discretion of the organization and in compliance with federal and organizational policies. Reports occur at appropriate intervals to transmit security and privacy information about systems or common controls but not so frequently as to generate unnecessary work or expense. Authorizing officials use the security and privacy posture reports and consult with the senior accountable official for risk management or risk executive (function), senior agency information security officer, and senior agency official for privacy to determine if a reauthorization action is necessary.

Security and privacy posture reports are marked, protected, and handled in accordance with federal and organizational policies. Security and privacy posture reports can be used to satisfy FISMA reporting requirements for documenting remediation actions for security and privacy weaknesses or deficiencies. Reporting on security and privacy posture is intended to be ongoing and should not be interpreted as requiring the time, expense, and formality associated with the information provided for the initial authorization. Rather, reporting is conducted in a cost-effective manner consistent with achieving the reporting objectives.

References: [SP 800-53A]; [SP 800-137]; [NIST CSF] (Core [Identify, Protect, Detect, Respond, Recover Functions]).

EXERCISE 11.5

Why is reporting in this task important?

_____

_____

_____

_____

TASK M-6 ONGOING AUTHORIZATION

Responsibilities	
Primary Responsibility	Supporting Roles
- Authorizing Official	- Senior Accountable Official for Risk Management or Risk Executive (Function) - Chief Information Officer - Senior Agency Information Security Officer - Senior Agency Official for Privacy - Authorizing Official Designated Representative

SDLC Alignment	
New Systems	Legacy Systems
- Operations/Maintenance	- Operations/Maintenance

CSF Alignment	
CSF Number	CSF Task

Task Flow

Inputs	Outputs
- Risk tolerance; security and privacy posture reports - Plans of action and milestones - Organization- and system-level risk assessment results - Security and privacy plans	- A determination of risk - Ongoing authorization to operate, ongoing authorization to use, ongoing common control authorization - Denial of ongoing authorization to operate, denial of ongoing authorization to use, denial of ongoing common control authorization

Organization should strive to achieve ongoing authorization with their information systems and common control sets. This means that authorizations to operate, or authorizations to use do not have a specific end date but are instead monitored for changes to security posture or risk profile, continually monitored to ensure only approved changes are made, and an accurate reporting program is established to ensure that the authorizing official and other key risk leaders are kept abreast of changes to the security or risk status of the information system.

Changes maybe driven my external providers such as manufacturers of operating systems or hardware, user requirement changes, or changes to the threat landscape. These and other things can change the risk posture of both the information system and the enterprise as a whole.

The authorizing the official will validate through assessments and reports the information systems operation does not impact the risk tolerance or appetite of the organization. If this can be maintained the organization can benefit from the use of ongoing authorization. To be effective the authorizing of official must validate that ongoing risk determination and risk acceptance is being made and officially document this acceptance.

Control authorizations that change over time must be communicated to the information system owner or common control provider by the authorized official indicating what has changed in the systems authorization. This could be as simple as requiring additional mitigations, requiring the System or common control set to undergo a new authorization process restarting the RMF, or as extreme as revoking the authorization to operate.

Ongoing authorizations reduce the cost of securing and maintaining systems and common control sets while increasing the security posture of the information system and maintaining the correct risk level.

NIST SP 800-37 Text
ONGOING AUTHORIZATION **Task M-6** Review the security and privacy posture of the system on an ongoing basis to determine whether the risk remains acceptable. **Potential Inputs:** Risk tolerance; security and privacy posture reports; plans of action and milestones; organization- and system-level risk assessment results; security and privacy plans. **Expected Outputs:** A determination of risk; ongoing authorization to operate, ongoing authorization to

use, ongoing common control authorization; denial of ongoing authorization to operate, denial of ongoing authorization to use, denial of ongoing common control authorization.

Primary Responsibility: Authorizing Official.

Supporting Roles: Senior Accountable Official for Risk Management or Risk Executive (Function); Chief Information Officer; Senior Agency Information Security Officer; Senior Agency Official for Privacy; Authorizing Official Designated Representative.

System Development Life Cycle Phase: New – Operations/Maintenance.
Existing – Operations/Maintenance.

Discussion: To employ an ongoing authorization approach, organizations have in place an organization-level and system-level continuous monitoring process to assess implemented controls on an ongoing basis. Task R-4, the authorizing official or designated representative reviews the security and privacy posture of the system (including the effectiveness of the implemented controls) on an ongoing basis to determine the current risk to organizational operations and assets, individuals, other organizations, and the Nation. The authorizing official determines whether the current risk is acceptable and provides appropriate direction to the system owner or common control provider. The authorizing official may determine that the risk remains at an acceptable level for continued operation or that the risk is no longer at an acceptable level for continued operation, and may issue a denial of authorization to operate, authorization to use, or common control authorization. 111 The findings or results from the continuous monitoring process provides useful information to authorizing officials to support near-real time risk-based decision making. In accordance with the guidance in
The risks may change based on the information provided in the security and privacy posture reports because the reports may indicate changes to the security or privacy risk factors. Determining how changing conditions affect organizational and individual risk is essential for managing privacy risk and maintaining adequate security. By carrying out ongoing risk determination and risk acceptance, authorizing officials can maintain system and common control authorizations over time and transition to ongoing authorization. Reauthorization actions occur only in accordance with federal or organizational policies. The authorizing official conveys updated risk determination and acceptance results to the senior accountable official for risk management or the risk executive (function).
The use of automated support tools to capture, organize, quantify, visually display, and maintain security and privacy posture information promotes near real-time risk management regarding the risk posture of the organization. The use of metrics and dashboards increases an organization's capability to make risk-based decisions by consolidating data in an automated fashion and providing the data to decision makers at different levels within the organization in an easy-to-understand format.

References: [SP 800-30]; [SP 800-39] (Organization, Mission/Business Process, and System Levels); [SP 800-55]; [SP 800-160 v1] (Risk Management Process); [IR 8011 v1]; [IR 8062].

EXERCISE #.#

What role(s) can authorize the continued operation of a system or common control set?

_____

_____

_____

_____

TASK M-7 SYSTEM DISPOSAL

Responsibilities	
Primary Responsibility	Supporting Roles
- System Owner	- Authorizing Official
	- Authorizing Official Designated Representative
	- Information Owner or Steward; System Security Officer
	- System Privacy Officer
	- Senior Accountable Official for Risk Management or Risk Executive (Function)
	- Senior Agency Information Security Officer
	- Senior Agency Official for Privacy

SDLC Alignment	
New Systems	Existing Systems
- N/A	- Disposal

CSF Alignment	
CSF Number	CSF Task

Task Flow	
Inputs	Outputs
- Security and privacy plans	Disposal strategy
- Organization- and system-level risk assessment results	- Updated system component inventory
- System component inventory	- Updated security and privacy plans

When a system or common control set is no longer needed it should be removed from operation. It is important that key actions take place when removing, or decommissioning, systems or control sets. Care should be taken to treat media as required by the organization classification and media handling policies. It may be required the data is retained after the system is decommissioned to ensure legal or regulatory requirements on the retention of specific types of information are followed. Is also important to ensure that in media containing Data or information does not leave organizational control without being properly sanitized in accordance with the organization's sanitization requirements.

It's also important to notify organizational officials including the authorizing official that the system or control set will be decommissioned. Users of the information system Core system owners that are inheriting controls from the system or common control set should be notified of the decommissioning of the system prior to the decommissioning taking place.

Organizations have flexibility in determining the method of decommissioning and reporting on the decommissioning of systems including the status of information and media but must ensure that legal and regulatory requirements are met.

The disposition of system hardware and software should be processed through a central organizational entity that can determine if these assets can be reused on other projects.

NIST SP 800-37 Text

SYSTEM DISPOSAL

Task M-7 Implement a system disposal strategy and execute required actions when a system is removed from operation.

Potential Inputs: Security and privacy plans; organization- and system-level risk assessment results; system component inventory.

Expected Outputs: Disposal strategy; updated system component inventory; updated security and privacy plans.

Primary Responsibility: System Owner.
Supporting Roles: Authorizing Official or Authorizing Official Designated Representative; Information Owner or Steward; System Security Officer; System Privacy Officer; Senior Accountable Official for Risk Management or Risk Executive (Function); Senior Agency Information Security Officer; Senior Agency Official for Privacy.

System Development Life Cycle Phase: New – Not Applicable.
Existing – Disposal.

Discussion: When a system is removed from operation, several risk management actions are required. Organizations ensure that controls addressing system disposal are implemented. Examples include media sanitization; configuration management and control; component authenticity; and record retention. Organizational tracking and management systems (including inventory systems) are updated to indicate the system that is being removed from service. Security and privacy posture reports reflect the security and privacy status of the system. Users and application owners hosted on the disposed system are notified as appropriate, and any control inheritance relationships are reviewed and assessed for impact. This task also applies to system elements that are removed from operation. Organizations removing a system from operation update the inventory of information systems to reflect the removal. System owners and security personnel ensure that disposed systems comply with relevant federal laws, regulations, directives, policies, and standards.

References: [SP 800-30]; [SP 800-88]; [IR 8062].

EXERCISE 11.7

What are some important considerations for data/information when decommissioning a system?

_____

_____

_____

_____

INDEX